W9-BZW-245

IN HOCK

Ledger from John Simpson's New York City pawnshop. First page of entries for August 15, 1838. Collection of the New-York Historical Society.

IN HOCK

*Pawning in America from Independence
through the Great Depression*

WENDY A. WOLOSON

The University of Chicago Press
CHICAGO AND LONDON

WENDY A. WOLOSON

is an independent scholar and consulting historian living in Philadelphia.
She is the author of *Refined Tastes: Sugar, Consumers, and Confectionery in
Nineteenth-Century American Culture.*

The University of Chicago Press, Chicago 60637
The University of Chicago Press, Ltd., London
© 2009 by The University of Chicago
All rights reserved. Published 2009
Printed in the United States of America

18 17 16 15 14 13 12 11 10 09   1 2 3 4 5

ISBN-13: 978-0-226-90567-9 (cloth)
ISBN-10: 0-226-90567-5 (cloth)

Library of Congress Catloging-in-Publication Data

Woloson, Wendy A., 1964–
    In hock: pawning in America from independence through the Great
Depression / Wendy A. Woloson.
        p.   cm.
    Includes bibliographical references and index.
    ISBN-13: 978-0-226-90567-9 (cloth: alk. paper)
    ISBN-10: 0-226-90567-5 (cloth: alk. peper)   1. Pawnbroking—United
States—History.
I. Title.
    HG2101.W656   2010
    332.3′40973—dc22

                                                        2009018828

TO DAD

AND TO THE MEMORY OF MY GRANDPARENTS—
They taught me that things matter

CONTENTS

Acknowledgments :: *ix*

ONE: In Hock

1

TWO: The "Jew Broker" in American Culture

21

THREE: In Defense of Pawnbrokers

54

FOUR: The Economies of Everyday Life

86

FIVE: Pawnbroking and Criminal Activity

122

SIX: Loan Societies and the Legitimation of Pawnbroking

154

SEVEN: Unredeemed

182

Notes :: *195*   Index :: *233*

ACKNOWLEDGMENTS

Writing this book has left me deeply in debt. Many people offered their insights and advice, their support and encouragement. And they demanded nothing in return—not collateral to demonstrate my worthiness or interest payments to compensate for their efforts. The debts I accrued were wholly unsecured, part of an economy characterized by a commerce of ideas rather than material things. Being engaged in such a robust extramarket economy has been one of the great pleasures of this project. The credits I extend here can go only a small way toward settling my accounts.

Among my creditors are friends and fellow historians who providentially share an interest in exploring and bringing to light the real and typically unglamorous economic lives of average, ordinary, and too often anonymous Americans. Special thanks go to Brian Luskey, who early on (when "In Hock" was not yet even the title of a conference paper) shored up my confidence to pursue the subject of pawnbroking at a time when studies of "marginal" economies were not yet fashionable. He has been an unflagging supporter, an incisive critic, and, most important, a good friend. Many others along the way also contributed in myriad fashions, giving encouragement and advice and sharing their thoughts and source material. In sum, their contributions helped me maintain the momentum I needed to see this through. Their belief in the worthiness of this project has been essential to its completion, their faith in me particularly humbling. They are Paul Erickson, Josh Greenberg, Ellen Hartigan-O'Connor, Alison Isenberg, Bruce Mann, John McCusker, Michelle Craig McDonald, Roderick McDonald, Stephen Mihm, Marina Moskowitz, Rich Newman, Dan Richter, Seth Rockman, and Bob Zecker. Peter Stallybrass deserves special mention for his infectious enthusiasm and generosity in sharing his own rich research materials on early pawnbroking in Great Britain.

I first met many of these people in my capacity as a curator at the Library Company of Philadelphia. My former colleagues, many of whom I am fortunate to count as friends, have also made contributions to this book: Jenny Ambrose,

Linda August, Alice Austin, Rachel D'Agostino, Ruth Hughes, Connie King, Charlene Knight, Andrea Krupp, Holly Phelps, Erika Piola, Jennifer Woods Rosner, and Sarah Weatherwax. In addition to being on the lookout for relevant primary sources they might encounter working with special collections, they also eagerly tracked the progress of my work, even though research trips often took me out of the building (thanks to the flexibility extended by the director, John Van Horne). Charlene Peacock and Linda Wisniewski deserve particular mention for helping me assemble many of the visual sources that appear in the following chapters. They arranged photography, hunted down sources, and co-ordinated the requisite paperwork. And they were always good-natured about it. Others I met during my time at the Library Company—David Doret, Steve Finer, Bill Helfand, Peter Masi, Charles Rosenberg, and Michael Zinman—also have my thanks for their support, kindness, and sharing of source materials.

Staff at other institutions also count among the people I am indebted to. Original documentation on the history of pawnbroking is measured by the fragment rather than the linear foot, and it often remains well hidden in library stacks. Without the efforts of curators, archivists, and librarians across the country—who often searched unpublished finding aids, scoured obscure collections, and willingly sent me scans and photocopies—much of the evidence that undergirds and enriches this work would have never surfaced. Barbara Austen, manuscript archivist and cataloger at the Connecticut Historical Society, found one of the few pieces of nineteenth-century correspondence that refers to pawning. Jim Baggett, head of the Archives Department at the Birmingham (Alabama) Public Library, spent time with me during my visit to the archive, making accessible the ledger books of the Steel City Pawn Shop (one of the few surviving collections of historical pawnbroking business records) and pointing me to secondary sources on the history of the region.

Ted O'Reilly, manuscript reference librarian at the New-York Historical Society, unearthed John Simpson's ledger book, the only existing nineteenth-century American pawnbroking ledger that I know of. It had been lost in the stacks for many years, and its rediscovery allowed me to quantify many of my suppositions about early pawning and redemption patterns, helped me identify a few of the tens of thousands of New Yorkers who patronized pawnshops in the early nineteenth century, and made much more poignant the daily struggles of ordinary Americans to stay afloat. Dale Rosengarten, curator of the Jewish Heritage Collection at the College of Charleston, made available to me images of the I. D. Rubin family, including views of their early twentieth-century pawnshop. Cheryl Schnirring, curator of manuscripts at the Abraham Lincoln Presidential Library, hunted down both the pawn ticket belonging to Ulysses S. Grant and also documentation about how it arrived at the repository. Shan Sutton, head of the Holt-Atherton Special Collections at the University of the Pacific Libraries, located, surveyed, and sent photocopies of correspondence from the Hands Loan Company, the only such business correspondence of pawnbrokers I have been able to find. Helen Wykle, special collections coordinator at the University of North Carolina at Asheville, made available to me a copy of the oral history of Leo Finkelstein, whose accounts describe how a pawnbroker living down south survived the Depression and helped his customers do the same. While on a Kate B. and Hall J. Peterson Fellowship at the American Antiquarian Society, I was in the capable hands of Gigi Barnhill, Joanne Chaison, Tom Knoles, Marie Lamoureux, Dennis Laurie, and Jackie Donovan Penny. I came away from that month in Worcester, "working under its generous dome," feeling refreshed, filled with new ideas, and well stocked with source material for this and future projects.

Like historical documents and oral histories, graphic images have served as important primary source material in addition to enlivening the story of pawnbroking. Marshaling images and permissions was no small matter and involved many people working at several institutions. Jon Benoit coordinated the process of obtaining several reproductions from the American Antiquarian Society, and Coi Drummond-Gehrig of the Denver Public Library, Western History and Genealogy, helped me secure a photograph of an early western pawnshop. RA Friedman similarly helped with reproductions of pawn tickets from the collection of the Historical Society of Pennsylvania. And for sheet music images I worked with Kelly Spring of Johns Hopkins University.

Because the fundamentals of pawnbroking have changed little over time, today's professionals working in the industry helped me understand historical aspects of the business, from the mechanics of keeping books and making appraisals to pawnbrokers' relationships with authorities and customers. The proprietors of McGarry's allowed me access to their small but invaluable business archives, setting aside a private space in their shop to accommodate me every Friday for an entire winter. They also put me in contact with the head of the Pawnshop Investigation Unit of the Philadelphia Police Department, an important source for learning about stolen goods. Ric Blum, who runs the Dayton Loan Office, has been part of this project nearly since its inception, serving as a conduit between me and professional pawnbrokers working today, including members of the National Pawnbrokers Association. Although we have still not met face to face, he has continued to send me relevant clippings, answered my often naive questions, and maintained correspondence even during personally trying times. Working with these thoughtful and generous people has caused me to defend the honor of ("my") pawnbrokers all the more passionately.

The people at the University of Chicago Press transformed *In Hock* from a clunky manuscript into a polished, well-conceived, and well-organized book. Most of the credit goes to the patience and thoughtfulness of my editor Robert Devens, who I cannot thank enough. In addition to helping me endure the many and often grueling phases of writing, he applied his extremely good judgment to choosing anonymous readers whose insightful feedback—ranging from the finer points of legal and economic history to aspects of material culture studies—made this a much better book. I have also been the beneficiary of Robert's supremely able and forbearing assistants, Emilie Sandoz and Anne Summers Goldberg. As manuscript editor, Alice Bennett smoothed out the text, resulting in a more readable and better organized work.

Credit also goes to my family and friends, who put up with hearing more about pawnbroking past and present than they ever deserved to. My many friends—Bruce Compton, Sharon Hildebrand, Mary Anne Hines, Dave Jacobson, Terry Snyder, Linda Stanley, and Donald and JoAnn Stilwell—tolerated my preoccupation for many years, providing welcome levity and necessary diversions along the way. My mother, Joan Woloson, continues to be my most ardent fan, making me feel that with her support I can do just about anything. Thanks also go to my brother, Blake Woloson, one of the smartest and funniest people I know.

David Miller, my loyal companion, has remained close by my side. More than anyone else, he has made accommodations for this project, from turning countless Friday happy hours over to discussions about the latest pawnbroking discoveries and theories to sharing space at the dinner table with growing piles of manuscript pages. In addition to providing general emotional support, he has put up with my jokes, read and commented on shaky drafts, and provided technical assistance. I am happy to have him in my life. Dogs Cecil and Dean-O (who, incredibly, lived and slept through another book) provided convenient excuses to turn away from the computer screen and go for walks that, salutarily, brought me into contact with the outside world.

In our own ways we historians are all writing autobiographies, and *In Hock* is no exception. This book grows out of my experience of being raised in a family that was passionate about, and perhaps obsessed with, the material world. They are to be credited with fostering my interest in used goods and secondary economies. My grandmother, Leah, was a successful antiques dealer, expert in early American primitives—braided rag rugs, wrought iron lighting devices, hand-hammered pewter dishware, needlework samplers, and the like. She ran her shop out of the modest stone house built by my grandfather, Peter, who was himself an accomplished tinsmith and woodworker. Like early pawnshops, his shop was a mysterious place, dim and grimy. It was jammed with wood and metal lathes, worktables, and metal-fashioning devices with cogs and cranks. The stone walls were festooned with hundreds of pairs of specialized tin snips, hammers, embossing tools, and screwdrivers, with jars of nails and bolts and rivets hanging from the wooden ceiling beams. The place (along with my grandfather's blackened hands—permanently stained from his work) enchanted me as a kid.

They instilled in my father, Kent Woloson, an appreciation for material objects. For as long as I can remember, he too has amassed old things (stuff with which his wonderful and wonderfully tolerant wife Linda cohabitates). I cherish memories of getting out of school early to go with him on road trips to antique toy and train shows in distant cities. Today, "doing" antique shows, flea markets, and eBay remain some of our favorite pastimes, and together we continue to look for hidden treasures, searching for something new in the old. Because their sensibility has so informed my research and writing, I dedicate *In Hock* to my father and to the memory of my grandparents, with the deepest love and gratitude.

CHAPTER ONE

IN HOCK

On my first visit to my local pawnshop Tracy welcomed me with a bright smile. She oversees McGarry's, one of the oldest pawnshops in the United States, and was happy to show me around and tell me about the business. Her staff, including jewelry repairers, appraisers, and bookkeepers, is composed of family members who have worked there for years. In keeping with tradition, she learned the profession from her father, Walter, who himself was trained from a young age to be a pawnbroker.

Like almost all pawnshops today, this one also sells new and used jewelry and watches, functioning as both a retail outlet and a loan office. The shop is fronted with two show windows that display choice items, and a signboard propped on the sidewalk advertises jewelry repair. The generously sized planters near the street are filled with seasonal flowers, and the door is embellished with paper decorations of turkeys, shamrocks, or bunnies, depending on the time of year. The interior looks like any other jewelry shop—bordered by long glass display cases containing rings, necklaces, earrings, watches, and more. The place is neat and clean, the atmosphere relaxed and friendly. The radio is tuned to NPR.

You wouldn't know simply from appearances that this place is a pawnshop. The pawnbroker's traditional sign of the three golden balls is nowhere in sight, and save for a two-line listing in the yellow pages under pawnbrokers, the operation identifies itself as a jewelry store selling new, custom-made, and estate pieces. First-time customers find their way here primarily by word of mouth. The shop's core clientele consists of dedicated regulars who have been coming for years and whose families have been patrons over many generations. People are loyal: after their first visit, they keep coming back.

Pawnbrokers and their staff are not unlike bartenders and beauticians, whose relations with their clients are at once professional and personal. For many the place plays a special role in both economic and social aspects of their lives. People come to this particular pawnshop when they are in need, and the staff helps them out whenever possible. Customers share intimate details about themselves with Tracy and explain what has brought them to her place at this particular time. She often sees her clients weekly and cannot help getting to know them; she has been invited to christenings, weddings, and funerals.

I came here seeking historical materials, and Tracy generously shared her modest business archives, setting aside space for me to work in a side office every Friday for a few months. At the same time, she fiercely protected her customers' privacy, quickly ushering me past the showroom whenever I came. She introduced me to the police detectives running the Pawnshop Investigation Unit, with whom she is on surprisingly friendly terms. But she has also, like many other pawnbrokers, pushed for legislation that would protect her customers' privacy by limiting authorities' access to her rich database of pawners' personal information.

Why is it remarkable that a pawnshop might be clean and tidy? Or that the pawnbroker might be personable? Or that she is on amiable terms with the people charged with surveillance of her shop? Or that pawners might demonstrate customer loyalty by returning time and again and by passing on the name of their pawnbroker to friends, coworkers, neighbors, and relatives who might also need such services? Or that, despite all this, she would prefer that I use only her first name?

Very few professionals (besides perhaps lawyers, used car salesmen, and politicians) are subjected to the close scrutiny and harsh judgment experienced by pawnbrokers. Many people react viscerally to pawnbroking, even if they have had no firsthand experience as pawners. Some of this apprehension is understandable. Pawnbroking defies easy categorizing. The movement of consumer goods in pawning is unlike ordinary retail exchange—pawnbrokers deal in material items but are not merchants, and though they lend money, they are not bankers. Pawners too evade easy taxonomy. Some have possessions valuable enough to secure a loan but may not have enough capital to obtain alternative forms of credit such as credit cards. Small-business owners, whose cash is tied up in company assets, might hock their watches and fine jewelry in order to make payroll. Others, waiting for the next payday, bring in a gold chain or an MP3 player to get cash to cover a utility bill, dodging service disruptions, late charges, and reconnection fees. Some pawners have such a distrust of financial institutions that they would rather go to check-cashing outlets, payday lenders, and pawnshops than keep their money in banks. Still others, with drug habits, bring in household items they have stolen from their own families in hopes of getting cash for a quick fix.

Most of our antipathy toward pawnbroking does not come from direct experience (which might make us more tolerant) but has arisen instead from centuries of systematic and targeted stigmatizing of pawning, a major focus of this book. *In Hock* traces the history of pawnbroking in the United States from its beginnings as a distinct profession around the time of American independence through the Great Depression, when pawnbroking was in decline. (In recent years the profession has experienced a resurgence, in part because of tightening economic times and in part because of the rise in immigrant populations who tend not to use banks.) The book discusses how the many misconceptions about the profession came about and why negative characterizations of the business continue to resonate.

Significantly, pawnbroking in America emerged with the modern economy and was dependent on the working poor and the unemployed and underemployed who made industrial capitalism possible. With the vibrant postrevolutionary commercial world apparently humming with wholesale and retail trade, pawnbroking and other "marginal" economies were visible reminders that not everyone enjoyed the same economic prosperity. Pawnbroking was a business that occasionally intersected with, sometimes subverted, and often circumvented wholesale and retail exchange. Rather than seeing pawnshops as outgrowths of the inequities created by a new economic system, commentators blamed pawnshops for myriad social ills, including poverty, crime, and intemperance. They continued to revise and refine their criticism throughout the nineteenth century, creating negative associations about pawnshops and pawnbrokers that still vex the industry today.

In Hock is also in part a response to traditional economic historians who, smitten with the success stories of wholesale and retail merchants, have all but ignored the lives of ordinary individuals. Indeed, active secondary and tertiary markets were by-products of industrial capitalism. The many thousands of people living in developing urban areas who daily struggled to get by relied on the services and products provided by pawnbrokers, junk dealers, and used goods vendors. Economic ventures dismissed at the time (and by many today) as aberrant or marginal were in fact normal and common. The pages of historical newspapers were crowded with advertisements documenting the robust used goods markets in American cities. Pawning was an important component of these markets and central to the daily economic lives of countless individuals.

Mutually dependent, professional pawnbroking and industrial capitalism matured together during the nineteenth century. Although pawnbroking in one form or another might have arisen within some other economic structure, it certainly would not have thrived as it did. Without laborers' ready access to cash loans from pawnshops, merchants and manufacturers could not have as effectively maximized profits by charging so much for retail goods and could not have avoided paying workers a living wage for their time and labor. Pawnshop loans were crucial stopgaps that helped people make ends meet from one payday to the next, because income was often not enough to cover expenses.

Nevertheless, reformers, politicians, businessmen, xenophobes, and others continually vilified pawnbrokers, pawners, and pawnshops. *In Hock* asks readers to reconsider the traditional negative campaigns by demonstrating how crucial pawnbroking—and its demonizing—was to the emergence and eventual triumph of industrial capitalism. Often-scathing critiques of the business dogged pawnbrokers throughout the nineteenth century, in lectures, sermons, newspaper editorials, reports of philanthropic organizations, popular fiction, cartoons, and even scientific treatises. Cultural commentators blamed the country's chronic underclass on its supposed exploitation by pawnbrokers instead of acknowledging that that underclass was created by, and necessary to, the emerging—and exploitative—economic system. Although the collective efforts of those who decried pawning did not in fact eradicate pawnshops, their disparagement, finely honed and calcified over the decades, created negative impressions of pawnbrokers and their customers that continue to reverberate.

In Hock takes readers through the many familiar criticisms of pawnbroking and analyzes them, weighing their legitimacy against historical facts: the story of American pawning habits is more complicated and significant than has been thought. This is an economic history that traces the American economy from its early iteration as a relatively informal and highly social system based on mutual dependence to a structured, top-down model energized by the profit motive. It is also a business history that describes the development of pawnbroking as a profession distinct from other brokering and lending operations. A social history as well, the book describes how all classes, and especially the working poor, turned to collateral loans when faced with untenable financial circumstances. The history of law enforcement and government control are also important components of the story, since pawnbrokers—as suspected receivers of stolen goods—were among the few professionals required to report their business dealings to authorities. Because pawners used personal possessions as collateral, the history of pawning is linked to the development of large-scale consumer culture during the nineteenth century, especially in its final decades. Philanthropic endeavors are also relevant here, because reformers—always outspoken—early on blamed pawnbroking for a variety of social ills yet later established semiphilanthropic pawnshops themselves when it suited their economic interests. Finally, any analysis of pawnbroking has to take into account the social and economic impact of anti-Semitic sentiment on individual proprietors and the profession as a whole. The formative years of American anti-Semitism and pawnbrokers both occurred during the era covered in this book, and anti-Semitism is a theme that regrettably yet inescapably recurs throughout.

Because pawnbroking has always been situated at the nexus of so many goods, people, and dominant economic institutions, *In Hock* is a social history of capitalism that considers more than merely the commercial transactions of the rich, famous, and easily accessible. It is puzzling that most studies in economic history have ignored or dismissed "fringe" economic activity even though it appears throughout the historical record. Indeed, rather than being "fringe" or "marginal," pawning played a central role in the lives of millions of Americans, although, curiously, the most recent scholarly treatment of the subject was published in 1899.[1] Shifting focus away from the stories of the most successful and vocal historical personalities will inevitably lead the inquisitive to other equally important forms of "petty" entrepreneurialism. The rich source material below the surface reveals a far more robust and complete picture of economic enterprise on all levels, well beyond the transactions of the merchant elite. It is imperative that American historians in general, and economic historians in particular, spend more time uncovering these rich layers and reconsidering their social and economic impact: transactions in secondary and tertiary markets were as essential to the emergence of capitalism in America as wholesale and retail exchange.

Perhaps one of the reasons pawnbroking has been understudied is that people do not really understand exactly what pawning is. Fortunately for this endeavor, much about pawning has not changed significantly over time, so what was true for nineteenth-century pawners and pawnbrokers remains much the same today. Pawning involves the simple act of using a *pawn*—a piece of movable property (something small enough to take to a pawnshop)—as collateral to secure a short-term cash loan. While writing *In Hock* I pawned a gold necklace at Simpson's Loan Company in Philadelphia and will use my experience to explain what takes place.

Decidedly more downscale than McGarry's, Simpson's looks slightly shabby and feels a bit depressing inside. The exterior is designed to intimidate, the entrance fortified by a wrought iron gate and two locked metal security doors. The woman behind the counter at Simpson's is no less accommodating, though. She introduces herself as Ilona and explains the loan terms, as the Truth in Lending Act requires. Until the banking reform legislation of the Depression era, limits on the interest rates pawnbrokers could charge in the United States were set locally. Throughout the nineteenth century, therefore, it was not uncommon for pawnbrokers operating in different cities of the same state to charge their customers radically different interest rates. Even today, interest rates and fees are not uniform across the country but vary significantly from state to state. The rates in Pennsylvania (where I live) are among the lowest, at an annual percentage rate (APR) of 36%. If I lived in a high-interest state such as Alabama, however, I might be charged as much as 300% APR to borrow the same amount of money.[2] If I do not pay back my loan within the specified time with interest and additional fees, my gold chain will be *unredeemed*—forfeited to Simpson's for resale. Ilona will lend me $40 on the chain, and if I wait until the end of my five-month loan term, I will need to come up with $46 to get it back. If I never enter Simpson's again, I will forfeit legal custody of the collateral. Our mutual obligations cease at the expiration of the loan or upon its repayment.

As a first-time *pawner*, I am required to provide personal details that will become part of an electronic database accessible to the police. In the nineteenth century, pawnbrokers' clerks would have recorded similar identifying details, inscribing their pen-and-ink notations in massive ledgers made available to police and city officials. Today my driver's license provides some information, but Ilona also needs a daytime phone number in addition to my weight, my date of birth, and, disconcertingly, my Social Security number. After keying my particulars into the computer she returns my identification and pushes the button on a surprisingly dated dot matrix printer that generates a wide slip of paper. This is my *pawn ticket*, which in the precomputer era would have been a printed form completed by hand (as shown in fig. 4.5). Pen poised above the form, Ilona decodes the language of the ticket, confirming my personal information, a description of what I have brought in ("14K YG GUCCI LINK NECKLACE 10.0 DWT"), and the interest rate accruing on the loan, which she also writes boldly at the top "3%—month." I can renew the loan (have it extended) by paying the interest accrued at the end of the initial five-month term.

Pawn tickets are transferable, so anyone who has this ticket, *my* ticket, in addition to having all the particulars necessary to steal my identity, can redeem my chain "without you even knowing it," I am cautioned. (This, too, is nothing new. Fringe entrepreneurs of the late nineteenth century engaged in a brisk trade of real and forged pawn tickets.) The white copy of the ticket stays at Simpson's. The pink copy goes to the police. And I keep the yellow copy. As I sign on the line, agreeing to forfeit the property if I default, Ilona, friendly and attentive, slides the cash across the counter with my pawn ticket and buzzes me out, wishing me a nice day. In less than ten minutes I am light one gold necklace but carry two extra twenties in my pocket.

Simpson's displays the three golden balls, the iconic sign of pawnbrokers everywhere (save upscale places that prefer not to advertise so conspicuously). Still recognizable to many, the sign emerged not in fifth-century China, where pawnbroking is thought to have originated, but in medieval Europe, a representation of money as golden balls or disks.[3] Some theorize that the balls symbolize the coin-filled purses that Saint Nicholas gave to a man so destitute he considered selling his three daughters into prostitution. The saint left the purses at the poor man's house by night—enough of a dowry to make each daughter a suitable bride.[4]

More likely the symbol of the three balls derived from motifs decorating medieval coats of arms. They might have been appropriated from the Flemish van der Beurse family, whose crest was embellished with three purses representing the bill and commission brokering profession. Or perhaps the three balls were taken more directly from the motifs ornamenting the Medici coat of arms, although as international merchant bankers they, like the van der Beurses, were not directly involved with pawnbroking. "It may be," as historian Raymond de Roover has noted, "that a shield bearing a gold chevron between three bezants [coins] was first displayed as a sign above the door of an Italian pawnshop in Lombard Street" (fig. 1.1).[5]

DURING THE MIDDLE AGES, pawnbroking emerged as a distinct profession, functioning in large measure, according to Kenneth Hudson, "to meet the needs of powerful and ambitious rulers, who required money to finance wars and the building of castles, palaces, and churches, and to maintain a standard of living which they considered appropriate to their rank, power and social position."[6] Because the aristocracy was so dependent on loans from pawnbrokers, they resented the power these debtor-creditor relationships gave to the lenders, and so pawnbrokers' place in society remained perpetually uncertain and unstable. In 1199 Richard I set the legal interest rate at 10%, giving the clergy cause to pursue usurers with the weight of the law behind them. Such usury was the pretext for expelling the Jews from Great Britain in 1290 when lenders were simply trying to collect money owed to them. Often "licentious monks and clergy" pawned the very church property they were entrusted to care for in order to pay for luxuries.[7] The only ones who accepted this kind of property as collateral—Jews—therefore not only gained control of sacred artifacts but also possessed firsthand knowledge of their customers' profligate habits.

After the Jews' expulsion, the Lombards from Italy stepped in as Great Britain's moneylenders. They too extended loans to the rich and powerful. And they too waited years to be repaid. Extending large loans on highly prized collateral should have been a boon to the Lombards' business, but their debtors had luxu-

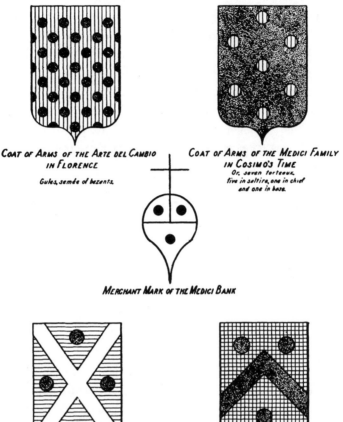

COAT OF ARMS OF THE ARTE DEL CAMBIO
IN FLORENCE

Gules, semée of bezants.

COAT OF ARMS OF THE MEDICI FAMILY
IN COSIMO'S TIME

Or, seven torteaux,
five in saltire, one in chief
and one in base.

MERCHANT MARK OF THE MEDICI BANK

COAT OF ARMS OF THE BANK OF SCOTLAND

Azure, a saltire argent
between four bezants.

COAT OF ARMS OF THE PAWNBROKERS
IN GREAT BRITAIN

Sable, a chevron or
between three bezants.

FIGURE 1.1. "Balls or Roundels as a Symbol of the Money-Lenders," in Raymond de Roover, "The Three Golden Balls of the Pawnbrokers," *Bulletin of the Business Historical Society* 20, 4 (October 1946): 123.

rious lifestyles to maintain and were not always fiscally prudent. Slow to repay, pawners tied up large amounts of Lombard money for years.[8] The Lombards were themselves expelled in 1530, leaving it to private British pawnbrokers to carry on the pawnbroking business alone.[9]

On the Continent organized pawnbroking emerged from philanthropic efforts. By the early 1600s Belgium, Holland, France, and Italy had all established "monts-de-piété" (a phrase variously interpreted as "mountains of charity," "hills of piety," and "banks of charity").[10] The monts-de-piété offered secured loans to the poor at much lower interest rates than those charged by private pawnbrokers. The institutions were organized and overseen by state governments and local charities. Belgium's first was founded by a Flemish priest in Ypres in 1534. Holland's Groote Banck van Leening was established in Amsterdam in 1614.[11] France saw its first nonprofit pawnshop in 1577, and Louis XVI issued an official decree to establish a mont-de-piété in Paris in 1777.[12] Because England's many attempts to establish nonprofit pawnshops were unsuccessful (thwarted every time by corruption among organizers and investors), private pawnbrokers continued to flourish and often loaned at usurious rates because authorities did not enforce existing regulations.

Though they operated in premodern society, independent pawnbrokers found their customer base greatly expanded with the ascent of industrial capitalism. The number of independent pawnbrokers grew during the eighteenth century not only in London but also in the rapidly industrializing city of Manchester. Patrick Colquhoun (merchant, statistician, and creator of the modern police force) acknowledged that "labouring people" often needed a pawnbroker's services, for example, "when they marry, and first enter upon life, to raise money upon whatever can be offered as a pledge." Yet Colquhoun also realized that pawnbrokers, free of any effective surveillance, were at liberty to take advantage of the neediest. Certainly the nominal £10 license fee did not deter the "*Sharpers* who . . . bring disgrace upon the reputable part of the trade" by acting primarily as receivers of stolen goods. At the end of the eighteenth century Colquhoun estimated that over 640 people were working as licensed pawnbrokers in and around London alone, then a city of over one million people.[13]

In Colquhoun's Britain the sign of the three balls was ubiquitous. It also appeared in popular culture, perhaps most notably to symbolize the state of society in William Hogarth's series of engravings *The Four Stages of Cruelty*, widely circulated on both sides of the Atlantic. "Beer Street" and "Gin Lane," first published in 1751, portrayed Londoners under the influence of two kinds of alcohol (figs. 1.2 and 1.3). Hogarth showed denizens of Beer Street, comfortably buzzed, as a healthy, active, and merry group of fishmongers, painters, and builders— happy people doing honest work. Here "good" businesses prosper. A beer saloon has taken over N. Pinch's pawnshop, the teetering three balls its only vestige. All is right with the world. In contrast, Hogarth's Gin Lane looked like a postapocalyptic eighteenth-century society. Here the devastating effects of drinking gin include chaos, starvation, and death. A baby falls from the arms of an inebriated woman. A man has hanged himself from a rafter. Collapsed buildings lit-

FIGURE 1.2. The health of pawnbrokers correlated inversely with the health of society. William Hogarth, "Beer Street" ([London]: Published according to act of Parliament, February 1, 1751); reissued as plate 53 in *The Original Works of William Hogarth* (London: John and Josiah Boydell, 1790). Library Company of Philadelphia.

FIGURE 1.3. William Hogarth. "Gin Lane" ([London]: Published according to act of Parliament, February 1, 1751); reissued as plate 54 in *The Original Works of William Hogarth* (London: John and Josiah Boydell, 1790). Library Company of Philadelphia.

ter the landscape. The gin peddlers, the pawnbroker, and the undertaker alone continue to flourish. Pawnbroker S. Gripe, smartly peruked, enjoys a healthy trade in one of the few buildings still standing.[14] His attention remains fixed on the goods offered up, oblivious to the disruption around him. As collateral, the scene implies, the possessions of the desperately poor will fund a few more gin binges. Hogarth's prints incisively critiqued the government's policies favoring manufacturers of cheap gin and exposed the harm it did to the populace.[15] The works also condemned the trades that apparently profited from societal decline and dislocation—the ones that made people drunk, took their things, then buried the owners.

To Americans, London seemed like both a cosmopolitan city that provided a steady stream of new goods and ideas and also a harbinger of evils that might visit themselves upon the new nation. Hogarth's prints, Colquhoun's writings, and other reports from across the Atlantic were warnings. Expressing this creeping anxiety was, for example, a broadside printed in Philadelphia in 1772 supporting public auctions (a contentious issue at the time), which noted that giving people the opportunity to purchase goods cheaply at auctions would keep out the "evils" of pawnbroking. Taxing or abolishing auctions, on the other hand, "will probably introduce Pawn-Brokers, as in London."[16] Although organized pawnbroking would not appear in America until the early nineteenth century, it was already a business people were wary of, representing yet another aspect of Old World urban life that Americans did not wish to import.

Certainly there were many worrying things about the industrializing of cities—overcrowding, crime, vice, and pollution among them. That pawnbrokers might also flourish with industrial expansion was particularly vexing, especially because the morality of lending money at interest—usury—had been preoccupying philosophers, religious thinkers, and political economists for centuries. They tackled the issue from many perspectives, yet by the end of the eighteenth century, when professional pawnbrokers were more visible than ever before, there was still no consensus, or even agreement on whether usury actually existed and, if it did, whether it was to be governed by the laws of nature, religion, or economics. An early (and seemingly eccentric) take on usury was Aristotle's. He believed that money was "sterile"—that it could not reproduce. Therefore if borrowers were compelled to pay back more than they owed, lenders were acting against nature by creating money from money. According to Aristotle, money could rightly be put only to a higher purpose, something useful and productive. In other words, the generation and use of money was to be "subservient to household management" and not an end in itself.[17]

Religious thinkers, in contrast, preoccupied themselves not with the metaphysical nature of money but rather with its moral dimensions, and theological issues regarding usury have been particularly contentious. For example, scholars disagree about whether the Bible deems all usury sinful or whether it provides an exemption in the case of Jews lending to non-Jews.[18] The most often quoted verses appear in Deuteronomy:

> Deuteronomy 23:19–20. Thou shalt not lend upon usury [*neshek* (interest)] to thy brother [*l'ahika*]; usury of money, usury of victuals, usury of anything that is lent upon usury. Unto a stranger [*nokri*] thou mayest lend upon usury; but unto thy brother thou shalt not lend upon usury, that the Lord thy God may bless thee in all thou settest thine hand to in the land whither thou goest to possess it.

Jews, then, were prohibited from charging each other interest, but they could charge outsiders. (This "double-edged sword," as Benjamin Nelson referred to it in *The Idea of Usury*, resulted in Christians and Jews operating under parallel, independent economic and religious systems governed by separate laws.) Others have argued that if usury was always a sin, God would have proscribed it altogether rather than providing loopholes. According to the Bible, usury was permissible not only when Jews were charging gentiles, but also when borrowers were not destitute:

> Exodus 22:25. If thou lend money to any of my people with thee that is poor, thou shalt not be to him as a creditor; neither shall you lay upon him usury.

> Leviticus 25:35–37. And if thy brother be waxen poor . . . take thou no usury of him, or increase: but fear thy God; that thy brother may live with thee. Thou shalt not give him thy money upon usury, nor give him thy victuals for increase.

Tribal law and universal law therefore remained in conflict: Were usurers sinners, outsiders, or both?

The clergy weighed in as well, such as the Reverend Henry Smith, who delivered a sermon against usury to Londoners in the mid-eighteenth century. The sermon proved so popular that it was reprinted in the Colonies. His definition of usury was capacious: usury was not simply charging simple interest on loans (though it was that too). Using a borrower's assets (such as land, ships, and livestock) until he repaid the loan also qualified as usury. Making collateral loans of any sort that deprived the borrower of the use of his possessions was usury. And charging more for goods bought on credit than for cash counted as usury. Smith's vision of this particular sin was fully formed: he saw the hand of the devil at work in people he considered usurers, who "lurk about the City like Rats and We[a]sels."[19]

Smith articulated the creeping anxieties that attended moneylending. All the myriad problems besetting the early modern city, Smith insisted, stemmed from usury: "Usury is a Kind of Cruelty, and a Kind of Extortion, and a Kind of Persecution. . . . if there were Love, there would be no Usury, no Deceit, no Extortion, no Slandering, no Revenging, no Oppression."[20] Christians living in the ever-changing eighteenth-century world drew on religious doctrine to reconcile morality and money, good citizenship and good business.

Economic theorists had a different perspective, looking not to the musty past of biblical pronouncements but to the bright future of prosperity made possible by robust entrepreneurship. These men debated how to harness the potential of expanding national and international trade and how to deftly negotiate an increasingly complex material and commercial world. Concerned about how rates of interest could best be managed to generate wealth and create widespread prosperity, they sought to unshackle market decisions from Deuteronomic law so people would feel free to pursue entrepreneurial endeavors and make as much money as they wished. To these economic theorists, concerns about usury, rooted in the past, were nuisances that thwarted economic and social progress. Religion—quaint and largely irrelevant to commerce—could not and should not stand in the way of making money. Laws of the marketplace increasingly trumped biblical law.[21] Depending on how one looked at it, profiting from someone else's need by charging interest might be sinful and unjust. But loans at interest rates determined by the market might also enable unfettered economic growth by encouraging entrepreneurs to take more risks with their own money, lending it to others who themselves were inspired to embark on expansive (if expensive) commercial ventures.[22]

Scottish Enlightenment thinkers—John Locke, David Hume, and Adam Smith among them—introduced modern economic theory to the Anglo-American world. For them, religious and moral law did not govern market forces. Optimal rates of interest, not whether loans at interest should be extended at all, remained their central focus. Interest rates, economic theorists realized, could be manipulated according to the needs of the market. Loans at low interest rates, for instance, might encourage the circulation of money and contribute to overall economic health and prosperity, "the surest sign of the flourishing state of the country's trade."[23] In his seminal *Wealth of Nations*, first published in 1776, Adam Smith advised reasonable caps on interest rates, slightly above prevailing market rates (between 3% and 5% in Great Britain in the last decades of the eighteenth century) so that men of capital, the "sober people," would be financially motivated to "venture into the competition." Yet interest rates, if left unregulated, might ensnare the foolish, the "prodigals and projectors" willing to pay such exorbitant rates.[24]

In contrast, Jeremy Bentham asserted that a truly free market should not place any limits on interest; in such a market usury as such would no longer exist, because any interest rate would be legal. Like everyone else, Adam Smith's "prodigals and projectors" had the right to make their own decisions, argued Bentham, even if those decisions were ill-advised and ultimately self-destructive. Free enterprise meant "the *liberty of making one's own terms in money-bargains.*"[25] People's visceral responses, their "imaginations and passions," rather than rational thought caused them to condemn usury, to believe that "usury is a bad thing . . . usurers are a bad sort of men, a very bad sort of men, and as such ought to be punished and suppressed."[26]

Bentham was on to something: popular beliefs about usury generally and usurers specifically (who were often personified as pawnbrokers) were grounded in emotion, not reason. The public viewed economic issues from religious and moral perspectives, continuing to grapple with reconciling Christian principles of fairness and charity with the profit motives of commercial enterprise. These debates permeated American thought, whether brought over with Old World immigrants or broadcast on native soil through popular print. Although average Americans likely did not understand the finer religious and economic aspects of the ongoing debates, they knew in their hearts that usury was a bad thing. Even the accumulation of wealth by charging legal interest remained suspect, since it was a way of earning money without having to produce anything (shades of Aristotle's belief that it was unnatural for money to beget money). The public felt so strongly about usury, in fact, that as late as the 1830s the author John Bolles remarked that potential readers would probably not even lift the cover of his *Treatise on Usury and Usury Laws* because of lingering "prejudice and ill-will." Instead, he surmised that they preferred to remain uninformed and would "continue faithful to their ancient doubts, fears, and disbelief."[27]

Prevailing social and economic conditions did not change popular opinion about moneylending and moneymaking. For one thing, more and more immigrants were flocking to the major East Coast ports of Philadelphia, New York, Boston, and Baltimore in search of a better life. Yet these economies could not support the influx of people, who now in truth faced bleak prospects. The lives of laboring Americans were precarious and lacking in the most basic creature comforts. Their chances of moving up were slim. Many lived in "a perpetual cycle of subsistence migration."[28]

New immigrants and "native" Americans alike had to make their way in a country experiencing profound transformations. Territorial expansion, greater personal mobility, changing demographics owing to emigration and immigration, and extreme economic shifts were but a few of the factors creating a society in flux. Domestic manufacturers lobbied for protective tariffs so that entrepreneurs in the new nation could compete against their European rivals. Internal improvements such as roads, turnpikes, bridges, and canals connected formerly remote towns to each other and to bustling port cities. Peddlers tramped out into the hinterlands, selling goods supplied by urban wholesalers, linking city and country folk through shared material aspirations. The mechanisms of an industrial capitalist system were gearing up. And people tried to situate themselves within this shifting world by forming groups united by distinct ethnic, occupational, and religious affiliations while at the same time trying to weave themselves into the larger American fabric.

At this moment the character of commercial exchange was being transformed as well. Transactions once conducted by barter and credit among friends, neighbors, and fellow churchgoers were by necessity becoming more structured, since they more often took place among people who did not know each other, trust each other, or share ties created by mutual obligation. Many did not even speak the same language. When immigrants disembarked from their boats they searched for decent living quarters, then for work, then for money. Their capital often took the form of jewelry, linens, blankets, and silver. Needing cash, they looked not to friends and neighbors (who either had been left behind or were broke themselves) but for the familiar sign of the three balls, which by the 1820s appeared in advertisements and dangled over shop fronts in major American cities (fig. 1.4).

The economic gaps resulting from emergent capitalism created opportunity for some and brought deprivation for others. There is no denying that pawnbrokers, by now considered the same as usurers in the popular imagination, made their business from others' hardships (and in this sense can be considered the founders of the nation's poverty industry). Early on, it was men who dominated pawnbroking (later to be joined by surprising numbers of women), able to apply the skills they had developed as traders and brokers to the lending profession in particular. They situated their shops where their likeliest clientele lived and worked—the poorer sections of expanding cities. To survive, pawnbrokers required a steady pool of customers who belonged to the hordes of working poor: people who needed cash loans, who had some personal property of value to put up as collateral, and who would eventually earn enough money to get their belongings out of hock. (Pawnbrokers profited much more from redemption than from resale of collateral.) Luckily for them, expanding industrial capitalism provided these ready customers.

Opportunistic businessmen, pawnbrokers followed nineteenth-century

FIGURE 1.4. Advertisement for Stephen Blatchford's County Money Office, Philadelphia, showing the pawnbroker's sign of the three balls. *Desilver's Philadelphia City Directory and Stranger's Guide, for 1828* (Philadelphia: Robert Desilver, 1828), front matter. Library Company of Philadelphia.

westward expansion, setting up outposts in frontier towns. They made money primarily—but not solely—from the underclass in younger cities such as Pittsburgh, Cleveland, Cincinnati, and Chicago. Like a leading economic indicator, the rootedness of pawnbrokers in a particular area signaled the relative maturation of capitalism there. Without consumer goods and a sizable population of needy people to patronize them, there could be no pawnbrokers. Places with successful pawnshops were those experiencing significant shifts from artisan to factory labor, the erection of larger production facilities, deskilled, underpaid workers, labor cycles following commercial rather than natural seasons, and pools of the unemployed ready to enter the workforce.

Pawnbrokers had much in common with their customers, struggling through times of economic uncertainty, since they could not get paid if pawners had no money. And pawnbrokers were often treated as pariahs—working in a profession that profited neither from production nor from consumption.[29] Primarily

Jews who were barred from many other professions, pawnbrokers found that their experience in other fringe economies, selling used clothing, furniture, and jewelry, could be put to use in the more lucrative pawnbroking business, and so they sought opportunities in the promising milieus of emerging industrial cities. Because Jews were often unable to join the credit networks enjoyed by the cadre of elite Anglo-American merchants, they banded together, developing alliances with other Jewish families to provide some social and economic stability in an otherwise unfriendly environment.

Prejudice against Jews resounded beyond the business community, pervading popular culture. Comparisons to Shakespeare's Shylock dogged Jewish entrepreneurs, especially the moneylenders and pawnbrokers. As the decades of the nineteenth century passed, anti-Semitic stereotypes became more widely applied, more strident, more concrete, and more freely expressed. Critics accused pawnbrokers of contributing to crime and vice by taking in stolen goods and providing local drunkards with the cash for another round of drinks, both long-standing charges. Political cartoonist Edward Clay was certainly channeling William Hogarth's "Gin Lane" when he drew the political cartoon "The Times," a scathing commentary on life in the United States in 1837, the year of the worst financial crash to date (fig. 1.5).[30] Like Hogarth, Clay observed the toll poverty took on ordinary citizens. In his world, the unemployed loiter on the streets, idle, drunk, and desperate. But three businesses continue to do well: Peter Pillage's law office, S. Rumbottle's liquor store, and the pawnshop overseen by Shylock Graspall.[31] The bad reputation of pawnbrokers in particular and the negative reaction to Jews in general reinforced each other, confirming many Americans' anxieties and fears.

Reformers and critics saw what they wanted to see and interpreted pawning in ways that suited their own interests, whether to claim racial superiority, to excoriate the poor for being lazy and profligate, or to advocate temperance as a form of social control. Pawners themselves were rarely asked about their standards of living or their wants and needs, thus enabling critics to indulge their bourgeois prejudices and preoccupations. To pawners, the pawnbroker was a temporary fixer who could ease short-term financial problems. Often members of the underclass for whom eviction and hunger were chronic worries, pawners had few alternatives to the local pawnshop. Until the late nineteenth century, Americans established no other institutions that loaned money to the poor, not even savings banks. The pawner's story is that of the average American living and working during the nineteenth and early twentieth centuries, when it was often impossible to make ends meet without putting something in hock. Within an economic system that promised economic opportunity for all (in exchange for hard work

FIGURE 1.5. Detail. Edward Clay, "The Times" (New York: H. R. Robinson, 1837). Lithograph. Library Company of Philadelphia.

and clean living), having so many pawners and pawnshops belied the myth of Horatio Alger and his uplifting bootstraps.

The pawns themselves, from the humble cotton handkerchief to the flashy diamond breastpin, were also important actors in the story, speaking volumes about the uncertain place of goods in the emerging American consumer culture. Meanings collided. Sentimental value could not be quantified, bartered with, haggled over, or negotiated. To the perpetual vexation of cultural commentators, no matter how personally significant an item was, if it lacked market (resale) value, a pawnbroker would not lend money on it. Outsiders judged a pawnbroker's business-mindedness as hard-heartedness motivated by greed. Based purely on margins of profit and loss, however, his lending practices would have been deemed justifiable if carried out by "legitimate" entrepreneurs.

The lasting utility of pawnbroking throughout the century remained a perennial concern of those who did not need collateral loans. For one thing, critics of pawnbroking remained uneasy about what members of the underclass would do if allowed ready access to cash, having little faith that they would spend it responsibly. For another, critics feared pawnbrokers' role in providing that money, a position that empowered them economically and enabled them to empower their customers by giving them a degree of financial agency. Who was worthy of receiving credit was one issue. Who was worthy of extending credit was another.[32]

By the end of the nineteenth century many notable entrepreneurs, some of whom had decried pawnbroking in the past, had changed their minds, realizing its profit potential. There was certainly something to be said for an enterprise that not only continued to survive within a turbulent economy but also made inroads in newly established areas of the country. The nonprofit monts-de-piété that had been so successful throughout most of Europe for more than a century provided a template for late-century American philanthropists who established their own semiphilanthropic shops and thus "domesticated" pawnbroking, as they had gambling and stock speculation during this same era.[33] Capitalized by the industrial magnates of the Gilded Age and operated "on a business basis," pawnshops were sanitized and cleansed of their tawdry associations—stripped of the three balls and referred to as "loan societies." Thus did Cornelius Vanderbilt, J. P. Morgan, and others become pawnbrokers of a sort.

Pawnbrokers who ran their own shops were much like other businessmen. Some were honest and others were not. Some loaned to regular clients on favorable terms in certain circumstances, advancing money on collateral of little value, extending the duration of a loan, or freezing interest charges. Others exploited their customers by lending at usurious rates and tacking on extra fees. Some pawnbrokers actively cooperated with police to help recover stolen items and return them to their owners. Others worked as fences, funneling stolen goods through their shops and back onto the market.

For many reasons, justified and not, pawnbrokers have been looked on with suspicion and scorn. This prejudice is experienced by few other professionals. Tracing the formative years of pawnbroking in America and exploring the biases against the institution helps us see how people of all classes came to embrace the emerging capitalist ethos, despite its inherent inequities. Through the exigencies of industrialization and the resulting concentration of wealth in fewer hands, capitalism created a perpetual underclass and with it the need for small loans. Those who stood to benefit the most from capitalism necessarily demonized pawnbroking, characterizing pawning as "marginal," pawners as profligate spendthrifts, and pawnbrokers as avaricious profiteers.

Pawning itself is, and always has been, a simple process. When I pawned my gold necklace I was engaging in a form of borrowing that is centuries old;

the basic principles have not changed much over time. By pulling back and examining the wider scope of pawning, we can see that its rich tradition has been particularly conflicted in America, the mythical land of opportunity and wealth. Rather than charting a course for upward mobility through hard work, many Americans—possibly a majority—found themselves patrons of their local pawnshop, a place far away from the American dream. And rather than using their possessions to make life more comfortable, people found themselves drawing on their property—reserves of capital—to secure loans to purchase basic necessities and cover pressing expenses: food, rent, and medical bills. Pawnshops offered the elasticity people needed in a market society that was becoming increasingly inflexible.

Industrial capitalism begat wealth and poverty, winners and losers. It remained in the winners' collective self-interest to create consensus among the larger public that capitalism was good for all of society, that wholesale and retail exchange were the "normal" and "mainstream" ways of doing business, and that this particular economic system was the only one befitting a modern, civilized nation. By its continued existence, however, pawnbroking demonstrated quite clearly that the promise of capitalism was broken for countless Americans. The true character of emergent industrial capitalism can be found beyond the shiny surfaces of retail show windows and the smooth pages of ledgers, revealing life as it was actually lived by most Americans, not simply the privileged few.

Tellingly, pawning remained a popular coping strategy throughout the nineteenth century, from the very dawn of capitalism through the second Industrial Revolution. The endurance of pawnbroking through radical economic shifts and perennial boom and bust cycles was an indication both of its ability to adapt to changing times and, more important, of Americans' enduring need for such an institution. Regardless of the rhetoric championing capitalism as a democratizing force, it created the inequities that led pawners to their local pawnshops. Pawnbroking could not have survived without the continued expansion of capitalism. Yet at every turn pawners, pawnbrokers, and the institution of pawnbroking were denigrated and demonized. Why was this so? Counting the great number who put things in hock makes it evident that there were many more losers than winners. What did it say about capitalism that it generated so many pawners? The symbiosis of pawning and capitalism warrants further examination if we are to fully understand the living and working lives of those who came before us and comprehend the economic exigencies of the people who continue to struggle today.

CHAPTER TWO

THE "JEW BROKER" IN AMERICAN CULTURE

What we know about pawnbrokers comes primarily from popular culture. Television crime dramas show them fencing stolen goods. Newspaper and magazine articles describe how they thrive in floundering economies. And movies portray them as callous and detached, perhaps no more famously than in Sidney Lumet's screen adaptation of Edward Lewis Wallant's 1961 novel *The Pawnbroker*.

Although delivered through modern media, these stereotypes are part of a much longer tradition. As early as the 1760s—long before there were professional pawnbrokers in the country—Americans were presented with broad characterizations of them, typically elaborations on Shakespeare's Shylock. Tracing the origins and development of the pawnbroker's stereotypical qualities, however distorted, is essential to understanding the particular and paradoxical role they played within emerging industrial capitalism. Pawnbrokers were at once necessary to the continued well-being of this economic system and important scapegoats for the various social ills that attended the financial difficulties it brought. Loans from pawnshops supplemented substandard wages, enabling workers to continue to feed their families and producers to continue to exploit their workers. Although capitalists indirectly benefited from the services pawnbrokers provided, it was also in their interest to encourage the idea that pawnbrokers were fringe operators whose business had no place in the "mainstream" economic system. Depicting pawnbroking as aberrant and marginal made wholesale and retail exchange seem "normal" by comparison. So entrenched are stereotypes about pawnbrokers that we continue to internalize them. Even a seasoned historian who had never encountered a pawnbroker once asked me why I wanted to write a book about "those scumbags." Today's "scumbags" descended from pawnbrokers formerly identified as "N. Pinch," "Shylock Graspall," and simply "the Jew broker."

In order to promote the benefits of capitalism to the general public, businessmen and cultural commentators demonized pawnbroking by portraying it again and again as anathema to the emerging capitalist system. Anti-Semitic characterizations figured largely in this endeavor, defining pawnbrokers as threatening foreigners who looked strange, spoke an alien, barely intelligible dialect, and adopted shady or illegal business practices such as usury and fencing. Their profits never came from hard work or entrepreneurship, unlike those of most wholesalers and retailers. Not only were they were supposedly hard-hearted and greedy, but they supported their customers' profligacy, intemperance, and criminal inclinations.

These stereotypes calcified over the long nineteenth century but started surfacing in America in the eighteenth, borrowed from English popular culture. Early print sources became the first references American readers could draw on regarding the character of the pawnbroker (unless, of course, they had been pawners in the Old World). Printers often included humorous squibs in their almanacs, newspapers, and ephemeral pamphlets, including deprecating pieces about pawnbrokers. For example, the London publication *Mother Midnight's Comical Pocket-Book,* reprinted in Boston in 1763 for a domestic readership, contained "My Pawnbroker's *Epitaph,* " which described the interred as

> A composition of deceit
> A thief—a lyar—and a cheat;
> Who ne'er was easy, but when doing
> Something to help poor peoples ruin;
> Such were the fruits of Holdfast's labour,
> To plunder, rob, and strip his neighbor;
> He'd let 'em pawn their cloaths and rings,
> And swear he never had such things;
> He'd sell their rings, he'd wear their cloaths
> Himself—or lend 'em out to beaux.[1]

Another "Epitaph on a Pawnbroker" appeared in a 1790 issue of the *New-York Daily Gazette:*

> BENEATH this stone the vile remains are lain,
> Of *Gripus Grasp all Pinch,* a rogue in grain,
> Whose studies center'd in the hoard of gain.

Of needy indigence, for sums he'd lent,
The usurer extorted cent. per cent.
Yet wealth beheld him stranger to content.

Death, in his journey passing by that way,
Took him and pawn'd him to Old Nick one day,
Where other scoundrels like bad pledges lay.[2]

These and similar space fillers were suggestive, and their themes continued to re-verberate over time. The pawnbroker cheated his customers by robbing them of their hard-earned property, appropriating others' possessions for his own use. He was innately greedy, his "hoard of gain" a compulsion. He was forever in search of more profit, merely as an end in itself. Readers could only hope that, as suggested in the third verse, pawnbrokers would get what was coming to them in the after-life, their souls pawned to the devil like so many pieces of worthless collateral.

On stage, Shylock appeared in Shakespeare's *Merchant of Venice,* undoubt-edly the most famous and notorious Jewish character. Premiering in America in 1752 in Williamsburg, Virginia, the play helped disseminate "significant cultural baggage" about European Jews to Americans up and down the East Coast, from Albany to Charleston.[3] Shylock could easily be seen as symbolizing all Jews as unprincipled and godless. Their blind devotion to money might even drive them to mutilate and murder their own.[4]

The unflattering depictions of Jewish moneylenders in popular culture were expressions of real and increasing anxieties about issues ranging from immigra-tion and class status to legitimate employment and the morality of profit mak-ing. In 1782 financier and one-time treasurer of the United States Robert Morris wrote to a friend about the unusually high interest rates charged on cash loans during the Revolution, referencing Jewish moneylenders. "Mortifying as it is," he wrote, "the Jew Brokers and others have informed me in the course of my inquiries that *Sub Rosa* they frequently get 5 per Cent per month from good Substantial men for the use of Money with pledges lodged for the repayment."[5] Morris's use of "Jew broker" was likely meant to be descriptive rather than pe-jorative.[6] The moneylenders he referred to, members of an elite group, helped Morris broker deals with the French to finance the war, since the fledgling na-tion had no resources of its own. They were respected for their connections and resources.

Yet Morris's view of the "Jew broker" as a respectable figure remained a minority opinion. Most Americans had no firsthand experience with Jews (there were only about five thousand in the country in the 1820s) and therefore impressions—"Jews-in-the-abstract"—came from caricatures imported from across the Atlantic.[7] Shylock was one referent. Physical characteristics, including facial features and clothing, which would be increasingly exaggerated, were another. Early cartoonists' signifiers for Jews included large, hooked noses, wide hands with open palms, and what would become their recognized symbol—the sign of the three balls.[8] As the eighteenth century moved to the nineteenth, and again as the nineteenth century turned to the twentieth, the pawnbroker emerged as a prominent figure whose popular characterization was reshaped and redeployed to suit contemporary needs, embodying prevailing concerns as they changed over time.

The pawnbroker became a cultural figure who conveniently embodied marginal status both socially and economically. He was portrayed as a Jew, a member of a religious minority. And he came with the European legacy of being engaged in a bad business. It was a gift to propagandists that each of these generalizations, like all stereotypes, had some basis in truth.

Depictions of pawnbrokers in popular culture, whether in fictional or supposedly nonfictional accounts, were as a rule anti-Semitic. In the first decades of the nineteenth century Americans accepted as fact that moneylending and usury were Jewish practices. In short order people conflated ethnic or religious affiliations with unscrupulous economic practices, thus forging conceptual links between Jews, usury, and pawnbroking that prevail even today. Nineteenth-century stereotypes painted the Irish as ignorant drunks, African Americans as lazy pilferers, and Jews as greedy connivers. This was a marked change from the respect Robert Morris gave to the "Jew brokers" he dealt with just a few decades earlier. Increasingly, a pawnbroker's Jewishness, real or perceived, determined the way he was portrayed and what he symbolized. To the nativists he was a foreigner taking money from hardworking Americans. To racists he was a strange-looking figure whose habits were alien, mysterious, and threatening. To social reformers he was both the supplier of money for alcohol that led people to intemperance and someone who took away people's cherished possessions. And to fellow businessmen he was a rival who tended to trade among his own kind (perhaps more profitably, too). Many Americans felt "ambivalence" toward Jews, whom they considered enterprising yet opportunistic. Jews could be seen as displaying "an admirable keenness and resourcefulness in business," yet "keenness might mean cunning; enterprise might shade into greed."[9]

Articulated as "questions" and "concerns," ideas about Jews remained relatively unformed at the beginning of the nineteenth century, although the specter of Shylock continued to influence people's general perceptions. "Queries respecting the Jews" frequently appeared in American magazines and newspapers.

The writers wondered who Jews were, where they came from, and what they did. The Jews living in America at the time were still so few—and concentrated in the urban areas of the East Coast—that their habits and general character (assuming there was such a thing) were still mysterious and inscrutable to the predominantly Christian populace. The population of the United States increased from 3.9 million to 9.6 million between 1789 and 1839. The Jewish subpopulation (still less than 1% of the total) grew even faster, from about 1,350 people in 1790 to 15,000 in 1840. Outside the major cities on the eastern seaboard, though, Jews remained "only dots in a Protestant landscape."[10]

Most people's experience with Jews was mediated through popular literature, folk culture, and religious teachings, creating a disconnect between common perceptions (often misconceptions) of Jews collectively and individually. There was the "mythical Jew," who was looked on with suspicion, and the "Jew who was known," who was well regarded.[11] Americans remained uncertain about which Jews they might encounter and whether to welcome or fear them.[12] In one instance a reader calling himself "Biblicus" asked the editor of the *Monthly Magazine, and American Review* in 1800 "to obtain information concerning several points in the history and present state of the Jews." He continued, "Every believer in [C]hristianity must look upon that people with peculiar respect and attachment, when he recollects how intimately their selection and separation from the rest of the world and their future prospects, are connected with the religion which he professes."[13] Other inquisitive readers wanted to know how many Jews currently lived in the world and where; if they had a governing body and if so, how it was structured; whether they still had distinct "tribes"; and if any lineal descendants of David were still alive. In a subsequent issue of the *Monthly Magazine,* "Querist" asked a most elemental question "of no small importance": "What is a Jew?" The self-described "rational Christian" answered his own question, disavowing Judaism altogether. "In embracing [C]hristianity, the rational man believes that he is fulfilling the law and the prophets, and is conforming strictly to the directions of Jehovah and his servant Moses. But admitting that the creed of a proper Jew must *exclude* a belief in Christ, that negative alone does not make a Jew."[14] If Jewishness was a matter of lineage, the writer reasoned, then "it is impossible to ascertain the genuineness of a Jew." He asked plaintively, "If an indefinite pedigree be not necessary to make a Jew, what number of generations must pass before he acquires all the penalties and privileges annexed to his people? Are they five, ten, fifteen, or twenty generations?" And finally, "Where is to be found the tree of any Jew's pedigree?"[15]

Jews' affiliation with pawnbroking and related trades, such as dealing in used clothes and auctioneering, created among them a cohesive, commercially defined group; yet it also reinscribed outsiders' perceptions that they operated beyond the currents of mainstream trade. In the second decade of the nineteenth century the public was still trying to determine whether the "Jewishness" of such businesses should be cause for concern. Take this exchange between two rival New York City newspapers from 1817. On August 25 the *New York Evening Post* published a brief court report:

> J. Sommers, a Jew Pawn-Broker, in Chatham-street, was convicted and fined on Friday last, one hundred dollars, at the suit of the Mayor and Corporation of the city of New-York, for having charged on goods pawned with him at the rate of about 65 per cent per annum, instead of seven as allowed by law.[16]

The next day the *National Advocate* reprinted the report, for two reasons:

> First, in order to inform our readers that an extortioner has been justly punished; and, secondly, to give them to know . . . that the offender *is not a Jew.* This is a new and unique mode of attempting to designate men by their *religious persuasion,* whether for criminal or political offences. . . . This system would be very apt and common in London, or in any part of that country which is so much the object of Mr. Coleman's admiration and *imitation;* but he may have yet to know, that in the United States, the Jew is his equal in rights, privileges, talents, and *almost* his equal, we may say, in *moral character!*[17]

The *New York Evening Post* responded the next day, claiming that the paper was not referring to Sommers's religion when using the Jew "epithet." It is used, the paper explained, "in common parlence, however improperly, as synonimous with extortioner." Before ending the discussion, the paper also pointed out this technicality: "In regard to the religion of Mr. Sommers, it is pretty evident from his unconscionable usury that he is not possessed of any. But he is nevertheless the son of Jewish parents, and though he may not belong to the synagogue, is, in point of fact as well as principle, entitled to the denomination which we bestowed upon him."[18] Both papers tried to argue the case on its merits—the *National Advocate* asserted that one's Jewishness was irrelevant, while the *Evening Post* countered that "Jew" was popularly understood to be a synonym for usurer and not necessarily indicative of religious affiliation.

It mattered little whether or not individual pawnbrokers were Jewish. Because they were all assumed to be, people scrutinized pawnbrokers' business practices and questioned their ethics. Other businessmen objected to Jews' opening their shops on Sunday, the Christian Sabbath. For example, a menacing notice placed in an 1828 issue of the *New York Flagellator* called out one such operator: "Had not a certain *little* Pawnbroker in Chatham-street, better make up his mind whether he is Jew or Christian, and not keep open house both days [Saturday and Sunday]? We shall expose him if he does not mend [his ways]."[19] Critics argued that doing business on Sunday, a holy day, was an affront to Christians and a transgression against the accepted rules of commerce. But concerns likely also arose because Jews could make money on days when Christian merchants could not. (Jewish proprietors opened their pawnshops at sundown on Saturdays and did brisk business well into the night.) Economic and cultural insecurities together fomented anti-Semitic sentiment. Any profits made by Jews, "the medieval symbol of Mammon," were characterized as ill-gotten gains, a charge that allowed merchants and manufacturers (who underscored their Christian principles) to deflect criticism from their own profitable yet exploitative business practices.[20]

Time and again people claimed to be tolerant and open-minded. Yet they resorted to epithets and stereotypes when addressing matters of profit and loss. For example, a writer in an 1841 issue of the *Sunday Flash* began, "We are friends to toleration . . . and we would put a Jew on the same footing with a Christian." Yet he objected to the prohibition against newsboys' selling papers on Sundays "while a swarm of blackguard, ugly Israelites" were allowed to sell used clothing the entire weekend. If the Board of Assistants allowed business to be conducted on Sundays, then "we intend to hire a host of little Hebrews to sell the Flash on Sunday, as it seems to be lawful for them to break the Christian Sabbath."[21]

Because Jews tended to enter financial and commercial professions rather than artisanal trades, people associated them with money. At times Jews' reputed financial acumen worked to their advantage. Throughout the United States Jews experienced some form of legal discrimination in the eighteenth and early nineteenth centuries, and in many states they were barred from voting, holding office, and practicing law. Yet the contribution of Jewish merchants and traders to Maryland's economy helped realize the passage of the "Jew Bill" in 1826, which accorded them basic suffrage. The state's need for revenue rather than religious tolerance spurred the decision, because "restricting the vote to Christians not only tended to place limits on those who might contribute to the state's wealth, but also provided a reason for some Jews to seek other abodes."[22] When there was more at stake, such as the welfare of an entire state (or the funding of a Revolution), then anti-Semitism receded.

The ability to make money—celebrated in such figures as the wealthy banker Stephen Girard—more often proved a liability for Jewish businessmen, who could not escape being seen as nineteenth-century Shylocks, "vastly powerful, manipulative, corrupt, devious, cunning, greedy, tricky, materialistic, dishonest, shrewd, grasping, and close-fisted."[23] In addition, any economic success Jews enjoyed was assumed to have derived from crime. Commentators held up Christian merchants as exemplars of honesty and integrity. By that standard Jews (in opposition to Christians) could only be morally corrupt, and their commercial dealings must be highly suspect and unseemly. In 1846, for example, the *National Police Gazette* responded to criticism regarding an article titled "Crime among the Israelites." The *Gazette*'s editor admitted that the piece was "calculated to reflect improperly upon the general character of the Israelites of this city." He continued, "A different impression has been created by those who are not close observers, from the fact that in almost every instance where an Israelite has been arrested for an offence, it is noted in the police reports of our city press, as having been committed by a 'Jew,'" while the religion of other accused criminals was "rarely if ever given."[24]

Other supposedly reliable and objective sources reinforced these stereotypes, replacing the image of "the Sephardic merchant princes" with shabby and semi-literate German peddlers "as the prototypical American Jews," who were by association also "usurious villain[s]."[25] For example, Ben Israel Tchuda, the titular character of a supposedly nonfiction piece published in 1855, "The Jew-Broker of Damascus," loaned "large sums to the needy, at extravagant rates of interest. With an expression of candor and sympathy for those who were unfortunate," the article explained, "it was notorious, that he ground the faces of the poor without mercy."[26] Echoing this was a passage in Edwin Freedley's highly popular midcentury advice book for striving young professionals, *A Practical Treatise on Business.* Freedley proposed a commercial taxonomy with itinerant peddlers at the bottom and eminent men engaged in international commerce at the top. Merchants, he declared, could be "reduced to one denomination—*men who live by buying and selling.*" Moneylenders, however, inhabited a different category altogether, illustrated by the "Israelitish woman who sits behind a bench in her stall on the Rialto at Venice, changing gold into silver and copper, or loaning money to him who leaves hat, coat, and other *collaterals,*" and the "Israelitish man who sits at Frankfort-on-the-Maine," lending "millions to men who leave in pledge a mortgage on the States of the Church, on Austria, or Russia."[27] Unlike the moneylenders, who were identified by their religion and nationality, the "denomination" of merchants was defined solely by their entrepreneurial endeavors.

No matter what their specific profession, all businessmen intended to make money. "The nation's commerce is the merchant's trade, the merchant's trade is the farmer's barter—the farmer's barter is the jockey's swap—the jockey's swap is the usuer's exchange—the usuer's exchange is the foreigner's wrap, and so on. . . . The grand object is MONEY," according to the *New England Artisan* in 1833.[28] Even so, the tenacious double standard celebrated and honored the commercial exploits of "mainstream" wholesale and retail merchants while sharply criticizing pawnbrokers' business practices. Unlike pawnbrokers' gains, which allegedly came from usury, wholesalers' and retailers' profits were considered reasonable, justified, and essential to the continued success of the nation. Pawnbroker Abraham Laban, a fictional character in an 1855 novel, explained the double standard to one of his customers: "The merchants denounce us for charging four per cent. a month for our money, when they design to realize eight per cent. on it, and sometimes succeed." He continued, "With fifty thousand dollars, they sell to the amount of half-a-million. If they get ten per cent. profit on their sales, they receive eight per cent. per month on the capital invested. And yet they curse us, call us usurers, and pass laws to prevent us, if possible . . . from reaping more than six per cent. from *our* investments!"[29]

Presumably most businessmen were not inclined to detail their religious lives in their memoirs, since religion had no bearing on their economic success. Yet William Simpson, in his autobiography about life as a member of a prominent New York City pawnbroking family, took pains to correct any assumptions that his family was Jewish. The book's very first pages boast that the Simpson family "set new and rigid ethical standards for a profession that has never been praised for its integrity or its charity."[30] Simpson's book traced the family's lineage from a long line of Englishmen who were "gentile" and "Protestant."[31] The obituary of Robert Simpson, another member of the famous pawnbroking clan, described him as a former member of Trinity Church who had more recently attended Saint Andrew's Protestant Episcopal Church. Yet an article from the 1860s on the Simpsons' pawnshop presumed the proprietor's ethnicity, describing him as a "Hebraic chief" overseeing a staff of "young Shylocks" and "Israelitish clerks." The writer even gave Simpson the stereotypical German-Jewish dialect: "I gifs you only vifeen tollar on dat vatch."[32] Even gentile pawnbrokers were Jewish in the popular imagination.

Pawnbrokers were aliens in a commercial world populated by supposedly moral and upright Christian entrepreneurs, and the very nature of the business set it apart from "normal" economic dealings. The antithesis of merchants, pawnbrokers doled out money instead of taking it in, profiting from customers who lacked capital rather than possessed it. "His customers are not to be wheedled, coaxed, grinned at, protested to," noted nineteenth-century writer Douglas Jerrold, who elaborated, "No; *his* customers—the people who contribute to him thirty per cent.—for the most part address him with a respectful meekness; many with a shame-faced hesitation."[33] The ideal retail customer cared about fashion and purchased the latest goods to display status. Pawners, however, were "branded with the mark of necessity," and therefore pawnbrokers could practice "the usual uncourteous behavior" with their customers.[34] To observers, pawnbroking confounded the familiar relationship between customers and proprietors (or their surrogates, the clerks). Before the widespread appearance of fixed-price shops that charged everyone the same amount, customers negotiated what they would pay, and many factors determined an item's ultimate cost. Although one could get a better price by paying cash, consumers more often bought goods on credit. One's ability to obtain a line of store credit in turn depended on many things, including reputation and personal comportment—both considered accurate barometers of solvency. Flirting with the employees also helped with negotiations; conversely, difficult and overbearing customers who got on a clerk's bad side received few favors.

The purchases customers made in retail shops were optimistic in nature. They were also embodiments of their labor, the tangible rewards earned from an honest day's work. Fabric might become a suit of clothes. Food would be prepared for a nourishing meal. A trinket could become a status symbol and a keepsake to be handed down in the family. Inside pawnshops, by contrast, pawners dispossessed themselves of the things they had worked hard to own, an aberrant act when the marketplace privileged consumption. Items that were once indicators of hope, economic vitality, and physical comfort became, as collateral, markers of a downward fall, loss of prospects, alienation. Critics looking at the process from outside saw the antithesis of capitalism at work in both the pawns and pawning. A woman "presents a small trinket to the pawnbroker: how different the money-lender's manner from the oppressive obsequiousness of the jeweller who, five years since, sold the locket to her!"[35]

Authors of popular fiction amplified emerging anti-Semitic sentiment through their work, which reached broader audiences than did business literature. Pieces of fiction were serialized in the newspapers and in the magazines delivered to readers' doorsteps and hawked on street corners; they were also published as cheap soft-bound volumes that crowded booksellers' shelves and filled the packs of itinerant peddlers. As pawnshops became familiar fixtures in most American cities by the 1830s and 1840s, pawnbrokers became important stock characters in this popular fiction, figures onto which authors projected prevailing cultural anxieties.

Two related literary genres, the urban novel and the more factually based urban sketch, peeled back the veneer of respectability from modern American life, revealing the city's gritty recesses for genteel readers' prurient appetites. A successful series of urban sketches was written by George Foster, who spent his career primarily as a newspaper reporter and wrote for such publications as the *New York Tribune* and the *Philadelphia Sun*. His books ("a curious mixture of indictment and celebration"), *New York in Slices* (1849), *New York by Gas-Light*

(1850), and *New York Naked* (ca. 1854), were devoted to the greatest American city.[36] In *New York in Slices* the author both cautioned and promised his readers that life in the Five Points area would shock even "the practised eyes and hardened olfactories of a veteran New-Yorker." He described the area as "the great central ulcer of wretchedness—the very rotting Skeleton of Civilization, whence emanates an inexhaustible pestilence that spreads its poisonous influence through every vein and artery of the whole social system, and supplies every heart-throb of metropolitan life with a pulse of despair."[37]

The city's collective despair in fact captivated American novelists and their readers alike. Urban America supplied plenty of material—anguish, poverty, crime—that rivaled Dickens's London. New York City, for one, was "illuminated by a sickly lamp, while the street begins to fill with rowdies, negroes, drunken sailors, pick-pockets, burglars, and vagabonds of every description . . . [and] an intolerable stench of brandy, tobacco, and steaming carcasses, meets us."[38] The squalor of the American metropolis was now on par with that of major European cities and proof of the country's maturation. Foster and his peers celebrated the city as they inventoried its many indignities, obscenities, and depravities.

Seedy business establishments, characters in their own right, filled the pages of popular fiction and included such gray market enterprises as mock auction houses, gambling dens, oyster saloons, and gin shops. Pawnshops also frequently appeared. In a typical passage from *New York in Slices,* Foster wrote, "We don't know a much more melancholy thing than to ramble through one of the extensive pawnbroking establishments in Chatham-street or the Bowery, crammed with their inconceivable variety of articles of use and luxury. . . . each group tell[s] its own little domestic or personal romance."[39] From the frying pans and diamond rings he spotted in pawnshop windows Foster distilled tales of poverty and woe, adultery and debt. The pawnshop's evocative contents, including andirons and wicker baskets, constituted a digest of mid-nineteenth-century markers of financial success turned to failure.[40] He invited his comfortably middle-class readers to imagine the paths of ruin and degradation that led owners, clutching their possessions, through the pawnshop's doors. Similarly, the pawnshop in the anonymous 1855 novel *Estelle Grant* is "literally crammed with parcels each one of which contains a lamentable history of its own." The biography of a pawn was limited only by one's imagination and could have been "the rich dress of the flaunting frail one," "the starving mechanic's toolbox," "the failing courtezan's jewels," or "the unfortunate drunkard's last shirt."[41]

Pawnshops especially captivated readers whose lives, economically and geographically, were far removed from the teeming masses that comprised the pawners in most antebellum East Coast cities. Author and poet Eliza Cook's article

"Obscure City Life," for example, appeared in an 1852 issue of the Cincinnati woman's magazine the *Ladies' Repository*. Edited by Methodist ministers and reaching a circulation of 40,000, the magazine was intended to offer midwestern readers a "less worldly" alternative to *Godey's Lady's Book*, containing "sober, earnest," moral pieces of poetry and prose.[42] Although purportedly less cosmopolitan than *Godey's* and other similar publications, the *Repository* did not shy away from bringing tales of big city life westward for its readers' vicarious experience. Descriptions of the "lowly denizens" lurking in the city's "back streets" constituted armchair slumming for nineteenth-century readers living hundreds of miles away.

Eliza Cook offered observations from peering into a family's front window, revealing intimate scenes of urban life to thousands of avid readers. Acting as omniscient observer, Cook savored the "squalid and gloomy" lives of the people she saw and told of a "sickening display of varied poverty [that] exists in every thing there exhibited."[43] An essential stop on Cook's tawdry city tour was the pawnshop, infused with "desperate despair" and "sullen depravity." Each pawn, she insisted, embodied a tragic story. From her perspective, nothing was pawned by choice, and all pawners lacked agency. Who could help seeing herself in the pawned tea service that "could tell a tale of 'better days,' when decent friends met on a birthnight, and when the plum-cake garnished the blue and gold plate"? One moment the family is enjoying "shrimp and water-cresses" served on fine Staffordshire decorated with "fairy birds and Eden flowers." The next, the father has fallen ill and lost his job. The mother pawns a succession of prized possessions: the tea service, a sable gown, a ring. Pawns from another household fall victim to a son's errant ways. Having "become a dissolute idler, and step by step declined into the abyss of vice," he has pawned an inscribed Bible and a monogrammed silk handkerchief, both gifts from his mother.[44] Cook's lesson to readers was clear. Rather than being an integral part of a family's domestic economy—something they relied on to get them through the week—pawnshop transactions were part of a downward spiral leading ultimately to despair and death. In these accounts, neither pawns nor their owners were redeemed.

Pawnbrokers oversaw these dismal places, and the evil pawnbroker, almost always Jewish, appeared as a stock character in many popular novels. The short story "Cousin Fanny" appearing in *Graham's Magazine* in 1849 is one example. Having pawned everything else, Cousin Fanny had only her most precious possessions left—two masterfully hand-painted miniature portraits of her father and mother. She had forfeited the gold locket that encased them long ago but hoped to get something for the pictures, which were "worth at least one hundred dollars each, and infinitely precious to her." But the pawnbroker, a "hard, money-getting son of Israel," was inured to his customers' suffering. Seeing indigence day in and day out—"having look[ed] on misery three hundred and thirteen times in the year"—made the man callous and unfeeling. Predictably, he declared Fanny's precious miniatures to be worthless and wished her away. Only when she coughed up blood (which might stain the shop floor) did the pawnbroker reappraise the items, lending her four dollars on the portraits he knew to be "of much value" but a risky investment nonetheless: "Yes, pawnbroker and Jew that he was, he pitied her."[45]

Authors frequently characterized pawnbroking as a profession well suited to the Jews, for whom, according to the common stereotype, such distasteful work seemed fitting. "Most of the pawnbrokers are foreigners," observed one newspaper article, "chiefly Jews." "The fact that but few native American citizens are willing to engage in such a calling, is honorable to the character of our countrymen."[46] Commentators set up Jewish pawnbrokers as straw men: depicting them as bloodthirsty and rapacious profiteers made capitalists such as bankers, dry goods merchants, and retailers seem perfectly moral and reasonable. They did not have to justify their own financial pursuits—not being Jewish was defense enough.

Authors and publishers realized that the American audience wanted to read about lurid subjects; and with the explosion of book publishing and the increasing presence of pawnshops in the urban landscape, popular fiction more often featured pawnbrokers and pawnshops. Capitalizing on the sensational nature of the business in order to sell more copies, the promotional material for the 1849 fictional work *The Three Golden Balls, or The Diary of a Pawnbroker,* provides a case in point:

> THIS WORK presents a glowing picture of that epitome of human suffering and misery—the pawnbroker's office! What a view of life it unfolds! Crime, dissipation, folly, and too often unmerited destitution, meet at the pawnbroker's counter. The high and the low, the virtuous and the depraved, are alike the subjects of the cold, heartless, cent per cent usurer; who weighs with equal indifference the cherished token of affection which want wrings from the reluctant hand of suffering virtue, and the ill-got prize which successful villainy presents, and doles out his ducats with miserly hesitancy! Such are the scenes which, with the hand of a master, are portrayed here; and we venture the assertion, that it will be found a work of deep and intense interest.[47]

The advertisement appeared in diverse publications including *Godey's Lady's Book*—the mainstream periodical for well-heeled women, and the *Monthly Cosmopolite,* one of the many New York City rags published for the "sporting" crowd

FIGURE 2.1. (*left*) Advertisement for *The Three Golden Balls, or The Diary of a Pawnbroker, Monthly Cosmopolite* 4, 13 (April 1, 1850). Courtesy, American Antiquarian Society.

FIGURE 2.2. (*right*) Frontispiece, *The Three Golden Balls, or The Diary of a Pawnbroker* (New York: H. Long and Brother, 1849). Rare Book and Manuscript Library, University of Pennsylvania.

(young men who dedicated their leisure time to gambling, womanizing, and carousing). One version of the ad featured an illustration of the pawnbroker sitting behind his counter, scales at the ready, facing a downtrodden woman (fig. 2.1).

The promotional blurb, however, sensationally misrepresented the book's content, which was actually a collection of dull, unrelated anecdotes. And the narrator was not even a pawnbroker by trade but a lawyer who had inherited the business from his father (himself a lawyer who had acquired the shop from a client as payment). The book's frontispiece, titled "The Pawnbroker at Home"—shows an upstanding businessman with all the trappings of the genteel: he sits in his study, quill pen in hand, surrounded by book-lined shelves and a marble bust (fig. 2.2)—a far cry from the advertisement showing a curly-haired, hook-nosed man behind a counter. Clearly, publishers recognized that the reading public would be grabbed by the promise of lurid content about Jewish pawnbrokers exploiting vulnerable women (and getting their just deserts in the end).

The Three Golden Balls had nothing on Emerson Bennett's *The Artist's Bride, or Pawnbroker's Heir* of 1856, which contained one of the most virulently anti-Semitic portrayals of a pawnbroker to date and fortified it with the popular scientific systems of physiognomy and phrenology. This was no minor work—Bennett was an extremely popular and prolific novelist who wrote more than fifty novels and serialized works in addition to hundreds of short stories during his career.[48] Now almost forgotten, Bennett enjoyed a loyal readership throughout his life; his most popular works, such as the frontier tale *The Prairie Flower* (1849), sold over 100,000 copies and were reprinted in several editions. Although one historian described Bennett's productions as filled with "pasteboard heroes and heroines and occasionally interesting minor characters [who] go through melodramatic routines against an authentic backdrop," nineteenth-century readers adored his writing.[49]

Like his other novels, Bennett's *Artist's Bride* appeared in many forms and saw a wide readership. It was serialized in the Philadelphia newspaper the *Sunday Mercury* in 1856 and published as a novel in New York that same year, with a subsequent edition coming out three years later. Bennett's main character, ninety-five-year-old pawnbroker Isaac Jacobs, "had the same parentage" as his shop. With a "long, cadaverous, and wrinkled face," "bloodless lips," and "great, green, cold, goggle eyes that seemed to see dollars in everything," Jacobs was "the personification of Avarice."[50] The intensity of his drive for money was matched only by his deep hatred of Christians. The main story line revolves around Jacobs's lifelong pursuit, "his monomaniac idea of revenge," to obliterate every family member descended from his sister Hagar, because she married a Christian.[51] By the end of the story, four people were dead on Jacobs's orders, and heroine Villeta Linden, the last of Hagar's descendants, had been abducted by Jacobs's criminal partner, a man whose father had murdered her father at the pawnbroker' behest.

Bennett's pawnbroker is utterly corrupt and hateful. Had his plans come to fruition, "the Jew would have the treble satisfaction of getting one more of his hated relatives out of the way—of seeing the family of the murdered man crushed and blasted by sorrow and disgrace—and of having the family of the murderer more directly in his power."[52] Jacobs's Jewish radicalism drove his homicidal tendencies. He was rabidly intolerant, going so far as to kill his own family members because they were products of intermarriage. Being a Jew, he was also impelled to kill out of greed, pure and simple. When authorities came to arrest Jacobs they found him "counting his money and congratulating himself."[53] Overcome with shock and fear, he died just as the police crashed through his door. The pawnbroker's antithesis, Villeta Linden, the Christian "dove," inherited all Jacobs's money and lived happily ever after by helping the poor.

A reviewer in *Godey's Lady's Book* acknowledged that Bennett's pawnbroker "is perhaps too strongly drawn" and that the "baseness" of his character "might probably have been applied with as much justice to brokers of other religious denominations, as to a professor of Judaism." The reviewer continued, "We do not, we confess, approve of the practice adhered to by many of our popular writers, of choosing their characters from sects of religion or sections of country and, after making them as odious as possible, leaving them to be viewed as fair representatives of classes or bodies of men."[54] Yet the magazine continued to carry advertisements for Bennett's new book, undoubtedly because copies continued to sell in great numbers.

By midcentury works of popular culture, especially those depicting pawnbrokers, had fairly well established anti-Semitic stereotypes in the public mind. The presumed Jewish identity of pawnbrokers had become so accepted, in fact, that even fictional characters remarked on it. Charles Parkinson, featured in a novel about the Panic of 1857, was pleasantly surprised when, venturing into a pawnshop for the first time, he saw that "behind the counter stood not a black-eyed, long-bearded, sharp-visaged Jew, *as my imagination had pictured*, but an intelligent, business-like looking individual."[55] The "Jew broker" embodied an extreme form of capitalism whose purpose was the worship of money above everything else, including God.

These figures appeared again and again. Solomon Moses Simpson, the main character in *Our Chatham Street Uncle*, is caretaker for his niece Naomi, the product of a mixed marriage of Christian father and Jewish mother. Her religion is a constant source of tension in the Simpson household. Pure and principled, Naomi lectures the family about their lack of faith and their greediness. She tries to convert her cousin Hagar to Christianity, and the young girl asks, "But the Jews refuse Christ, and you say we can only get to heaven through him. Will there be no Jews in heaven, Naomi?" "Yes, indeed," she replies, "God will give them a better mind."[56] A true Christian, she is surrounded by the corrupting, materialistic forces of Judaism. Uncle Solomon admits, "I cares only for piles monish."[57] Naomi snaps at her cousin, "Don't talk to me about Jews and Gentiles. You all worship money; and it makes you hard as iron."[58] No matter that Simpson was a religious man who "kept the feasts, sent his family to synagogue, lived on good terms with his rabbi, [and] sometimes thought the holy city would be restored," he nevertheless "worshipped 'piles monish' with all his soul."[59] In the end Solomon Moses Simpson met the hellish fate that was coming to him—his shop went up in flames, the "stealthy foe" with "a little darting angry tongue like a serpent enraged . . . hissing for a troop of brother-demons."[60] The fire destroyed pawnbroker and pawnshop both. Even on the verge of death Simpson continued to fret about "mein shops" and "mein monish," and "With the name of his idol, mammon, on his lips, our uncle ventured into eternity."[61]

Nineteenth-century stories reinforced the prevailing notion that pawnbrokers, and not the society they lived and worked in, conspired to create and profit from profound economic disparities and social isolation that Americans often faced. Just as urban areas were characters in these works, so too were the pawnshops themselves. Repositories of tens of thousands of personal objects no longer in their owners' possession, pawnshops symbolized the tenuous and severed links between the present and past, the new country and the old, deep personal relationships and an impersonal world. Sometimes authors gave objects the power to reunite long-lost relatives, a trope that appeared throughout the century. In the 1843 *Godey's* story "The Mourning Ring," for example, a ring passes through the hands of several people before reaching the pawnshop. It belongs to an old woman whose granddaughter, an impoverished seamstress, takes it to a jeweler for repair. She loses it on an omnibus. A good Samaritan finds it and returns it to the wrong person, thinking it belongs to a wealthy passenger. The rich woman's servant steals it from her and eventually pawns it. The poor seamstress's father— the only survivor of a shipwreck but for years presumed dead—recognizes the ring when he happens to pass by the pawnshop. He makes inquiries and eventually finds his way back to his mother and daughter. The object, a shared possession, embodied the protagonists' common lineage, linking them when all other lines of communication had failed. In its state as a piece of collateral, the ring symbolized alienation. Without the object to bring them together, the characters would have remained strangers.[62] Similar stories appeared in other publications.[63] The only thing that made them at all plausible was the pawnshop, which provided a reason for disparate objects and people to converge. The lost-and-found structure of these stories enabled authors to introduce characters who were members of the noble poor—hardworking children who were the only caretakers of sick and elderly relatives and were trying to make their way in harsh circumstances.

Highly exaggerated depictions of pawnbrokers, pawners, and pawns articulated the growing anxieties of American life as immigration delivered more people to the country's shores and transportation networks increased mobility. Cultural and economic concerns intensified as people wondered who these new people were and what role they were to play. Works of popular culture had largely succeeded in creating a coherent, seemingly logical stereotype: the pawnbroker had become implicitly the *Jewish* pawnbroker—the Jew broker—and as Jews and pawnbrokers became increasingly stigmatized, the stereotypes reinforced each other.[64] People coming from small, cohesive towns as part of flows of transnational and internal migration soon joined thousands of others. Strangers now living together as neighbors and housemates, the newly transplanted did not necessarily look alike, maintain similar habits and customs, or speak the same language. It was easy to blame these strangers for problems arising from substandard living conditions and insufficient wages. And Jewish pawnbrokers often found themselves convenient scapegoats.

Ideas promulgated through popular culture influenced people's daily interactions and thus functioned as powerful social forces. For example, anti-Semitic stereotypes found their way into formal credit reports, which came into use in 1841 as a response to the widespread economic anxieties that lingered in the aftermath of the Panic of 1837, a crash bankrupting even the most prudent businessmen. Face-to-face intercourse and recommendations from friends and acquaintances no longer proved one's creditworthiness. Credit reporters, members of a wholly new profession, took into account a person's business *and* personal life when calculating how likely he was to repay a debt. Sobriety and marital status counted as much as capital and assets. Ethnicity and religion were also determining factors. In a Jewish businessman a credit reporter saw not a savvy entrepreneur but another incarnation of Shylock. He was tribalistic. Greedy. Ruthless. Coldhearted. Scheming. And these characteristics, based on credit reporters' perceptions rather than their actual experiences, ran counter to the Jeffersonian ideal of the yeoman farmer-entrepreneur—the independent individual who by his own merits rises and succeeds, helping to solidify the economic foundation of the entire nation. Even when credit reporters deemed a Jewish enterprise sound by all objective measures, they qualified their analyses to fit preconceptions of "Jewish business," which remained shady and suspect. A typical comment was, "He is a Jew and although in point of fact he may now be perfectly responsible, yet Jews have a wonderful faculty of becoming at almost any moment they choose entirely irresponsible."[65]

"Proper" business dealings of eminent merchants took place according to an established etiquette, discreetly behind the doors of banks and countinghouses, and among like-minded entrepreneurs. The moneymaking of Jews was different—unseemly, crass, public. Transactions occurred in the full light of day, often on the sidewalk and within the used clothing shop, auction house, and pawnshop. You could see, hear, and (some people claimed) even smell Jews. An auctioneer was, "generally speaking, a black, curly headed Jew, with a moustache on his lip or an imperial on his chin."[66] So fully formed was the stereotype that Jewish dealers were even ascribed an odor: "We *smell* Limburger cheese, and *feel* on our arm the gentle pressure of the hand of Moses," claimed one observer.[67] Similarly, the home of pawnbroker Solomon Moses Simpson in Julia McNair

FIGURE 2.3. Jews at the opera as a row of noses. *New York Picayune* 7, 48 (November 15, 1856): 381. Courtesy, American Antiquarian Society.

Wright's *Our Chatham Street Uncle* smelled "extensively of onions, mackerel, and fried mutton."[68]

Nineteenth-century American popular culture established and normalized the archetype of the Jew as "half-comic, half-hideous, with red wig and grotesque false nose," drawing it more finely and precisely over time.[69] Oversized noses, massive hands, and fractured English differentiated Jews from "native" and presumably more refined Anglo-Americans whose looks and behavior were taken as the norm against which everyone else was measured. A newspaper article about the opening of an Italian opera in 1856, for example, showed Jews in attendance as a row of noses (fig. 2.3).[70] In John Beauchamp Jones's 1855 novel *The Winkles, or The Merry Monomaniacs*, son Walter Winkle takes his friend George Parke out slumming one night and decides it would be an amusing "lark" to visit the shop of Abraham Laban, the "Jew pawnbroker." As Walter casually explains, it's "for the fun of the thing. Great Nose knows me."[71]

Such sweeping stereotypes gained even more credence when promulgated using "scientific" methods. The systems of physiognomy and phrenology, purportedly objective ways of determining people's character from their appearance, were widely accepted at the time. Marshaling what were believed to be concrete, readily observable data comforted those who remained anxious about a changing society and were searching for a reliable way to assess the strangers living in their midst. Physiognomy, conveniently, posited that one's countenance could not help but express character traits. Once learned, the structure of facial features could be read like a text and their underlying meanings clearly understood. Myriad books, pamphlets, and public lectures disseminated information about the systems across the country. Luminaries and murderers alike were the subjects of physiognomic and phrenologic analyses; many people accepted the theories as grounded in fact.

It so happens that "acquisitiveness"—the desire to possess things—was the personality trait written on Jewish faces based on their prominent noses. In his *Outlines of a New System of Physiognomy* James Redfield asserted, "This faculty is indicated by the breadth of the nose just above the wing of the nostril. . . . The sign, if large, gives a broad arch, as we see in the face of the negro, and in that of the Jew."[72] Redfield confirmed his findings in another study that compared the physiognomy of animals and humans. Benjamin Franklin's double chin was a sure sign of his thrift. According to Redfield: "'Poor Richard,' who was remarkable alike for his economy and his economical sayings," was like the cow, who was also "very full under the chin, and is careful to pick up every straw that is thrown out with the dirt." Conversely, Jews were analogous to goats in both temperament and appearance. Noting that both goats and (Orthodox) Jews had beards, Redfield joked, "The profession of a barber finds no followers among the Jews. And yet the Jew is a notorious *shave*, or there is no truth in the common opinion."[73] Redfield asserted that the Jew "takes the whole or none; figuratively speaking, he 'grinds the faces of the poor.' This kind of business is very thoroughly done in a pawnbroker's establishment, and the Jews are the people to do it." He added, gratuitously, "The smell in a pawnbroker's store is sickening; it nearly resembles what the Spaniards call *aroma de bacallo*" (the smell of dried codfish).[74] Admiring a painting of Shylock on exhibit at the Philadelphia Art Union in 1849, a writer for *Godey's Lady's Book* commented that the work successfully captured the "angry menaces" of the character: "The head of Shylock, with its enormous frontal developments, its broad base and perverted moral powers, is in fearful phrenological accordance with the character."[75]

By the later decades of the nineteenth century the accretion of words and images in popular culture had created a fully formed stereotype of the "Jew broker," well in line with the solidification of capitalism. Other businessmen were not singled out by their ethnic and religious affiliations. The behavior of Jewish businessmen, however, was judged by a different standard, and their entrepreneurial spirit and drive to make a buck were almost always seen as exploitative, motivated by a desire for money above everything else. The economic exploits of other businessmen seemed downright beneficent by comparison.

Authors of popular fiction, who were particularly effective at reinscribing these ideas, cast the Jew broker as hard-hearted, greedy, uncaring. (Emerson Bennett's blisteringly anti-Semitic *Artist's Bride* even found a favorable new audience and was republished in both 1874 and 1875 under the title *Villeta Linden*.)

Business literature and other so-called factual pieces also revitalized centuries-old depictions of the grasping Hebrew moneylender. And the racist pronouncements of the phrenologists and physiognomists provided even laymen with the "objective" indicators they needed to prove that one's "acquisitive" drive was as plain as the noses on Jewish faces. Seen favorably, the goatlike stubbornness Redfield assigned to the Jew could also manifest itself as respect for tradition, objectivity, and dispassion. One phrenologist itemized these traits: "He is religious; he is fond of trade; he is thrifty; he is conscientious, in his way"—all laudable qualities for any businessman. But all praise was tempered and qualified when it came to the *Jewish* businessman, because "his ideas of right and wrong are based on the Law of Moses, and his justice does not always admit the modifying influences of mercy" that, implicitly, Christian merchants possessed.[76]

Caricatures of pawnbrokers and references to pawning appeared in many forms and were quickly assimilated into new media. People who did not read novels or consult manuals of business advice might see cartoons in newspapers; those who did not read newspapers might sing satirical verses printed on songsheets; those who did not sing might be handed a comic trade card on the street. By the mid-nineteenth century pawning had become such a familiar act that publishers assumed audiences would understand more obscure references to the three balls. For example, a cartoon from the time simultaneously lampooned genteel women's needlework and pawning, a curious juxtaposition. Published under the heading "Our Fashions and Fancy Work" was a pattern to make a pocket watch case that looked exactly like the countless white-on-black stitchery patterns found in women's magazines. Once fabricated, the case was to be embroidered with a picture of the three balls and the rubric "MONEY LENT." It was "appropriate as a present to a young gentleman" because his watch would likely wind up in hock, its "manifest destiny" (fig. 2.4).[77]

By this time audiences were being entertained by humorous squibs about a pawnbroker's character and background. The comic monthly *Nick-Nax for All Creation*, for instance, published a long list of pawnbroking jokes. Several alluded to aspersions on the pawnbroker's religious and moral beliefs that it was assumed readers would get:

No dinners? None with him. It is Lent all the year round.
What does he not allow? He never allows you to pledge your word, your
    honor, your character, or your reputation—these being articles of no
    value in his estimation.
Is he a Christian? No; he cannot bear anything to be redeemed.
What is his store? The refuge of the robber with his gain—a place wherein

FIGURE 2.4. "Our Fashions and Fancy Work," *Nick-Nax for All Creation* 1, 7 (November 1856): 224. Courtesy, American Antiquarian Society.

poverty is obliged to witness the moral sucking of its blood, without the means of stopping the leech that draws it.[78]

Relatively straightforward representations of pawnbrokers and pawnshops referred to current events and, logically, to economic downturns. The cartoon "Love and Hard Times," for example, appeared in 1858, the year after a devastating economic panic. It depicts a woeful Cupid about to pawn his bow, arrow, and quiver (fig. 2.5).[79] And as a metaphor for the country's dire economic straits in the aftermath of another crash came the 1874 cartoon appearing in *Harper's Weekly,* "The Tendency of the Times: A Lesson to Heads of Families." Here Uncle Sam stands in tatters on the doorstep of Levi's pawnshop, about to pawn his pocket watch (fig. 2.6).[80]

Illustrated magazines published in the final decades of the nineteenth century returned to a focus on the Jewish aspect of pawnbroking and pushed the stereotype even further, refining the anti-Semitic portrayals of Jews appearing in popular print. Although by the 1880s the complexion of pawnbrokers had changed, especially as more Irish joined the profession, pawnbroking would always be a "Jewish" occupation in the public imagination.[81] The steady appearance of graphic imagery after the Civil War fixed these and other ethnic stereotypes in the American mind's eye. Germans were brute butchers, Irish women

FIGURE 2.5. "Love and Hard Times," *Nick-Nax for All Creation* 2, 10 (February 1858): 295. Courtesy, American Antiquarian Society.

FIGURE 2.6. "The Tendency of the Times: A Lesson to Heads of Families," *Harper's Weekly* 18, 891 (January 24, 1874): 88. Library Company of Philadelphia.

semiliterate domestics, and African Americans slack-jawed loafers. Jews were scheming criminals who, it was claimed, "had little respect for Christian laws, property, [and] even life."[82]

The printed and moving pictures appearing in the visual landscape of the late nineteenth century provided the public with images that were much more complex and fully realized than textual descriptions. Pictures concretized popular stereotypes. What was more, graphic illustrations reached unprecedented numbers of the population and, unlike written texts, could speak to the literate and illiterate, native and nonnative speakers equally. They were highly influential in creating more definitive characterizations across ethnicity, religion, and occupation, normalizing the stereotypes among mass audiences.

Although it is impossible to know with certainty how faithfully individual consumers read and internalized the xenophobic messages put before them, caricatures in popular culture undoubtedly both shaped and reflected common attitudes. Some have argued that popular portrayals of Jews were benign compared with the treatment of members of other religious and ethnic groups. Even though Jews were shown as obsessed with making money, they were at least "sharper than other groups, who tended to be portrayed as dim witted."[83] Yet "sharp" traders could as easily be considered scheming as smart.

These distinctions were articulated and reinforced by popular media, which saw terrific expansion in the decades following the Civil War. More efficient papermaking and bookmaking technologies along with extended distribution networks brought greater numbers of affordable books, newspapers, and periodicals—now highly illustrated—to an audience growing adept at reading words and images. Publishing houses also printed works in foreign languages to accommodate the aesthetic tastes and practical needs of new immigrants. Cheaply produced broadsides, circulars, trade cards, songsheets, and other printed ephemera also circulated widely. Perhaps most effectively, illustrated humor magazines such as *Puck* and *Judge* deployed visual imagery to unapologetically critique all aspects of American life, from fads to political scandals.

Puck was founded in 1877 (first published in both English and German), and by the 1890s nearly 90,000 people were reading the magazine, making it one of the most popular purveyors of comic images. And at the dawn of the twentieth century *Judge's Library* was reaching over 114,000 people.[84] Tellingly, *Puck* "did not regard itself, nor was it thought of in its time," as anti-Semitic; similarly, *Judge* represented itself as "scrupulous" and operating "within the bounds of modesty and good taste."[85] If that was truly the case, then Jewish stereotypes had become fully normalized, accepted, and acceptable. Take, for instance, the cartoon appearing in an 1888 issue of *Puck* captioned "At Miss Ahrenheim's Wed-

FIGURE 2.7. A Jewish father cruelly punishes his child by making him watch the pawnbroker charge less than legal interest. "A Case for Gerry," *Puck* (January 18, 1893): 348. Library Company of Philadelphia.

ding." The father of the bride prods his daughter to test the purity of her wedding ring in the middle of the ceremony. In broken English he whispers, "Here ish der acid, Leah. Drop a liddle on der ring to see uf it vas reel golt!" Wearing an ill-fitting suit and an oversized diamond ring, Ahrenheim is associated with ostentatious yet shabby display (suggesting he is either a used clothing dealer or an unscrupulous pawnbroker who puts his customers' collateral to personal use). Another *Puck* cartoon presents a baby's "Alarming Symptoms." Mother Cohnstein is concerned because her child lazes in its cradle all day "and don't dake no interest in anyding." Shocked, Father Cohnstein replies, "Vat! don't dake no interest? Mine Gracious, he must be teadt!" In the house of another yet cartoon family, the Hockstein parents debate how best to discipline their son. Pawnbroker Hockstein says, "I vos going to put him on der gounter and make him vatch me vile I scharge der next gustomer only six per cent." To which Mrs. Hockstein *"in motherly horror"* protests, "Oh Fadder! You vos *too* cruel!" (fig. 2.7).[86] All the cartoons utilize evocative surnames, broken English, and pictorial cues to present exaggerated depictions of Jews whose financial concerns take precedence over yet also define family bonds.

People bought illustrated magazines because of their "continuing popular fascination and delight with ethnic material." Magazines continued to deliver this content and package it in different ways, such as putting out special issues focusing on particular ethnic groups.[87] The characters also lived on in other forms, migrating from the pages of *Puck, Judge,* and *Life* to appear on trade cards and in comic almanacs and popular joke books.[88] Eugene Zimmerman (better known as "Zim"), whose cartoons regularly appeared in print, discussed the importance of rendering physical characteristics in his 1910 book *Cartoons and Caricatures, or Making the World Laugh.* Hebrew and Irish faces displayed the "two extremes for characteristic curves." "You already know," he wrote, "that to produce an Irish face you must give it a pug nose, and the Hebrew face the hook nose." While he acknowledged that not every face belonging to an ethnic group actually conformed to these characteristics, "to carry out the purpose of your picture you must stick to these" for broad audiences to comprehend the meaning.[89] The results expressed the "split personality" of popular comics, whose contents could be at once good-humored and corrosive.[90]

Defending itself against an attack by the *Jewish Messenger* over a particularly offensive cartoon in 1881, *Puck*'s editor responded,

> We have no prejudice against the Jews or the Jewish religion, . . . no prejudice against the Irish or the Irish Roman Catholics; and if mere caricature is objectionable, the Irish have surely much more reason to complain than the Jews, who have always found a champion in *Puck*. Our Hebrew friends must not be so sensitive. . . . If they do not wish to be made fun of, they should not intensify the traditional peculiarities that so often make them the subject of ridicule. They are clannish, and cling to their antiquated puerile Oriental customs and mummeries as a Chinaman clings to his pigtail.[91]

Jews should lighten up, *Puck*'s editors insisted, because their magazine was an equal-opportunity offender; Jews, in fact, were treated generously compared with other ethnic groups. And if the cartoons *did* step over the line, it was only because Jews brought it on themselves by resisting assimilation, stubbornly clinging to their "traditional peculiarities." In a contemporary essay Mark Twain defended the Jew thus: "He is not a loafer, he is not a sot, he is not noisy, he is not a brawler nor a rioter, he is not quarrelsome."[92] Yet he too equivocated, describing the group's "other side." The Jew, he wrote, "has a reputation for various small forms of cheating, and for practising oppressive usury, and for burning himself out to get the insurance."[93] So as a group Jews were known to be industrious yet occupied themselves by pursuing petty gains at the expense of others. Commentators never clarified how this diverged from the exploits of other (Christian) capitalists.

Manufacturers of consumer products themselves disseminated anti-Semitic imagery through promotional materials, embellishing their packaging, circulars, and trade cards with images of the Jew broker that were often printed in full color. Such advertising reached the masses—Americans could not avoid them. At Philadelphia's 1876 Centennial Exposition, for example, exhibitors gave away tens of thousands of colorful trade cards and advertising circulars, igniting a national collecting craze that brought advertising into the home. Agents also sent trade cards through the mail, storekeepers piled them on shop counters, manufacturers sealed them inside packages, and leafleters distributed them on sidewalks. Adults and children avidly collected serialized trade cards and other small pieces of advertising—the "new" popular culture—and spent hours pasting them into scrapbooks.[94]

Effective trade cards used novel images to capture people's attention, and some advertisers incorporated the figure of the Jew broker into their promotional materials. One advertising card for a patent medicine produced in the late 1880s claimed that Taylor's Sure Cure could calm even a pawnbroker's guilty upset stomach and allow him to sleep through the night. We recognize him by his unfashionably long beard, ostentatious jewelry, and the prominent nose that supports his pince-nez. He sleeps soundly, dreaming of the "Bill of Goods" he sold that day. Each of the three gold balls carries part of the product's name, and they are used as a convenient framing device to highlight Taylor's Sure Cure (fig. 2.8).

The pawnbroker appearing on the Bell's Pond Lily Soap trade card was drawn using the same visual vocabulary, appearing with exaggerated facial features and large hands, outfitted vulgarly in a shabby jacket and ill-fitting trousers and sporting garish jewelry (fig. 2.9). Here the meaning is even more evident. Personal hygiene, already a concern by the 1860s, had become an obsession of turn-of-the-century reformers. They believed that adopting the sanitary habits of "native" Americans was essential to immigrants' assimilation, improving both their physical condition and their moral bearing. To the middle class especially, cleanliness functioned as an important visual cue marking "moral superiority," while dirt was "a sign of degradation."[95] The message conveyed by the makers of Bell's Soap was anything but subtle: their soap could purify even the vulgar Jew broker, exemplar of the "great masses of filth" invading the country.[96]

Circulating the stereotype even further, including internationally, were postcards, wildly popular by the turn of the century. The U.S. Postal Service first issued prestamped postcards in 1873, and picture postcards gained popularity during the World's Columbian Exposition in 1893. Postcards could be personalized and mailed all over the world. Americans sent more than 770 million in 1906 alone and well over 900 million in 1913.[97] To meet consumer demand for novel cards, companies published countless designs. Any subject, from the patriotic to the pornographic, was commercially viable. Comic examples composed a large

FIGURE 2.8. (*left*) Taylor's Sure Cure is so good at treating indigestion that even a pawnbroker can sleep through the night. L. Crusius, illus., Richardson-Taylor Medicine Company (St. Louis, ca. 1888). Collection of the author.

FIGURE 2.9. (*right*) The stereotypical turn-of-the-century Jew has a large nose, lips, and hands and wears ill-fitting clothes and ostentatious jewelry. R. W. Bell Manufacturing Company (Buffalo: Gies, ca. 1890). Collection of the author.

part of the postcard market and included many examples satirizing pawnbrokers and pawnbroking drawn by some of the most famous comic illustrators of the era. Newspaper publisher William Randolph Hearst hired cartoonists to design comic postcards to be included as cutouts in the Sunday papers, commissioning among others Richard Felton Outcault (creator of Buster Brown), whose comic strips addressed social issues such as the hardships of tenement life.[98] Although the pawner is the butt of the joke in these postcard scenes, the pawnbroker remains his reliably stereotyped self (figs. 2.10, 2.11).

Stereotypical qualities, including those ascribed to the Jew broker, could not help but influence people's thinking, given the sheer volume of printed material in circulation by the end of the century and the vividness of its content. Even representations meant to be innocuous used exaggeration, like the depiction of an avuncular Solomon Rubenstein on the cover of the 1894 "New Comic Song: Hock Shop"[99] (fig. 2.12). Representations were often bizarre, such as another piece of sheet music, from 1909, titled "Big Chief Dynamite." The song is about a Jewish pawnbroker named Cohen who leaves his wife to go out West and become "a tough Jew Indian boy" who takes on "Tough Guy Levi" the "cowboy Jew." On the cover, against a background of the iconic three balls, is a profile of Cohen as the "Jew Indian." He has a grotesquely large nose and a curly beard, and on his lapel a diamond pin shines blindingly. On Cohen's head sits, improbably, a full Indian headdress (fig. 2.13).[100] Typically, though, the images

FIGURE 2.10. "Say Au Revoir but Not Good Bye," R. F. Outcault, illus. (New York: J. Ottmann, 1909). Collection of the author.

FIGURE 2.11. "I'm Passing the Time" (New York: Souvenir Post Card Company, 1905). Collection of the author.

FIGURE 2.12. Sheet music cover illustrating an avuncular pawn-broker. "A New Comic Song: Hock Shop" (Chicago: G. B. Brigham, 1894). The Lester S. Levy Collection of Sheet Music, Special Collections at the Sheridan Libraries, Johns Hopkins University.

FIGURE 2.13. Sheet music cover illustrating a Jewish cowboy. "Big Chief Dynamite" (Chicago: Will Rossiter, 1909). The Lester S. Levy Collection of Sheet Music, Special Collections at the Sheridan Libraries, Johns Hopkins University.

were simply damning, such as the cover story recounting the crimes of "The Shylock Pawnbroker" that appeared in an 1895 issue of the pulpy *Beadle's Dime Library* and showed a hunched, hook-nosed figure counting his lucre in a dark little garret.[101]

By the close of the nineteenth century pawnbrokers and pawnshops, familiar fixtures in big cities and small towns alike, easily found a place in the movies. Full of possibility, pawnshops provided a rich setting for a host of theatrical situations, as they had in popular fiction. The first American film about pawnbroking, *Love in a Broker's Office*, appeared in theaters in 1897. It was followed in the first decades of the twentieth century by *Dress Suits in Pawn*, *A Jewel in Pawn*, *The Marriage Ring* (also called *The Pawn*), *The Pawnbroker's Daughter*, *The Pawnbroker's Heart*, *Bill Tell Pawnbroker*, *She Loved Him Plenty*, and Mutt and Jeff's animated film from 1920, *The Pawnbrokers*.[102] Pawnshops were settings equally suited to comedies, dramas, and love stories.

A notable early film was the endearing 1916 comedy short *The Pawnshop*, a perfect showcase for Charlie Chaplin's talents. As a hapless pawnbroker's assistant, Chaplin dirties all the pawns in storage when he tries to dust, puts a customer's head through a cello, guts a clock that a man has brought to hock, and nearly poisons a goldfish. In the end, Chaplin's character foils a robbery attempt by a diamond broker courting the pawnbroker's daughter. The hero of the day, at the end of the film he gets the girl. Much different in tone was the 1908 silent *Old Isaacs, the Pawnbroker* (written by D. W. Griffith), an unusually poignant portrayal of a Jewish character.[103] In the story, a little girl needs money for her sick and starving mother. The "Amalgamated Association of Charities," which she approaches first, provides no assistance, so she turns to the pawnbroker. Isaacs's assistant refuses to accept the girl's worn shoes as collateral; when she returns with her doll, the pawnbroker himself deals with her and at once realizes her plight. Playing against type, he comes to the girl's aid, saving her mother from eviction, paying their medical bills, and giving them food. He even buys the girl a new doll. In its promotional material Biograph described the film as "dissipating 'the malignant calumnies launched at the Hebraic race.'"[104]

Correctives such as Biograph's *Old Isaacs* were not unheard of, but only rarely did people consider that pawnbrokers were presented unfairly in popular culture. In one exceptional instance, a writer in the early 1870s explained to his readers that "a thriving pawnbroker should be a man with no excess of sensibility." He continued, "So many stories of wretchedness, misfortune, and ghastly want must be poured into his ear, that if he were a tender-hearted man he would inevitably beggar himself every day."[105] Sentimentality never figured into people's estimation of wholesalers, retailers, manufacturers, and other "established" men of business. In fact, unlike pawnbrokers, who dealt with needy customers every day, they were often far removed from the daily exigencies of the working poor and therefore did not have to be mindful of their own "sensibilities." Another contemporary newspaper article also addressed popular misconceptions about pawnbroking; it was titled "Pawnbrokers' Clerks: Not So Unsympathetic and Heartless as They Seem." The featured clerk denied that people in his profession were "fond of taunting the poor." Pawnbroking was a business like any other. "Because we handle money and make loans," he remarked, "people seem to think we loan it out because we don't know what to do with it. This is a mistake. . . . I often get blue at seeing so much misery about me."[106] Pawnbrokers could not indulge their emotions if they hoped to run a profitable business.

Yet by the end of the century the few objective accounts of pawnbroking were no match for the deleterious words and images that over the century had created an indelible portrait of the Jew broker. The conflation of Jews and pawnbrokers in mass market forms distorted the public's impression of pawnbroking, disseminating and naturalizing anti-Semitic stereotypes. The stereotypes in turn helped promulgate ideas about "proper" and "improper" ways to make money: demonized, Jew brokers made most other capitalists look good by comparison. "Queries regarding the Jews" no longer appeared in newspapers because by the dawn of the twentieth century the character of Jews, as presented in popular culture and represented most clearly by the pawnbroker, had become established beyond contestation.

Purveyors of popular culture including publishers, marketers, and writers did end up making some concessions, realizing that they walked a fine line between lampooning and insulting patrons they were trying to attract. Having learned various trades, many Jews *were* economically successful and therefore enjoyed the power of the purse. Popular cartoonist E. C. Matthews, for instance, advised in his 1928 book *How to Draw Funny Pictures*, "Be careful not to offend the Jewish people in your cartoons, or you may be unable to get them published." He underscored the admonition by describing an experience of cartoonist Zim, who "tells of a time when he bore down a little too heavily on these characters— and was called upon by a delegation of pawnbrokers, who asked him to desist."[107] That advertisers nevertheless saw fit to incorporate such caricatures in their promotional materials, however, shows just how normalized the types had become and how acceptable it was to deploy them in the mass media.

The image we conjure today of the exploitative, greedy, thieving pawnbroker became fully realized in the nineteenth century. Yet there remained a great discrepancy between common (mis)perceptions and the truth. Instead of equal opportunity for all, capitalism was created and fueled by large pools of the working poor who constituted pawnbrokers' main customer base. Rather than pulling them out of poverty as promised, hard work left many battling with their personal budgets. For average Americans, as we will see, upward mobility remained a mirage, forever unattainable. To blame pawnbroking, one of the clearest manifestations of capitalism's inherent inequities, was much easier than taking on the economic system itself. The following chapters are devoted to presenting a more balanced view of pawnbroking in American history and to creating a more fully realized portrait of the Jew broker.

CHAPTER THREE

IN DEFENSE OF PAWNBROKERS

Much as people might have despised pawnbrokers, theirs was a necessary business that arose because of capitalism. Pawnbroking was able to respond and adapt to the country's radically changing social climate and economic needs from the time of the early republic through the Great Depression and beyond. We need to look beyond the persistent and pervasive stereotype of the "Jew broker" to understand the role pawnbrokers actually played in the development and eventual triumph of industrial capitalism. Like so many other businessmen, pawnbrokers identified and pursued economic opportunities that best suited their professional experience, while taking advantage of and solidifying social and family networks.

In early American cities, men of commerce relied on brokers to obtain credit. Distinct from pawnbrokers, general brokers who operated out of "intelligence offices" and local coffeehouses and taverns fostered a wide range of deals among the merchant elite. They acquired "superior expertise" in certain specialties and were able to exploit economies of scale, making it more efficient for merchants to seek out their services rather than arranging and negotiating such transactions themselves.[1] Brokers functioned as a city's financial "concierges," undertaking a number of services with the utmost discretion. They sometimes loaned money on physical collateral, as did the people Robert Morris referred to in 1782 who, illegally, "frequently get 5 per Cent per month from good Substantial men for the use of Money with pledges lodged for the repayment."[2] Others ventured into the lending business when they had extra funds, such as attorney John Coghill Knapp, whose 1769 advertisement read, "Cash often to be had on approval, real, or personal security."[3] High-stakes brokers accepted abstract forms of capital as security, such as financial instruments and stakes in ships' voyages, leaving much of the country's wealth underwritten by (sometimes literally) floating credit. The services offered by one of the first self-identified brokers in America were typical:

> Hendrick Oudenaarde, Broker, HAS to sell, all sorts of European and West-India Goods, at the cheapest Rates.
>
> He likewise charters Vessels for different Ports in Europe and the West-Indies.
>
> Also collects in Freight Money, manages the Transactions relating to the Accounts of Vessels and Cargoes, for both Masters and Owners.
>
> And, at his Office, is also Money to be LET upon Interest, on approved Security, from £.500 to £.1000, and supplies Orders in Town, Country, or elsewhere abroad, with the utmost Dispatch.[4]

Similarly, Jonas Phillips, boasting international connections, made his living as a broker, trader, and auctioneer. Certainly a useful person to know, he "BUYS and sells all sorts of goods on commissions, for persons at home or abroad, charters and freights vessels, procures money at interest, and transacts all other general business of a broker and auctioneer, with the greatest dispatch, integrity and secrecy."[5] Business transactions during this era were fluid and flexible, often involving complex webs of debtor and creditor relationships among many people. For example, customers bartered with shopkeepers and traded among neighbors the products they made with their own hands. Prices, too, varied depending on whether purchases were made on credit or with cash.[6] And personal credit relationships often enmeshed people inhabiting different classes, such as the large merchant planters in Virginia who loaned to their poorer neighbors, exercising an "etiquette of debt" that both engendered cooperation and reinforced social and economic hierarchies.[7]

People outside the social and financial milieu of the merchant elite, those whose investments rested in small material possessions rather than large-scale commercial enterprises, obtained loans by pawning, offering their modest capital as collateral. Part of the informal economy of the seventeenth and eighteenth centuries, pawning was something people resorted to when they needed cash they didn't have, when tax bills came due or accounts had to be settled in specie (gold and silver coins) rather than with paper currency or promissory notes. Neighbors often offered a horse, plow, or similar piece of valuable capital as collateral for a short-term loan. Innkeepers, who had cash at their fingertips and a diverse and mobile clientele traveling with all manner of personal belongings, also became de facto pawnbrokers in the eighteenth century.[8]

As more people of all classes and circumstances moved into and through large cities after the Revolution, there was an even greater need for lenders. Uprooted from economic and social relationships forged by geographic proximity, shared interests, and family connections, people new to the city found it increasingly difficult to turn to a neighbor, relative, or local publican for a loan. Hence people calling themselves "brokers," whose occupation was to lend money and perform other financial services, saw an opportunity to serve newcomers in straitened circumstances. Although they did not completely replace the informal credit relationships that continued to exist in urban communities, brokers did identify a market niche, formalizing services that were once provided by someone known personally, who might have extended a loan out of goodwill rather than for profit. It was only a matter of time before these professional lenders became crucial to the survival of the poorer classes in particular.

In the early nineteenth century, as cities grew in population, economic activity, and cultural life, occupations also expanded, becoming more numerous, diversified, and specialized. Brokers, like other businessmen, began directing their skills to ever narrower fields of commerce. City directories were now listing lottery brokers, exchange brokers, money brokers, and commission brokers, and real estate, cotton, hide and skin, hay, tea, wood, wool, and hardware brokers soon joined their ranks.[9] In addition, some people diversified. Intelligence offices such as Warne's in Philadelphia functioned as employment agents, real estate brokers, preparers of legal documents, mail deliverers, and moneylenders (for those interested in "OBTAINING MONEY, on . . . deposits of merchandize, watches, plate, jewels, &c.").[10] Gradually, people calling themselves pawnbrokers also appeared, not necessarily performing a new service but able to make a living from pawnbroking alone or as their primary occupation.

The first pawnbrokers qua pawnbrokers appeared in New York City at the dawn of the nineteenth century. A major port, New York saw its fair share of peripatetic seamen in need of money. The city also experienced massive influxes of immigrants who stayed put, even in the face of "misery, disease, and shameless exploitation."[11] New opportunities for some created anxieties for others. How were all these people of varied circumstances to be molded into a coherent, orderly society?

Regulations governing pawnbrokers, not surprisingly, started to be enacted in early republic cities at this time, during the first few decades of the nineteenth century. They articulated the growing concern about the role of pawnbroking in the country's increasingly complex market economy. The New York City Common Council first discussed regulating pawnbrokers in 1805 but ultimately did nothing. Four years later, the body revisited the pawnbroking issue after receiving a grievance that "'the great number of Pawnbrokers and the unrestrained manner in which they conduct themselves' had become a source of serious and alarming mischief."[12] At last, in 1812, the Common Council passed its first ordinance regulating pawnbrokers, and it became a model for subsequent control efforts in other municipalities. The statutes embodied assumptions beginning to appear in the popular press, that pawnbrokers not only were criminally minded themselves but also exacerbated poverty and encouraged theft in the neighborhoods where they lived and worked. Lumped with dealers in used goods and junk, pawnbrokers had to pay an annual license fee to "be used and applied in and towards the support of the poor." To discourage trafficking in stolen goods, and reinforce social hierarchies in the process, regulations prohibited pawnbrokers from accepting collateral from minors, servants, apprentices, or slaves. The law also required pawnbrokers to keep detailed ledgers, to be presented at the request of authorities, recording each transaction and providing, in addition to a physical description of the pawner, "an accurate account and description of the goods, article, or thing pawned, the amount of the sum loaned thereon, the time of pledging the same, the rate of interest to be paid on the said loan, and the name and residence of the person pawning or pledging such goods."[13] (Many of these requirements remain in place today.)

Pawnbrokers in growing cities hoped that the costly yet increasingly necessary expense of licenses would confer at least some legitimacy on their businesses by affirming that proprietors were "of good character" and could be tracked by officials. (Licensing arguably had the opposite effect, since "legitimate" businessmen, such as wholesalers and retailers, did not need official sanction to operate.) In 1812 John S. Sommer (or Sommers) became one of New York City's first pawnbrokers to be granted an official license after nearly a decade of running his pawnshop. Stephen Blatchford of Philadelphia had been running his pawnshop for five years before the city enacted its licensing ordinance in 1819. Baltimorean Simon Eytinge used his position as the city's first licensed pawnbroker to assure the public of his integrity, "having given ample security to the Mayor and City Council for the faithful performance of his duties."[14] Baltimore, population 80,600, supported enough pawnbrokers by 1828 to have ordinances controlling their business, and some regulations may have dated back to the 1810s.[15] Baltimore pawnbrokers initially paid $200 annually in addition to depositing a $500 bond with the mayor to cover court costs related to any claims of stolen goods.[16] A significant expense, licenses forced pawnbrokers to be fully committed to the business and weeded out smaller, possibly shady operators. In 1832 six people, "having had an opportunity of observing her deportment," attested to the mayor that Sarah Millem was "a sober, honest, industrious and active person."[17] As intended, licenses made it easy for officials to track where pawnbrokers had set up their shops, to control their daily business, and to pursue alleged offenders.

Today pawnbroking is regulated by each state (and pawnbrokers also fall under the federal Truth in Lending Act), but for much of the nineteenth century pawning was controlled at the local level. Municipal governments, often spurred by private citizens, continued to address pawnbroking "issues" and, when necessary, set rates of interest, loan terms, and licensing fees. Some locales implemented two-tier interest rate systems (higher rates for loans below a certain threshold and lower rates for those above), while others applied a uniform rate to all loans. Neighboring states frequently enacted very different pawnbroking regulations; cities within the same state also often did not operate under the same laws. For example, in New York in the late 1860s Albany was "let[ting] pawnbrokers pretty severely alone," while Buffalo pawnbrokers received 3% per month and collateral was forfeited after a year. Rochester pawnbrokers charged 20% annually, and collateral left unredeemed after six months could be sent off for sale. Other cities had similarly diverse pawnbroking regulations. Philadelphia's loans, for example, accrued 6% annual interest, and collateral was forfeited after one year from the original loan date. Baltimore's pawnbrokers charged the same interest rate but required monthly renewal of loans and could also charge a graduated ticket writing fee (6¼¢ for each loan under $3, 9¢ for loans greater than $3 and less than $5, and so on).[18] By the early twentieth century California pawnbrokers were charging annual interest rates of 24%, while Virginia pawnbrokers collected annual rates of 120% on loans below $25, 60% on loans between $25 and $100, and 36% on loans above. Extra fees for ticket writing and storage of collateral also varied from state to state, making pawning terms and *actual* interest rates (when considered as a total of all charges) wildly divergent across the country. Determining legal and ethical limits of pawning rates remained local issues.[19]

Pawnbrokers were hardworking people who offered what was fast becoming a necessary service in maturing American cities, providing short-term loans on modest forms of collateral. Yet their profession, like dogcatching, was not one that people aspired to. Unlike clerks and mechanics, who received education through apprenticelike training and shared social activities, pawnbrokers enjoyed neither professional prestige, identity, specialized education, nor occupational camaraderie. Many early pawnbrokers entered the trade by degrees, beginning their careers as general brokers, traders, or peddlers and making personal and business connections across wholesale, retail, and resale markets. These experiences taught them how to calculate the worth of different kinds of goods when traded in various exchange spheres and honed their skills as sharp appraisers. They became expert in determining the value of goods in many markets, their knowledge confined not to any single good or commodity but encompassing a range of items and materials in various exchange spheres.

Most early pawnbrokers developed expertise by working in other occupations, commonly the resale and petty goods trades. Benjamin Ford, the first man in New York City to call himself a pawnbroker, started out as a shipwright in 1799 and in 1803 opened his pawnshop at 98 James, near the lively commerce of the East River waterfront. That same year John Sommer was working as a clothier, and from 1804 to 1809 he added "broker & intelligence office," offering various complementary services like his eighteenth-century predecessors. From 1810 through 1818 (after which he disappears from the directories, likely because of his usury conviction in 1817), Sommer identified himself as a money broker.[20] David Cudlipp was a hatter for three years and then a furniture dealer for two more before he opened his New York City pawnshop in 1845. Similarly, the description of John M. Davies's New York business changed over time although he remained at the same address. He was first identified as a clothier, then a stocking cap manufacturer, then a dealer, then a clothier again, and finally a pawnbroker. Most likely he was engaged in all of these occupations between 1830 and 1850 when he was listed in the New York City directories.

This pattern held true for those working in other cities as well. Over the fifteen years of his career in early Philadelphia, Roswell Holmes called himself an exchange broker, a stockbroker, and a pawnbroker, likely performing all these functions at the same time. A decade later, Moses Vanderslice started as a Philadelphia clothing dealer, working at that occupation for thirteen years before becoming a pawnbroker in 1850. Baltimore pawnbrokers followed similar paths. James Lebrantlwaite began his career selling dry goods at the Lexington Market. By 1831 he had become a pawnbroker. Likewise, Jacob Aaron got his start as a secondhand clothing dealer and Levi Benjamin began as a used furniture dealer before they became pawnbrokers.[21] By 1831 Lewis Silver had made his way into pawnbroking, initially entering the world of commerce as a dealer in combs, jewelry, and variety goods. Pittsburgh pawnbroker Henry Cimiotti started out as a watchmaker in 1847 before opening his pawnshop and loan office some ten years later, as did Barnhard (or Bernard) Heinemann in Boston about a decade later.[22]

Although later pawnbrokers tended to learn the profession from their grandfathers, fathers, and uncles, newcomers could still become pawnbrokers if they were savvy about retail and resale markets. For example, Greenville, South Carolina, pawnbroker George Chaplin (trained in the business by his father) reminisced about the elder Chaplin's becoming a pawnbroker in the early twentieth century:

He had worked for the shoe factories in Boston, been a peddler, and opened a small, hole in the wall, retail store. . . . My Dad knew that he couldn't compete with the jewelry stores, where you make so much a week, and pay out in a year, or with the Stein Brothers clothes, a good suit costs all of fifteen dollars in those days. . . . so he opened a pawnshop, had no experience whatever. Took in a fair number of pieces of glass, before he learned how to tell whether it was a real diamond or not. But [he] hired a Mr. Sam . . . a Jewish guy with a big bow. He was a professional pawnbroker, and my dad gradually learned the business, very bright, and was very good at it.[23]

A lasting and successful career in pawnbroking rested on one's ability to identify local market niches and to accurately appraise a miscellany of goods.

These and other pawnbrokers came to American cities when conditions were right: when enough of a concentrated underclass emerged to support the profession and when petty (and typically peripatetic) entrepreneurs amassed enough capital to set up stationary shops. As urban areas became economically viable, able to support manufacturing operations and the populations to run them, the more these places were able to support pawnbrokers—and the more they needed them. In most American cities the spread of pawnshops kept pace with population increases, geographical expansion, and the maturation of capitalist economic structures. Unemployment, "one expression of the power of ownership and the dependence of employees in a market economy," created a labor reserve that enabled industrial capitalism's low wages and provided ready customers for pawnshops.[24] And the more people became enmeshed in the market economy, the less flexibility they had to seek out new opportunities or to return to traditional occupations such as farming. This was no less true out West. By the early 1880s, for example, the Leadville Loan Office occupied a storefront in the business district of what was then Colorado's second largest city. The city's population—some 40,000 at the time—comprised thousands of enterprising gold and silver miners and thousands more hangers-on who profited in various service industries, from pawnbrokers and surveyors to prostitutes and saloon operators (fig. 3.1).

Pawnbroking was in fact an essential service that would not have existed without the economic inequities inherent in the emerging capitalist system. The New York Society for the Prevention of Pauperism counted ten licensed pawnbrokers in the city in 1820 (about one for every 12,000 people). Just six years later, forty-one were licensed (one pawnbroker for every 4,800 people).[25] And these figures did not include the many unlicensed pawnbrokers whose shadowy operations inhabited basements and back alleys in violation of local ordinances. Responding to what they thought were unfairly high license fees, New York City pawnbrokers in 1818 appealed to the Common Council for a reduction in the rate.

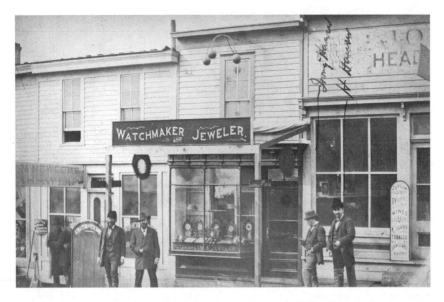

FIGURE 3.1. Herman Hauser's Jewelry Store, Chestnut Street, Leadville, Colorado, between 1880 and 1882. Denver Public Library, Western History Collection, X-380.

They objected to the $50 fee (almost 15% of a skilled worker's annual wages at the time and 20% of an unskilled worker's).[26] They also complained that police did not enforce the law, insisting, "We can name A greater number of those who cary on the business without Lycense, than there is of those who have Lycense at this time."[27] Increased license fees and tougher regulations notwithstanding, by midcentury New Yorkers were walking around the city with about half a million dollars of local pawnbrokers' money in their pockets, spending it on tools and faro, rent and gin.[28]

Pawnbrokers, to put it in contemporary terms, "gave something back" to their communities. By the 1830s and 1840s they had put down roots, opening family-run shops, increasing their capital investments, developing business and social networks, and forging relationships with regular customers from the neighborhood. Once established, they stayed. In all cities, the number of pawnbrokers continued to rise during the nineteenth century; they kept up with and sometimes outpaced overall rates of population growth, indicating the persistent economic needs of the working poor. City directories indicate broad trends. New York and Philadelphia maintained fairly consistent numbers of pawnbrokers per capita in the middle decades of the nineteenth century. But other cities saw increases: in Boston, for example, there were two and a half times as many pawnbrokers for each person at the end of the 1850s as at the beginning (1:22,200 vs. 1:8,900), and in Cincinnati there were almost three times as many (1:38,500 vs. 1:13,400). Per capita figures for the end of the century were as follows: Boston, 1:5,200; Providence, 1:16,500; and Chicago, 1:16,200. The statistics counted only licensed pawnbrokers; many more calling themselves used clothing and used goods dealers also loaned on collateral. In the case of Chicago one observer estimated that there were "perhaps two hundred others pursuing the trade" who did not appear on the official books.[29] By the first decades of the twentieth century there were almost two thousand licensed pawnshops in the country, clustered in localities with "a thickly crowded population of wage-earners."[30] The cities supporting the most pawnbrokers by the early twentieth century were those with the highest populations. While absolute numbers of pawnbrokers were larger in the big cities, the populations of smaller cities supported relatively more pawnbrokers (see table).[31] Once they reached critical mass, the number of pawnshops in major American cities remained fairly steady.

Pawnbrokers strategically situated their shops near their likeliest customers in vibrant, densely populated areas. These neighborhoods tended to be sites of intense commercial activity—involving legal and extralegal transactions, retail and secondhand selling, gray and black market exchange—and crucial to the survival of local neighborhood economies.[32] According to a commercial geography that organized most cities into distinct areas of wholesale, retail, and resale commerce, pawnshops tended to cluster in what we might today consider fringe neighborhoods.

Philadelphia and New York saw the most pronounced concentration of pawnshops in what were considered marginal neighborhoods—spaces also characterized by population density and diversity, extralegal activities, and a liberal choice of popular amusements. In New York City in the 1820s and 1830s, pawnbrokers and dealers in secondhand goods anchored Chatham Street, on the edge of what would become the notorious Five Points. The area's unsavory reputation was well deserved. One nineteenth-century account described the place as populated "principally, with Jews and low class foreigners." Unseemly businesses flourished, including "cheap hotels and lodging houses, several pawnbroker's shops, and half a dozen concert saloons."[33] The prudent and street-smart avoided Chatham Street after dark. Junius Henri Browne thought even the weather was different there, the sun "a little obscured," the wind possessing "the sense of taint."[34]

By the end of the 1840s there were four pawnbrokers working on Chatham Street and several others clustered in the surrounding blocks. Just around the corner on Orange (later Baxter Street) stood the neighborhood's main retail corridor, catering to the area's mostly impoverished residents. Secondhand shops and clothing dealers occupied twenty storefronts along Orange, leaving little

TABLE 3.1. Number of Pawnbrokers in Relation to Population, 1911

City	Population (in thousands)	Pawnbrokers	Population/broker (in thousands)
New York	4,700	201	23.4
Chicago	2,100	77	27.3
Philadelphia	1,500	102	14.7
St. Louis	687	23	29.9
Boston	670	72	9.3
Cleveland	561	37	15.2
Pittsburgh	534	24	22.3
San Francisco	416	47	8.9
New Orleans	339	25	13.6
Minneapolis	301	23	13.1
Indianapolis	234	15	15.6
Louisville	224	6	37.3
Providence	224	18	12.4
Denver	213	21	10.1
Portland, OR	207	35	5.9
Columbus	181	25	7.2
Toledo	168	20	8.4
Memphis	131	12	10.9
Omaha	124	30	4.1
Troy, NY	77	9	8.6
Harrisburg	64	8	8.0
Jacksonville	58	8	7.3
South Bend	54	4	13.5
Lincoln	44	5	8.8
Topeka	44	5	8.8
Austin	30	3	10.0
Council Bluffs	29	4	7.3
Shreveport	28	2	14.0
Wilmington, NC	26	1	26.0
Ogden City, UT	26	4	6.5
Burlington, VT	20	1	20.0
Guthrie, OK	12	5	2.4
Total	14,026	872	16.1
Total <100,000 ($n = 13$)	499	59	8.5
Total 100,000 to 500,000 ($n = 12$)	2,772	277	10.0
Total 500,000 to 750,000 ($n = 4$)	2,452	156	15.7
Total >750,000 ($n = 3$)	8,300	380	21.8

room for other kinds of trade.[35] Shoppers sharpened their elbows, vying for space on the narrow, overcrowded streets as they endeavored to purchase clothes, furniture, and food. Blocking their way were not only fellow consumers but also pushy tailors and used clothing dealers hawking their "fresh" goods. It was here that many unredeemed pawns entered secondary exchange, finding new owners and new uses through the resale market.

That pawnbrokers, secondhand clothing shops, and used furniture establishments (along with a thriving "service" sector) grew in clusters made perfect business sense. Like the countinghouses of wholesale merchants that faced the docks and the retail stores lining so many "market" streets of American cities, used goods dealers, beer saloon operators, dance hall proprietors, and like entrepreneurs increased their viability by situating their establishments in areas with vibrant complementary commerce. And so Philadelphia's pawnbrokers remained concentrated along the city's northern and southern borders, away from the "legitimate" wholesale and retail cores flourishing along the river near Market (High) and Chestnut Streets. Proprietors of other fringe enterprises also set up shop along these urban borders.

While the heart of Philadelphia was rich in commerce, its northern and southern edges needed improvement. Journalist George Foster characterized the "suburbs" of Northern Liberties, Kensington, and Spring Garden to the north and Southwark and Moyamensing to the south as lawless places free from government surveillance and control. "It must be remembered," he emphasized, "that the *City* of Philadelphia extends only from Lombard-street on the South to Vine-street on the North. . . . Within this space riots and mobs are unknown, and even disorderly scenes of the mildest character extremely rare." Areas beyond the city limits, though, were "infested with a set of the most graceless vagabonds and unmitigated ruffians." Foster meant the menacing gangs that roved the streets looking for cheap thrills and petty plunder. Indeed, Philadelphia's suburbs, especially along South Street, were dangerous places, "swarm[ing] with these loafers, who, brave only in gangs, herd together in squads or clubs."[36]

Unburdened by any systematic police control, the diverse population and its many activities brought a liveliness to these areas.[37] The very rich and the very poor mingled freely, as did members of various ethnicities and races. While this social mixing may have been scandalous to outside observers, residents themselves shared the collective ambition of getting ahead.[38] The neighborhood's mixed population at midcentury engaged in many enterprises. They drank, whored, pilfered, and occasionally rioted their way down South Street. By 1839 there were at least sixty-two taverns in the ten-block area.[39] Men had their pick of brothels. A guidebook listing Philadelphia's "Gay Houses and Ladies of Pleasure" pointed its readers to many on or near South Street, ranging from the very best to the commonest. Some back alleys harbored "houses of prostitution of the lowest grade, the resort of pickpockets and thieves of every description." Strangers were "earnestly admonished to not go there." In contrast, another brothel only a few blocks away was home to a respectable "swarm of yellow [mulatto] girls, who promenade up and down Chestnut Street every evening, with their faces well powdered."[40] The lower sorts needed pawnbrokers to get them through the exigencies of the day and to fund their debauchery at night. Ten of the city's thirteen pawnbrokers in 1850 were on South Street or within one block of the corridor.[41] Rooted, the shops continued to hem the southern and northern fringes of the city until the end of the century.

In other cities pawnbrokers were also at a remove from areas conducting wholesale and upscale retail trades, usually around the port, and could be found in or on the edges of middle-income neighborhoods. In Boston, for example, pawnshops started out clustered northwest of the harbor along Union and Sudbury Streets and Brattle Square. By the beginning of the twentieth century they had moved to the seedy Dudley Street area, a neighborhood also "infested" with "quack doctors, dime-novel exchanges, . . . cheap tailors, dentists, and furniture dealers."[42] And Baltimore's pawnshops, too, stood well away from the city's harbor life. Occupying storefronts on Baltimore, Gay, Pratt, and Charles from the 1840s through the Civil War, pawnbrokers such as Solomon and Levi Benjamin, Joseph Blimline, Isaac Lobe, and Benjamin Ulman situated their shops in congested areas with thriving retail business.[43]

Chicago pawnbrokers, who began appearing in meaningful numbers during the mid-1850s, fringed the Loop, settling along Wells and Randolph and also in "the Patch," a slum thick with Irish immigrants who frequented the neighborhood's many whorehouses and taverns.[44] During the second half of the nineteenth century they continued to occupy stretches of Wells and Randolph and established themselves on State Street as well, just a few blocks from the city's most impoverished "ghetto," as one reformer called the area. A block away from many of the city's pawnshops, the buildings sitting back-to-back on State and Plymouth Streets, for example, were home to nearly twenty brothels and to families making between $5 and $10 a week in the 1890s.[45] Observers noted that because people were so poor, amassing a livable income required every family member to contribute, including women who took in washing, did piecework, and picked rags, boys who shined shoes and sold newspapers, girls who worked in factories, and even toddlers, who could "sew buttons on knee-pants and shirtwaists, each bringing in a trifle to fill out the scanty income."[46] Through the mid-twentieth century pawnshops and secondhand dealers remained concentrated in the poorer areas of most American cities and gradually extended their reach into newly impoverished sections. Chicago again is a case in point. By 1910 pawnshops began appearing in "the emerging African-American neighborhoods of the Near South Side."[47] Marked by homemade signs and the nearly worthless goods in their windows, many operated as general used goods stores that were also, undoubtedly, unlicensed pawnshops. Only with late twentieth-century sprawl did pawnshops move away from urban cores and into the suburbs.

In many ways the interiors of pawnshops, too, reminded people that, although they were filled with goods, their purpose was not the same as department stores and dry goods shops. Retail spaces were light, spacious, and airy, with items tastefully arrayed in cases and on shelves. Ever-attentive clerks might flatter shoppers, offer personal service, and extol their wares. What was more, customers who wielded the power of the pocketbook often wheedled samples from clerks and cajoled them into giving discounts. Clothing emporiums and dry goods stores were places to see and be seen—bustling with genteel women decked out in the most fashionable attire, their good taste on display for other shoppers. Such venues created, reinforced, and amplified class distinctions among customers and articulated "the prestige of the business community" as a whole.[48] Goods moved out of shops as artfully and effortlessly as possible.

The seductive trappings of retail shops, however, were irrelevant to pawnbrokers. Most pawnshops ran efficiently with one or two helpers, without the retinue of clerks catering to the immediate needs of individual customers. Pawners would wait. Behind the long pawnshop counter rested hundreds of pawned items swaddled in paper and tagged with identification numbers, like corpses in a morgue. Glass cases held choice unredeemed pawns and used goods up for sale, but they were not arrayed with an eye for modern display. Items not neatly tucked away were stored in any available space. They dangled from ceilings, hung from walls, rested on floors, and spilled out onto the street (figs. 3.2 and 3.3).

Commentators interpreted pawnshops as they wished. Some saw the goods inside as the sad detritus of capitalism, material embodiments of once happy lives now shabby and hopeless. A writer for the *San Francisco Evening Bulletin* called pawnshops "the grand depot for all the squalor and misery of a large city," an inversion of John Wanamaker's retail oasis.[49] Others felt wonder and awe as in an old curiosity shop. And some could not decide. In *The Great Metropolis*, Junius Henri Browne described pawnshops as "dismal," "unclean," and "musty." "They reek with unwelcome odors. But sometimes," he admitted, "they affect cheerfulness and pleasantness."[50]

Except for upscale loan offices, pawnshops lacked the ordinary comforts of retail spaces, such as places to sit and corps of solicitous clerks. Pawnbrokers made

FIGURE 3.2. (*top*) Collateral and used goods often could not be contained within the confines of the pawnshop and flowed out onto the sidewalk. From "The Pawnbrokers of New York," *Great Republic Monthly* 2, 1 (July 1859): 19. Collection of the author.

FIGURE 3.3. (*left*) Pawnshop exterior showing typical pawns in the windows. B. Berkowitz Loan Office. New York, ca. 1924. George Grantham Bain Collection, Library of Congress, Prints and Photographs Division.

no pretense that they did anything other than lend money, and in this way many have been more honest professionals than the retailers pushing goods on the other side of the city. The pawnbroker "places no quick-eyed shopman at the door, no tenacious solicitor of the lingering customer to enter and trade. . . . he need not bow his back, or crush his face up into smiling wrinkles," observed one writer.[51] Counters separating pawners and pawnbrokers also served as thresholds over which items were transformed from personal possessions to units of capital, entering a state of suspended animation. Underscoring the dangerous aspects of the business, wrought iron bars and metal screening (the equivalent of today's bulletproof glass) often segregated pawners from pawnbrokers and helped protect and hide the valuable goods and cash that constituted the pawnbroker's capital.

Unlike retail consumers, pawners took visits to the pawnbroker in stride, employing euphemisms such as "going to see Uncle" and fibbing that their possessions were "in the shop." The genteel made concerted efforts to frequent pawnshops across town to avoid being seen by people they knew. Although not in the form of flattery and discounts, pawnbrokers *did* offer their customers something for their patronage: privacy. To protect pawners' identities, except when pressured by the authorities, pawnbrokers built separate cubicles (described by one nineteenth-century writer as "coffin-like") and maintained side entrances for people wanting to avoid public embarrassment.[52] A Philadelphia reporter writing as the "Night Hawk" in the late 1820s visited a pawnshop as part of his series on the city's demimonde and talked with the proprietor behind a screen that hid pawners' identities from the journalist.[53] For a long time, McGarry's in Philadelphia had a separate door for women around the corner from its main entrance to protect their privacy and spare them from walking through the storeroom for men's clothing, where they might be exposed to the opposite sex trying on or shedding pants and jackets. Philadelphia pawnbroker Phillip Nathans's advertisements promised, "All business transactions strictly confidential." He directed people to the "Private entrance . . . where applicants can transact their business confidentially."[54] In these spaces pawners tended to behave according to their social and economic class, apparent in the illustration published in the *National Police Gazette* in 1860 showing the interior of Simpson's famous New York City pawnshop. The riffraff elbowed each other, clamoring for their chance at the counter. In contrast, a demure, well-dressed woman standing in a privacy cubicle received personal attention (fig. 3.4).

A pawnbroker, though, could do only so much to shield customers from each other or, more to the point, from their own shame. Most pawnshops, small and close, were crammed with countless bundled goods and hordes of people, any daylight obscured because windows were festooned with secondhand goods

FIGURE 3.4. Pawnshop interior showing a genteel woman using a cubicle; the rabble at the counter have no concern about privacy. "Interior view of Mr. Simpson's Pawnbroking Establishment, Where Justice Matsell First Met Laura DeVere," *National Police Gazette*, March 3, 1860. Courtesy, American Antiquarian Society.

FIGURE 3.5. Running a pawnshop, often a family affair, required that every bit of storage space be used efficiently. "At the Pawnbroker," *Every Saturday*, 2, 62 (March 4, 1871): 209. Collection of the author.

for sale. Pawns that could not readily be stored close at hand were wrapped up and tied to a string, then hoisted "up the spout" to a floor above. (The clerk standing to the right in fig. 3.5 is doing just this.) Pawnshops smelled, too, redolent with the body odor of so many day laborers and the scent of the thousands of goods, many of them items of clothing, stored in back rooms. "The air seemed reeking with the foul breathings" of pawners over the decades, the floors worn down, the counters burnished, the walls tattooed with the graffiti of the bored, "scrawled over with names, songs, and rude drawings."[55]

Whatever their drawbacks, pawnshops provided a necessary service by supplementing many Americans' incomes. And they benefited more than just individuals and families. Loans also supported small-scale businessmen who needed to make payroll or buy new stock and supplies. These were typically "the petty entrepreneurs, people doing business on a 'shoestring,' street peddlers turned shopkeeper, sandwich stand operators, haberdashers, sweatshop owners, and the like, whose bank credit is worth little but who have something of value to pledge."[56] What was more, by funneling fresh used goods to secondary and tertiary markets through sales of unredeemed collateral, pawnbrokers contributed to a trickle-down economy that recirculated "preowned" goods. Auctioneers specializing in used goods earned valuable commissions by staging regular sales where bidders purchased unredeemed jewelry, clothing, furniture, tools, linens, and household implements.

Even regular pawnshop customers, hoping to find a bargain in others' unredeemed collateral, attended these sales to buy household accoutrements they could not otherwise afford. Proprietors of used goods shops also bid at auctions, purchasing stock to refinish, repair, and reupholster. Clothiers too found vast inventories of garments in all sizes, fabrics, and styles. Slightly worn items needed only to be cleaned. Other pieces could be restyled and dyed, while the shoddiest could be cut up and sold in bulk as rags. Jewelers, watchmakers, and metalsmiths went to sales of unredeemed collateral in search of raw materials—pieces of jewelry whose gems could be reset and metal melted down to create more fashionable objects. Watchmakers found fancy cases without parts and replacement parts without cases. Profit could even be found in the scrap metal of broken sadirons and tools selling below prevailing commodities prices. An account from 1905 estimated that over $1 million changed hands each year at auctions of unredeemed collateral in New York City. The volume of goods was so vast that separate sales (often staged by different auction houses) handled different kinds of goods including the miscellaneous ("a mass of flotsam and jetsam from homes, shops, offices, and places of amusement"), cheap jewelry, precious gemstones, and clothing.[57]

Contrary to popular perceptions, in most cities pawnbrokers' ethnicity became more diverse as time passed. Eventually, Jews who remained in the business were joined by the Irish, who had gained essential market experience in related but less lucrative trades such as scrap dealing. Pushed out of their native homes by the famine in the nineteenth century, the Irish met economic hardship in most American cities, offered little in the way of fruitful work and living wages. Facing discrimination on par with that facing African Americans (and in some cases even harsher), many Irish could only secure positions as unskilled laborers. Ditchdigging, hauling, and carting were all backbreaking, mind-numbing, unreliable work. The Irish with cash reserves (and those who immigrated with items they could pawn or sell) sometimes had enough money to rent a storefront and set up a junk shop. Junk dealing, which required knowledge of the markets in various raw materials such as copper, brass, rags, iron, and tallow, often served as a springboard to the more lucrative, reliable, and relatively stable pawnbroking trade. The Gearys, Bohans, and Clanceys set up shop right next door to the Goldsmids, Levys, and Isaacses.

In Chicago the pattern was reversed: most of the city's early pawnbrokers were Irish. Reformers estimated that only two Jewish families lived in the city in the 1840s; there were perhaps 1,500 Jews (out of a total population of about 112,000) by the 1860s (and already four times as many Irish by 1850) and nearly 40,000 Irish by the 1870s, constituting the fourth-largest Irish population in the country.[58] By the end of the century, Chicago's Jewish population was still catching up, numbering about 35,000 in 1895.[59] The Irish, by then long established, were moving on from pawnbroking, creating new entrepreneurial opportunities for Jewish immigrants in a business that in other cities had been dominated by Jews for decades. By the end of the nineteenth century Chicago saw the Caseys, Cunninghams, and Hogans getting out of pawnbroking and the Eppensteins, Lichtenstadts, and Lipmans taking it up.

Jews' involvement with pawnbroking resulted not from any inherent character flaws or moral failings, as the popular press often posited. Rather, they took up pawnbroking and like occupations largely because they were barred from other trades, especially the mechanical and artisanal, and so necessarily developed an acumen dealing in consumer goods as peddlers, used clothing dealers, and auctioneers. While not confined specifically to these trades, Jews began populating them in greater numbers by the 1840s and 1850s, because "they had been forbidden by law in many European countries from which they came to own land, to work in any but a very few of the handicraft trades, to engage in any but a very few kinds of businesses."[60] In addition, long apprenticeships with unsympathetic employers would have required observant Jews to break the Sabbath. Meanwhile, since charging interest on loans was not proscribed by the Jewish religion as it was for Christians, Jews had historically been the moneylenders, even to the Christian church itself.[61]

By midcentury pawnbrokers and resale traders in most cities were predominantly Jewish, and extended inter- and intrafamilial involvement in various sectors of the used goods business was fairly common. Although this pattern may have reinforced common perceptions that Jews were "tribalistic," such arrangements were often necessary for the survival of all and were actually no different from those of elite Anglo-American families whose wealth was the product of profitable and convenient economic alliances. The most successful and long-standing pawnbroking establishments flourished alongside, and grew apace with, other family members' businesses. The Goldbergs in Cincinnati during the 1850s were peddlers, brokers, and clothiers. The entrepreneurial pursuits of New York City's Levy family spanned the entire nineteenth century: Aaron was a successful merchant, auctioneer, and clothier. Abraham was a card manufacturer, clothier, and merchant. Arthur, Barnet, and David were all tailors, while Asher, Eleazer, Israel, J. H., Simeon, and Solomon were merchants. John J., Joseph, Louis, and Saul J. were all pawnbrokers.[62]

Families working in the same or related trades—often in close proximity—had common goals. Their enterprises endured because they cooperated with one another and shared economic resources and business connections. For instance, William Frank arrived in Philadelphia from Bavaria in the 1840s, "using $3.00 borrowed from a cousin." His stepbrother, a shoemaker, loaned Frank miscellaneous goods left over from his days as a peddler. This was enough to get Frank started in the used goods business, and when he arrived in Pittsburgh in 1846, he was able to start a pawnshop with two partners.[63]

Branches of the Nathans family of Philadelphia and the Seixas family of New York allied themselves by engaging in complementary businesses. By law a pawnbroker could not auction his customers' unredeemed collateral. Family branches running pawnshops and auction houses—often next door to or across the street from one another—kept the pawnbroker's returns in the family's coffers.[64]

For Jews in particular, access to family-based credit networks was crucial. As Bruce Mann has succinctly stated, "credit and reputation were inseparable."[65] It was extremely difficult for Jews to get credit because stereotypes, fostering widely held misapprehensions about their business practices, labeled them "non-producers" and "predators." Reports from Dun and Bradstreet would assess a businessman's trustworthiness according to his Jewishness, such as "Good, but Hebrew good"; and "No more than Jewish honesty.[66] Many Jews, already trading on the margins (financially and socially) as peddlers, secondhand clothiers, and used goods dealers, capitalized on extended family networks to the benefit of everyone involved. Outsiders extended credit to Jews only "cautiously," no matter the longevity of their success.[67]

Established, successful pawnshops were often passed down through single families rather than being taken over by outside partners; younger generations grew up in the trade and learned from fathers, uncles, and brothers, thus providing steady income to families over generations and contributing to social and economic stability where pawnbrokers resided. (See, for example, fig. 4.6, which shows four members of the Rubin family overseeing Uncle Dave's Pawnshop in Charleston, South Carolina.) The Benjamins, an early Baltimore pawnbroking family, began with Levi Benjamin. In the mid-1850s his sons Solomon and Jacob took over the business and eventually were operating three shops in the city. They hoped their father's regular customers would continue to patronize the sons, advertising their shop as "formerly occupied by Levi Benjamin," adding, "We solicit a continuance of the patronage so liberally bestowed on the old Establishment."[68] Pawners came to trust long-standing shops run by members of the same family and felt more comfortable getting their loans at the same place from familiar, reliable pawnbrokers.

A few women operated pawnshops, usually entering the trade through their husbands, who trained them in record keeping and appraising. Elizabeth Brooker, for example, took over her husband's eight-year-old Philadelphia pawnshop after his death in 1831 and continued to run it until 1853, when her son became proprietor. In 1833 widow Sarah Millem placed an ad in the *Baltimore American* attesting to her status as a fully licensed pawnbroker: "Mrs. MILLEM has given ample security to the Mayor and City council, for the faithful discharge of the trusts confided to her. . . . She particularly invites all such as require TEMPORARY RELIEF."[69] Located at 14½ Harrison Street, Millem's shop shared space with Jacob Aaron's secondhand clothing store. (By 1837 he had taken over the pawnshop.) Baltimore's city ordinance assumed pawnbroking was an equal-opportunity occupation, stating that applicants needed to provide "satisfactory evidence of his, her, or their good character."[70] According to city directories, Elizabeth Hart ran a pawnshop in New York City for at least five years, from 1810 to 1815, and may have been related to the Harts who operated as clothiers/pawnbrokers/liquor dealers on the same street through the early 1840s. Ellen Cunningham began operating a pawnshop and secondhand furniture store in Chicago in the mid-1850s.

Yet pawnbroking was still considered a man's business. Virginia Penny, for one, in her book *Five Hundred Employments Adapted to Women,* was not very hopeful about female pawnbrokers' prospects. She interviewed "an intelligent

Irish pawnbroker" who knew of only one woman in the business. Like Elizabeth Brooker and Sarah Millem, the proprietress was "nominally a widow, and employed a young man to stay in the shop." More often, women functioned as "auxiliaries" and made their way into pawnshops as wives, sisters, and daughters of proprietors. Penny's informant stressed that pawnbroking, an occupation not without its dangerous clientele, was better suited to "a strong man" who could deal with rude, drunk, and profane customers.[71] Yet in Chicago, and in a few other cities, females edged into the business: of the fifty-two pawnbrokers listed in the 1880 Chicago city directory, five were women.[72]

Most pawnbrokers remained as anonymous as their customers, leaving no personal papers or business archives. There were a few exceptions, however. The Simpson family, for instance, whose New York City pawnbroking business spanned five generations from the 1820s to the 1950s, embraced their professional heritage, calling themselves the "emperors of pawnbroking." According to the entry on pawnbrokers in the 1892 edition of *Appleton's Dictionary of New York*, "Simpson's is the trade name in New York most widely known in connection with pawnbroking, a large family of that name having long been identified with the business in this city."[73] Simpson's pawnshops were scattered through the area. Even though shops were independently owned by individual family members, the familiar name created a brand identity that raised the profile and reputation of them all, and pawners assumed they were branches of the same concern. A writer for *Harper's New Monthly Magazine* in 1859 created the composite of "Messrs. Timson and Co." in an article titled "Up the Spout."[74] In 1937 the *Saturday Evening Post* asked its readers, "Is Your Watch at Simpson's?"[75] And *Good Housekeeping* called the Simpsons "our royal family of American pawnbroking."[76]

Like many other pawnbrokers, the Simpsons relied on family connections to bankroll initial enterprises and passed their shops down through the generations. Brothers John B. and William took over their uncle Walter Stevenson Simpson's shop and then split up to form separate businesses. William's eventually went to William Jr., then William Joseph, and finally to William R., who wrote proudly about the family enterprise in his memoir *Hockshop*.[77] Cousin Robert owned another pawnshop emblazoned with the family name. And although the men did not enter into formal partnerships, they did enjoy the prestige, reputation, and respect of the Simpson name, which was so well known that "shops with which they are no longer connected carry on business under their names."[78]

The Simpson reputation thus resonated with generations of New Yorkers. An important source of the Simpson prestige was the family's emphatically non-Jewish ancestry. As *Appleton's* noted, "Although pawnbroking is supposed to be a business affected exclusively by Jews, yet the Simpsons are of Irish origin."[79] In *Hockshop* William Simpson referred to his "gentile Protestant family" lest readers make the wrong assumptions about the background of this pawn-broking clan.[80] The Simpsons' ethnicity was not the only thing atypical about them. When founding patriarch William Simpson died in 1879 after spending nearly half a century in the family pawnshop, he was said to be worth about $3 million, amassed through shrewd investments in real estate and manufacturing. Along with brother J. B., William spent his retirement on a rural estate in West Farms, outside the city.

A few other pawnbrokers also did well for themselves. Brothers Mitchell and Henry Hart were reportedly worth $12 million in the early 1870s. They accumulated their fortune over a lifetime of frugal living and shrewd investing in real estate and railroads. But rather than celebrate them for their entrepreneurship, the press depicted the brothers as a curiosity. Bachelors, the Harts lived above their shop in a "dingy garret" (also described as a "queer old house") and rarely ventured beyond Chatham Street. One writer found it remarkable that the pawnbrokers "did not hide their hoard, where, at the dead of night, they could rouse from their sleep to count the glittering gold and shining silver, but like business men kept a bank account, and several well-known banks were proud to have them as depositors."[81] More modest but still substantial were Elizabeth Brooker's assets, estimated at $225 in 1830, most likely the value of her deceased husband's property. As head of household, she was supporting not only herself but at least three other people.[82] Better capitalized was New York City pawnbroker John Levy. Thirty years old in 1850, he owned $20,000 in real property and supported six people.[83]

However, the earnings of those in the public record did not represent the average member of the pawnbroking fraternity. Like many other businessmen operating in interstitial markets, most pawnbrokers worked the margins. Once they reached their professional apex, they typically did not advance much beyond the class of their customers and failed to accumulate enough capital to invest in larger financial endeavors that would have elevated them socially and economically. A pawnbroker's profits were tied to the economic fortunes of his customers, and he often suffered losses at auctions of unredeemed collateral, especially during economic crunches. Pawnbrokers running shops in smaller cities necessarily supplemented the lending business with other petty entrepreneurial activities.[84] Average pawnbrokers made enough money to support their families and to keep the business going, but probably not much more.

Yet the misconception that most pawnbrokers were wealthy is understandable. They were, after all, the ones with the cash, and at any one time over the years Americans have been walking around with hundreds of thousands of dollars borrowed from pawnbrokers in their pockets. In 1828 the *National Advocate* reported an estimated $540,000 in outstanding loans in New York City alone ($2.74 per capita).[85] According to *Hunt's Merchants' Magazine*, in 1860 pawnbrokers on the East Side of the city held more than 1,750,000 outstanding pledges securing $1,237,000 in loans (an estimated 6.66 pledges per person for everyone in the immediate vicinity and 71¢ per loan).[86] The Provident Loan Society, New York City's nonprofit pawnshop, reportedly made $765,000 in loans to 36,000 people in 1897 alone.[87] Pawning in other cities followed the same pattern. Statistics for 1899 reveal that Chicago pawners, for instance, had over 24,000 items in hock, constituting more than $124,000 in outstanding loans averaging $5.08 each. During that same year pawnbrokers in Washington, DC, recorded over 4,000 pawns on their books for a total of over $32,000 in outstanding loans averaging $7.92 each.[88] In 1930 pawnbrokers' loans accounted for almost one-quarter of all consumer credit, and later in the decade between $140 and $600 million (estimates varied widely) was owed to pawnbrokers.[89]

Yet these figures, suggesting a wealthy pawnbroking industry, belie the reality of pawnbroking's economics. With so much money owed to them, pawnbrokers should have been swimming in cash. In truth, they were as vulnerable to fluctuating economic cycles as their customers. The cash that pawnbrokers loaned out did not necessarily equal cash coming back in. Loan interest, fees (for ticket writing, storage, and loan renewals), and proceeds from sales of unredeemed collateral made up a pawnbroker's income. Expenses recorded on the other side of the balance sheet included rent or mortgage payments for the shop and property taxes, clerks' wages, clerical expenses, security, storage, license fees, costs related to organizing auction sales (advertising, transporting goods to the site, the auctioneer's commission), losses from forfeiting stolen goods to the police, and depressed auction sales.

To get a sense of how well pawnbrokers did, it is possible to calculate the average profit made on each loan, dividing a pawnbroker's annual expenses by the number of pawns for the year. Profits and losses are determined by the difference between the cost to make each loan and the amount of interest coming back in over time (sometimes months or years). If a pawn is never redeemed, a pawnbroker collects no interest. Although he will eventually auction off the collateral, if it sells for far below market value, a pawnbroker might suffer a loss on that loan, unable to recoup the initial amount he extended and any interest he might have gained. If a pawner does redeem his property, the loan is profitable only if the additional interest exceeds the expense of granting the loan in the first place. Small loans over short terms are not very lucrative, even if made every week, such as the Monday morning pawning of Sunday clothes. In a study on pawnbrokers at the end of the nineteenth century, Champion Bissell noted that the "nondescript, bulky, dirty, and almost worthless pledges of the poorer classes" were especially unprofitable. A pawnbroker made next to nothing from a 50¢ loan on an article with little value and redeemed in a week: 63¢ (3¢ interest and a dime charged, "outside the statute," for storage). Bissell asked his readers, "What is it really worth to handle and examine a flat-iron, a vest, a chemise, a veil, and a feather, to tie them up in a bundle, number the bundle, ticket it, issue a duplicate ticket, and enter the transaction in a book? Would you want to do it, or hire an assistant to do it, for much less than thirteen cents?"[90]

In *The Business of Pawnbroking* Samuel Levine provides an example of a watch and a coat, each pawned for $1. The watch incurs a 3¢ interest charge per week, the coat 9¢ (3¢ interest plus 6¢ for storage). At the end of the year the pawner would have paid a total of $1.56 to pawn and redeem the watch weekly (52 × 3¢, or 156%), and $4.68 (52 × 9¢, or 468%) for the coat. "If this were all there was to these transactions," Levine maintained, "it would justify the opinion that the pawnbroker is making enormous profits."[91] But he then calculated a pawnbroker's average expenses for each loan by dividing the annual costs of running the operation by the total number of transactions for the year, thus arriving at the pawnbroker's average cost per loan. For New York City pawnbrokers in 1913 this figure was about 15¢. By Levine's estimates (which he squared against the Provident Loan Society's official reports for their own presumably accurate transaction costs), a pawnbroker typically lost money on smaller loans, garnering $1.56 in interest for the watch that over a year cost him $8.80 in transaction expenses, leaving a deficit of $6.24. He would have lost $3.12 on the coat over the same period. Midsize loans over long terms and large loans of any duration produced the most income and offset losses from the smaller loans. In *The Principles of Economics*, published in 1904, Frank A. Fetter provided yet another illustration of the economics of pawnbroking: "Five thousand dollars loaned in sums averaging ten dollars represents five hundred transactions, and yet if placed at five per cent. it yields but two hundred and fifty dollars a year. . . . the lender must credit a large part of the gross interest to the labor he expends in carrying on the business."[92] A pawnbroker counted his profits in pennies.

What was more, pawnbrokers did not prevail during the country's desperate economic times but were as likely to fail as other businessmen. Because cash (and the interest derived from it) was their stock in trade, pawnbrokers relied on the inflow of capital from pawners redeeming their goods so that they could loan it out again. Stored collateral did not count as a business asset, and if short on cash, pawnbrokers resorted to bank loans, possibly paying higher interest than they could legally charge their own customers for use of that very same money. Making matters worse, periods of economic depression affected the resale market in unredeemed collateral, so even when pawns could be liquidated, they might bring only a fraction of their former worth and much less than the amount initially loaned. In October 1876 Simpson's, for instance, had over $250,000 in outstanding loans: a quarter of a million dollars in, essentially, speculation—money invested on the chance that pawners would redeem their collateral.[93] Still reeling from the depression, a pawnbroker in 1876 "says his business was never so dull as it is at present . . . all his clients have pawned everything they have, and have no money to redeem what they have in pawn."[94] Trying to maintain a broad customer base, support regular customers, and minimize risk by not lending too much to any one pawner, pawnbrokers often had to cap loans during hard times, thus choking their profits even more.

Depressions also brought a higher class of clientele as economic hardship ascended to the upper classes, putting most pawnbrokers in a difficult bind. The quality of pawns coming in from the moneyed classes was generally higher—silver sets, precious gemstones, Civil War medals—and people therefore expected (and needed) more money for them. Pawnbroker James T. Waite observed in 1877 that the pledges "are much more valuable than New York pawnbrokers have been in the habit of receiving. Here is a silver snuff-box that belonged to a well-known politician. . . . This pair of gold suspender buckles belonged to a Tammany police justice."[95] And these objects likely were more difficult to sell at auction, unattractive to bidders because the reserve was too high or the objects themselves too peculiar.

Like other businessmen, pawnbrokers could also become the victims of unwise investments. During the depression year of 1893 the Taylor Brothers, for example, were forced to sell their pawnshop. "The trouble of the firm," according to one account, "was not due to anything in the pawnbroking business." Rather, the owners invested in a tannery (co-owned by a brother-in-law of one of the Taylors), which suffered liabilities amounting to some $125,000. Before overextending themselves in what became a failed concern, Taylor Brothers had a net capital of $88,000 and made an average of $1,000 worth of loans each day.[96] Bernard Berman similarly was forced to relinquish his pawnshop in early 1895; he sold it to Harris Ablowich, who intended to liquidate Berman's stock of diamonds, a more certain business proposition than taking on the pawnshop. "The cause of Mr. Berman's failure," a newspaper reported, "is attributed to losses on the sales of diamonds on the installment plan." If people, still recovering from the 1893 crash, were not able to redeem their pawns of tools and clothing, it was far less likely that they could continue paying off their diamonds.[97] The New York City nonprofit Provident Loan Society also felt the effects of the crash.

Although its robber baron organizers had ready access to capital, they nonetheless halted construction on new branch buildings. And in the wake of the Panic of 1907, officers decided to lower the cap on loans from $1,000 to $50.[98]

The effects of the Great Depression on pawnbrokers, like so many other Americans, were catastrophic. Diamonds depreciated to less than a third of their value, and shops specializing in loans on gemstones lost between $250,000 and $600,000 each year during the 1930s. The Provident Loan Society reportedly lost over $1 million in 1933 alone.[99] Leo Finkelstein's most vivid recollections of his time as a pawnbroker in North Carolina emerge from the years of the Great Depression when, possessing little operating capital, he continued to loan money and cash payroll checks. It was a difficult time: three local bankers committed suicide; a customer bought a gun at his shop, then killed himself on the spot. When the warmer months came, people pawned their overcoats for between $5 and $8. The wool coats invited moths, so Finkelstein filled the pockets with mothballs, sprayed the garments with DDT, and took them to the drycleaner's. By 1933 Finkelstein's shop was overflowing with more than eight hundred hocked overcoats. When cold weather gripped the area once again, people had no money to redeem their collateral, but the pawnbroker gave the coats back anyway—poor and cold, his customers needed them. Besides, he remarked in an interview, he wouldn't have been able to sell them to anyone else.[100] Estimated outstanding loans for all pawnbrokers in the country in 1933 alone amounted to $400 million.[101]

Other private pawnshops experienced similar difficulties. The Steel City Pawnshop, whose ledgers still exist, is a case in point. During the 1930s Birmingham was home to fourteen pawnshops (one for every 18,000 people), plus two additional pawnshops in the outlying mining town of Ensley, one of which was Steel City. Its ledgers, while not comprehensive (covering only a little over a year of business), do provide a sense of the way pawnshop owners and their customers were both trying to piece together a living. Money broker J. S. Keith opened Steel City in 1918. In 1931 Keith left the shop to run a furniture store across the street and William E. Daniel, a former tailor, was named proprietor. Mines owned by Tennessee Coal, Iron and Railroad, Sloss, Republic, Woodward, and Pratt Consolidated helped cushion the blow of the Depression, offering steady if low-paying work to the people in and around Birmingham. Annual wages fell from $924 in 1919 to $727 in the early 1930s; yet 31,000 people remained employed, working not only in the mines but also in textile factories and other occupations that supported the city.[102] Despite that, Steel City couldn't survive, and sometime in 1933 the shop went under. Former Steel City clerks and managers became salesmen, collectors, and gas station attendants.

However fragmentary, the transactions recorded in Steel City's surviving books show just how crucial pawnshop loans could be during times of increasing economic uncertainty among a population—in this case, many miners living in company towns—barely making ends meet. A pawnshop's bottom line often teetered between the red and the black, solely reliant on customers' ability to pay back their loans. One "nife" pawned for 50¢ was redeemed a week later. Another was not, the outstanding amount entered in red in the debit column. The clerks at Steel City accepted a range of pawns from things with true resale value to items taken as collateral for "courtesy" loans. The former included sewing machines, diamond rings, earrings, clocks, suits, fishing tackle, and guns. The latter, underwear, "sox," a piece of rosin, and a rain hat. The ledger pages document pawners who faithfully paid off loans on very humble items over many weeks. Such was the case with I. C. Bell, an African American laborer living in Ensley: "He is the best pay on the book," a clerk wrote approvingly on his account page. And because of his good credit history, Steel City would have extended many future loans to him. Likewise, Ensley laborer Frederick Hendrix (also African American) was "good for $500." Dollie Lee, who lived in nearby Fairfield, paid "monthly." And J. Clyde Vandiver, a switchman from Wylam, would "pay when can."

Correspondence from the Hands Loan Company in Stockton, California, tells a similar story, that pawnbrokers often worked with customers to get their money back, revealing a more dynamic and mutually dependent relationship than is typically thought. After receiving a "friendly reminder" from Mr. Hands in 1938 about the $10.90 still outstanding on his loan, Joe Williams replied,

> My Dear Ralph,
> We enclose $2.50 to apply on this balance we will knock the remainder off soon but boy has been out of work and my expenses have been heavy I tried to see you last two times I was in Stockton but you were closed late Sat. night & Sunday so I did not get to see you.[103]

In need of "a great favor," David Carr wrote the Hands Loan Company from Reno in 1937: "I wonder if you would put my suit, which you are holding, in a box and ship it C.O.D. for all charges due to me. . . . I have an office job here—but I can't go to work until I get my suit."[104]

Ultimately it was in pawnbrokers' best interests to remain flexible with their customers, since accommodating pawners' economic hardships and health crises increased the likelihood that they would make good on their loans and continue patronizing the shop. When she wrote to Mr. Hands, Emma Mitchell promised to be at his shop within the month to pay off her loan, pleading, "Please don't sell my rings, as I have been sick with my teeth."[105] James Davis couldn't redeem his suit coat on time because "I got my shoulder broke and haven't been able to work."[106] Mrs. Blackiston dispatched a letter on her husband's behalf about the watch he was "a couple days late" making payments on, explaining that "due to the serious illness of our little girl every thing but her sickness was forgotten." "I realize," she continued, "the watch is perhaps not worth as much as the loan and interest paid but the watch was a gift to Mr. Blackiston from his mother, who has passed on and of course is as treasured as a keepsake. You've been most kind in your past dealings and I sincerely hope that every thing is O.K. about the watch and that you have not sold it."[107] We do not know how Mr. Hands responded, but other correspondence suggests that customers often relied on his generosity. A letter from Glenn Foley requesting return of his Gladstone bag concluded, "Thank you kindly for the loan and also for the many favors you have done me in the past."[108] W. P. Holmes sent his son to Mr. Hands with a note reading, "This is my boy Jack. What you can do for him is alright. He wants to get some thing's for school before Tuesday. I do not get paid before Tuesday."[109].

Regulations notwithstanding, pawning continued to be a highly social and flexible form of borrowing, harking back to earlier, less formal credit economies. Because pawnshops were anchored in local communities, customers were often friends and neighbors as well. Mr. Hands and other pawnbrokers who extended generous terms, granting "many favors" over time, were both decent people and smart businessmen. They not only understood how difficult it was for people to weather financial storms but were also keenly aware of how essential pawners' loan repayments were to their own survival.

Indeed, extending favors unwisely could lead to a pawnbroker's downfall, especially in hard economic times like the Great Depression. No matter how many pawners faithfully paid off their $6 debts on pairs of pants or $1.50 on fishing tackle, there were many more who did not make good on their loans and left pawnbrokers surrounded by shelves packed with worthless stuff. The bad risks recorded in Steel City's ledgers included:

A. B. Barfoot, "Gone"
Walter Bailey, "Gone"
Sam Bennett, "Bankrupt, 8/13/29"
A. B. Blackstone, "Don't loan"
John Chandler, "Gone"
D. J. Coleman, "Don't Loan"
C. H. Cleveland, "Don't Loan"
Willie Clanton, "Gone"
Frank Dorsey, "Don't loan by order of W. E. Daniel"
Abraham Daniels, "Dead"

J. Edwards, "Don't loan"
Will Evans, "B.K. [bankrupt] 5/22/30"
Walter Freeman, "Bk"
Ben Fritz, "Bankrupt 5/24/30"
Ben Goodloe, "Aint no good"
William Glasgow, "Bank Rupt dont know when so he says"
L. Z. Green, "Gone"
John L. Henniger, "Dont Loan"
Elijah Howard, "Bankrupt 7/28/31"
J. H. Hayes, "Gone"
Mack Hunter, "Dead. Shot"
Primo Johnson, "Died Apr 9, 1931"
Will Johnson, "Moved," "Lost"
Jed Kirksy, "Dead"
John King, "Don't Loan"
W. L. Kilpatrick, "No good"
Martin King, "Dead"
Renty Mitchell, "Gone," "Come back"
Boss Mathews, "Bankrupt 7/10/31"
W. L. Milner, "Dont Loan. Said he would Trade with Bronson from now on"
Will Pittman, "Dont Loan"
Prince Smith, "BK 3–9–1931"
Andrew Thompson, "BK. 6–16–31"
G. C. Whatley, "Moved get address" "Bank Rupt 3/30/1931"[110]

It is no wonder that Steel City did not survive the Depression. Typical of so many other pawnshops, the Steel City story contradicts the popular belief that pawnbrokers did well during lean times. In fact, they experienced the personal fallout of economic crises more than most other businessmen. They saw the face of impoverishment every day. New York pawnbroker Irving Berg, who in 1954 reminisced about his professional life, "was reluctant" to discuss the Depression in much detail. "Business is best in normal times" was all he would say.[111]

Over time, pawnbrokers also found themselves responding to overarching shifts in the American economy. The second Industrial Revolution at the end of the nineteenth century delivered more consumer goods, faster and cheaper, than ever before, and pawners found it more convenient and affordable to buy new goods than to get their old things out of hock. "The good days of pawnbroking are over," declared one pawnbroker at the beginning of the twentieth century.[112] At the dawn of the century many pawnbrokers were limiting the items they accepted as collateral to those goods with higher and more stable value—watches, jewelry, gemstones, objects made from precious metals, cameras, fine musical instruments. They could both concentrate on a more exclusive clientele, especially if they also sold used goods in the same line, and hone their expertise and appraisal skills in just a few fields to better avoid being taken in by counterfeits.

Pawnbrokers catering to the upper classes (considered "a very delicate branch of the business") were also found in most major cities, located in tony parts of the city, "nestle[d] among the more aristocratic neighborhoods."[113] They held positions of economic and social power, knowing full well that their clients, whose reputations were in jeopardy, relied on confidential transactions. Operating discreetly—the three balls nowhere in sight—these men euphemistically called themselves "diamond brokers" and "loan agents."[114] Spared the typical dank and crowded pawnshop environs, genteel pawners conducted their affairs in comfortable, luxuriously appointed rooms furnished with overstuffed sofas and gilt-framed paintings, much like their own homes. Many loan agents, who held respectable day jobs as auctioneers, attorneys, and gem brokers, operated illegally in the underground economy, serving society's elite. Unlicensed dealers who escaped the notice of the authorities, they serviced the uppermost strata of society. "The loan office," observed one contemporary, "is an independent sort of affair, that charges anything the proprietor chooses, and sells the borrower up if he does not pay the accrued interest at the end of thirty days."[115]

Not that pawnbrokers asked, but the loans they extended to the upper crust underwrote vacations, helped maintain fashionable lifestyles, and funded gambling habits. Customers were the "mushroomery and upstarts generally, who have fluttered, and soared, and fallen; people of pretension without balancing qualities, and destitute of ballast in coin."[116] Whereas poor and middling customers, the "old skirt and petticoat army," pawned Sunday clothes on Monday and redeemed them Saturday night, upper-class pawners, the "watch and ulster brigade," did the opposite: they pawned their goods on Saturday night for quick cash and got them out of hock early the next week.[117] Upscale customers who needed cash also required discretion. Reputations (and credit extended on them) could quickly crumble owing to rumors of financial embarrassment or insolvency. One New York City diamond broker worked above a florist's shop. His customers, all "fashionable ladies," gained access through a hidden door while pretending to buy flowers.[118] Carver Reed and Company emphasized the "prominent position" and "ample capital" of its Philadelphia establishment, adding that "the Loan business is more of a confidential character than otherwise, and this feature is strictly maintained at this place."[119] The two branches run by Robert Simpson ("the Tiffany's of the pawnbroking business") on West Forty-second

Street and on Broadway, boasted of personal service in a milieu meant "to inspire confidence and respect." Entering by the private ladies' passageway on the side of the building, a woman could not but appreciate "the tactful manner in which you find yourself whisked through a grilled door into one of a series of small, soundproof private rooms, where you see no one and no one sees you except a Simpson's clerk who waits with dignity upon you."[120]

Upper-class pawners highly valued a pawnbroker's seeming indifference. And shrewd pawnbrokers leveraged their clients' indebtedness to acquire more customers and press for loan repayments, which were much preferred over forfeitures. "The lender," explained one account, "has double security for repayment. He has a moral, as well as financial guarantee."[121] One pawnbroker in 1881 described the "recent craze" for investing in mining company stocks. Calling to mind Internet day trading, the "rage for stock gambling" at the end of the nineteenth century induced "ladies of undoubted respectability who move in good society" to invest thousands of dollars that they obtained from private loan offices, since their husbands would never approve of such risky activity.[122] The names of these same women might well have constituted a loan broker's list of people to be cultivated, "ladies whose tastes and habits are known to be extravagant."[123] Such brokers even approached servants, who, for a price, acted as "useful agents in giving points in regard to future customers."[124]

Shrewd loan brokers could make hundreds, if not thousands, on each high-roller transaction. But their risks were high, as loan redemption rates hovered around 75%, a full 15% below the 90% average. Upscale pawnbrokers mitigated their risks by leveraging their knowledge. By going to a diamond broker for a loan, a wife was acting behind her husband's back. If for collateral she used a special piece of jewelry expected to make an appearance at a public event, she had to try to borrow it back from her lender. The favor came at a price—in exchange, she might be asked to provide names of "other ladies who are hard up for funds." In this way the woman, "after two or three experiences of the same kind," became "an agent of the man from whom she had borrowed money."[125] Unlicensed high-end pawnbrokers circumvented municipal regulations by operating under the radar, charging whatever interest rates the underground market would bear, and sometimes pressuring their customers. Being privy to highly delicate financial situations empowered these brokers, because they could use that sensitive information to their advantage.

Pawnbroking was not the brutish, unsophisticated profession that critics made it out to be. Rather, it required finesse from borrowers and lenders alike. Pawnbrokers were called on hundreds of times a week (and sometimes each day) to make fine distinctions about the quality of goods presented to them as collateral in order to make sound appraisals. They also had to stay abreast of prevailing markets and make valuations based on what they determined the future worth of a particular item to be. In addition, pawnbrokers made judgments in anticipation of the market's future climate. They endured the American economy's perpetual boom and bust cycles along with everyone else and helped their customers get through seasons of unemployment and other personal financial crises. Pawnbrokers were constantly adapting to the continual transformations of the country's macro- and microeconomies.

Although pawnbroking played a crucial role in the development of capitalism, it harked back to earlier economies in which economic and social relationships were interlinked. As lenders, pawnbrokers judged pawners with the same critical eye they used to assess their collateral. The relative creditworthiness of customers, established over long periods of repeat business, allowed pawnbrokers to grant higher loans and to remain somewhat flexible about terms of repayment while also minimizing risk. Remaining at the same location for several generations, pawnshops were part of the local fabric, and pawnbrokers came to know intimately the communities where they lived and worked. Their loans not only helped maintain individual household economies but supported small businesses that also anchored the neighborhood.

Undeniably, pawnbrokers held positions of power because they had reserves of much-needed cash and determined to whom it would be dispensed and on what terms. They also derived power from the sensitive financial information they gathered about their pawners, in particular members of the elite. For this class more than any other, social status, reputation, and the ability to obtain credit—to maintain increasingly materialistic standards of living—were interlinked.

Yet because they worked in the fringe economy, pawnbrokers rarely saw the kinds of wealth amassed by the famous Simpson clan. Although it is surely surprising to some, the average pawnbroker occupied a place among the middling. And because his livelihood was so closely tied to their rising and falling fortunes, he was also at the mercy of his customers, whom he relied on to repay their loans. There was give-and-take on both sides of the counter.

CHAPTER FOUR

THE ECONOMIES OF
EVERYDAY LIFE

The ledger from John Simpson's New York City pawnshop is massive, over five hundred pages logging more than 27,000 transactions. Even the most successful businesses likely did not complete 27,000 transactions in their lifetimes. This ledger, covering early August 1838 through the middle of February 1839, accounts for only a half a year's pawning for a single pawnshop. As the earliest and only nineteenth-century example still existing, it is remarkable.[1] At the same time, Simpson's ledger is quite ordinary in that it is representative of the quantity and quality of pawnshop transactions through time.

It contains just the facts: date, name, address, item pawned, and amount loaned. Yet the often cryptic information is still illuminating. A few pawns stand out because they are unique or unusual, such as the gold watch pawned for a hefty $110 and the accordion for $3. Most pawns are remarkable, though, only because of their utter humbleness. Hundreds of handkerchiefs ("hdcf"), petticoats ("pt"), and gowns appear on the books, pawned for as little as 6½¢. They were most often brought in by women who, when they did not elude compilers of the city directories, were listed as widows. These poignant entries present the stark realities faced by most people living in urban America, which already by the late 1830s experienced the results of solidifying capitalist structures. The average American's relationship with her (or his) pawnbroker tells us much about the exigencies—the economies—of ordinary daily life in the emergent American economy (see frontispiece).

People went to pawnbrokers because they needed money, of course. They secured their loans using what collateral they had—small, "movable" pieces of personal property. Pawners had to make decisions about what, of all the things they owned, to use as collateral. These material items inhabited flexible spheres of value, often simultaneously. Tracked over time, the kind of things people pawned indicates the fluctuating availability of goods during the development of the Industrial Revolution and the concomitant maturation of consumer culture. Perhaps not surprisingly, the most disenfranchised Americans—those with little property, cash, or steady labor—had to make extremely astute decisions about when and what to pawn. (Their financial balancing act mirrored that of the pawnbrokers, who similarly calculated loan values and creditworthiness.) Pawners had an easier time than cultural commentators did in understanding that objects could inhabit competing spheres of value—sentimental and monetary—at the same time. Those who frequented pawnshops did not have the luxury of compartmentalizing the functions of their objects—possessions had to do double if not triple duty as practical things with use value, repositories of emotion with sentimental value, and viable pawns with exchange value.

Pawning was an economic coping strategy well suited to the transformations occurring throughout the nineteenth century as the country experienced the shift to industrial capitalism and the intense boom and bust cycles that resulted. The pawnbroker provided access to credit that was otherwise unavailable to the working poor. Pawning was also responsive to often immediate financial need, providing short-term loans at a moment's notice. What was more, pawning offered flexibility (in what was acceptable collateral, the duration of the loan, and so on) to households experiencing extremely inflexible and straitened circumstances. Significantly, pawning was essential to the development of industrial capitalism and was particularly adaptive to larger economic changes over time. Its role in this regard cannot be underestimated. Evidence from the Simpson ledger alone tells us that tens of thousands of things were pawned each year—a rate of borrowing that did not abate in the subsequent decades.

For their part, pawners—not the victims that critics assumed—exercised a great deal of personal agency about what they pawned and how they integrated these loans into their regular household economies. Decisions regarding what to pawn varied among families, among individuals within families, and with the same person depending on particular circumstance. The people in line at the pawnbroker's counter and what they brought through the pawnshop's doors reveal much about the material and emotional properties of goods throughout the nineteenth century and the place of pawnbroking in economies at micro and macro levels.

The items taken in by John Simpson and other pawnbrokers fit the legal definition of a pawn as any piece of property used to secure a loan.[2] Pawns possess a few essential characteristics. They are "visible and tangible."[3] They have to be "movable," that is, able to be physically taken to a pawnshop, where they remain under the pawnbroker's physical control. A few things cannot be pawned. They include objects not able to be stored at the pawnshop, sacred items, and living things. Stakes in corporations, real estate, securities, bonds, and other financial instruments (the purview of bankers and securities dealers) also do not enter pawnshops as loan collateral. Property presumed to be stolen cannot be accepted as legal pawns. There have also historically been restrictions on pawners: loans cannot be made to intoxicated people, minors, and servants (the last more applicable to centuries past).

All loans, in effect, sell time: time to be able to use someone else's money. Many economic historians have cited liberal access to credit as an important reason for capitalism's early and rapid development in America, allowing merchants to buy stock on credit and enabling them in turn to extend credit to cash-strapped customers. Although many people were uneasy about the abstract and fluid nature of credit, "the lure of expanded credit was universally irresistible."[4] Credit was the only feasible way to fund large-scale commercial ventures. Men of capital parlayed their reputations, forged and reinforced through social and family relationships, into credit relationships. Eighteenth- and nineteenth-century merchants enjoyed generous credit terms, including low interest rates payable over long periods, often several years. They typically paid about 7% annual interest on various financial obligations (although this too was negotiable) and were allowed flexible repayment schedules. Business obligations were often inseparable from social relationships, and a man's ability to enter and remain in these relationships determined his access to capital.

Credit was extended on all economic levels. Chronically short on capital, colonists and, later, citizens of the United States relied on credit for most commercial transactions. Rarely documented, individuals often extended credit to one another informally, "Friend to friend, neighbor to neighbor," in "costly" and "inefficient" loans. These "private loans" enabled people to "start a farm, expand a small business, or ride out an unanticipated financial crisis."[5]

A different class of borrower was the pawner, who needed credit not to embark on empire building but simply to make ends meet. In contrast to the large-scale credit networks constructed among groups of merchants, pawnshop loans were discrete transactions requiring of pawners nothing more than to offer an item as collateral and repay the loan plus interest to get that item back. Local legislation enacted during the first decades of the nineteenth century fixed loan terms. Rates were set at, typically, about 6% in most cities, and renewal and repayment dates were also set down in writing.[6] Yet pawnbrokers exercised their own discretion and were often more flexible about these transactions, extending the duration of some loans, lending more than the collateral was worth, and waiving extra fees. Pawnshop loans suited the temporal needs of pawners, who could borrow money for a week, a month, or longer. People were, in effect, buying time.

Successful and well-connected merchants enjoyed the long-term credit cycle offered by the mainstream market. People with less money and fewer connections ("everybody but capitalists," according to one commentator) obtained cash from the pawnbroker and worked within shorter and more costly credit cycles to meet the crushing immediacy of weekly rent and daily food purchases.[7] Poorer people sought out loans of short duration, while those with an array of financial resources and options (whether access to credit networks or movable collateral) could buy more time to use others' money by securing larger, longer-term loans at lower interest rates.

Financial stability was often a matter of time. And time mapped onto class. With more time came more freedom. Their lack of cash and access to traditional credit networks handicapped the working poor, making their already inflexible economies even less able to withstand income drops and unforeseen expenses. Even people with steady employment found that paying for basic necessities was a chronic concern, dictating what they ate, where they lived, and how they behaved. Not unlike today, for instance, wealth decided the temporality of urban rent payments: successful merchants and artisans in New York City paid their landlords quarterly; less skilled artisans paid by the month; and others, engaged in occupations unknown or too obscure to merit recording in the rent books, paid every two weeks.[8] (Per diem, monthly rentals were cheaper than weekly rentals, but the working poor were not able to pay out such sums at any one time.[9] To cover the cost of potential vacancies, landlords charged a premium for shorter leases.)

Pawnshop transactions clearly show the necessity of buying time. Calculated over seasons rather than years, a craftsman's borrowing cycles with the pawnbroker were shorter than the loans a bank would grant to a merchant, reflecting and responding to the seasonal nature of much antebellum employment. Rivers frozen in winter closed opportunities to sailors and shipbuilders. Inclement weather often kept carpenters from their work, and the productivity of shoemakers and tailors depended on fickle consumer demand.[10] In an 1836 proposal for a nonprofit pawnshop, physician and philanthropist James Mease stressed to the Philadelphia Common Council "the very high rates of interest paid by some mechanics and others . . . during pressing distress, to pawnbrokers, for pecuniary advances on their tools of trade."[11] Pawnbrokers helped craftsmen get through slack times by accepting their tools as collateral and storing them securely during seasons of unemployment. A writer for *Harper's New Monthly Magazine* observed that "during the summer months the business of the pawnbrokers, though good, is not by any means pressing. The laboring classes are then, for the most part, well and profitably employed."[12] Artisans' collateral yielded relatively high loans—tools were precision-made implements, costly to replace, and the means of making one's livelihood. Carpenters' saws, masons' trowels, and leatherworkers' punches found easy conversion into capital during periodic lulls in work, often yielding enough money to tide families over entire seasons of unemployment.[13] When productivity resumed, employers often advanced wages so workers could get their tools out of hock and begin earning again.

Store owners also pawned cyclically, according to the rhythms of retail sales. It was common for small merchants to pawn goods from their stock to secure "money for the holiday trade," which would pay for specialty goods, advertisements, and store displays. A Boston merchant who did just that considered the three months' interest a reasonable fee "for the accommodation" of ready money.[14] Others, however, thought pawning a more dubious proposition, as lampooned in a late-century comic valentine, "Count Up the Interest":

> At the end of the season you're always dead broke,
> So to raise a few dollars your suit goes in soak.
> And the scheme is financially brilliant, you say,
> For your clothes get good care while thus laid away,
> And you in the meantime have use of the chink.
> A very few figures will show you, I think,
> That the man of three balls knows his "peesness" all right,
> And your scheme costs too much to be rated as bright.[15]

Unemployed and unskilled American workers, concentrated in ever-expanding urban areas, experienced very different material lives than did bankers, merchants, skilled artisans, and even small shopkeepers. Having little access to credit and practically no savings, laborers "tramped"—taking their labor on the road, stringing together a series of meager-paying jobs. They also relied on income from their wives' and children's work, pawning family possessions to tide them over during slack times. Christine Stansell writes of the "disintegrating family economies" among the poor and the countless housewives who "gave up altogether any lingering ambitions toward the role of household mistress and dedicated their energies instead to the makeshift housekeeping of the city." Even this "catch-as-catch-can routine of the destitute" was itself precarious, always at risk of further degradation if productive family members succumbed to illness or died.[16] Later in the nineteenth century the semiphilanthropic Provident Loan

Society stated that its various customers could not even cover the basics, seeking money "for food, shelter and clothing, and to meet emergencies arising from childbirth, sickness and death."[17]

Seamen, too, visited the pawnbroker when in port. For them pawning was one of a number of desperate economic transactions that kept them trapped in an endless cycle of poverty. On ship, sailors often had no choice but to purchase goods at inflated prices. While on board and in port, many drank and whored away their earnings (true to the stereotype) and had nowhere to go for more cash but to the pawnbroker:

> From the moment his vessel enters into port, he is surrounded by a set of men called crimps, who keep public, lodging, and boarding houses, of a description which would well suit the cities of Sodom and Gomorrah. These wretches, with the vile women they bring in their train, carry the irresistible bait of liquor and good cheer; advance a little money for present use; invite the weather-beaten voyager into their quarters; keep him in the commission of every sin and every excess until he has received his hard-earned pay; then stupify his every sense with liquor, rob him of his wages, and often strip him of his only jacket.[18]

Notorious for being bad debtors because they rarely redeemed their pawns, sailors suffered doubly because pawnbrokers gave them less than usual on security they had already paid above-market prices for on the ship.

Women made even more loyal pawners than seamen. For the fairer sex, money was especially tight. Their pawning cycles were the shortest, and their loans went to pay for urgent needs. Working in less skilled and often highly competitive occupations, women earned half or three-quarters what men did and owned fewer possessions with monetary value.[19] They were more likely to find themselves on their own and unable to meet their expenses, however modest. The women appearing in the Simpson ledger (35% of the identifiable pawners and possibly twice that), bear out Stansell's observation that "widowhood was virtually synonymous with impoverishment."[20]

Women employed various strategies to stretch their earnings. They scrimped on clothing, patching and mending and buying secondhand apparel. They ate less food and cooked with inferior ingredients. But rent, "the one unending terror of life," remained fixed—an absolute and constant yet utterly inflexible expense.[21] Pawning was often a woman's lifeline, the only way (save prostitution) she could make ends meet. Melanie Tebbutt notes that the customers frequenting Great Britain's pawnshops were most often women trying desperately to stretch a family income that stayed static as expenses grew. Women "were in the front line of the battle against inadequate resources," she writes, "and credit remained the only alternative to those for whom the recurring domestic crisis was more important than the high cost of borrowing."[22]

Pawning also allowed women a small amount of economic freedom, however circumscribed. Tebbutt points out that a woman often pawned domestic goods without her husband's knowledge, at times pawning *his* possessions. Even into the nineteenth century a married woman had little clear legal right to the products of her labor, and wages from much of women's work, legally designated as "house work," were considered an asset held jointly by husband and wife. A woman's income "mingled indistinguishably with her husband's in savings accounts or common household possessions." Her earnings, and the many things purchased with them, were not entirely hers.[23] Because the law of coverture required wives to relinquish all their property to their husbands upon marriage, it rendered a woman "economically passive, nearly powerless, and thoroughly dependent on her husband." Sadly, women could not presume equal partnership with men when they married, and too often husbands took advantage of their wives, declaring "open season on the property and earnings of the wife," according to historian Suzanne Lebsock.[24] Although the law varied from state to state over time, in many places coverture still applied in the late nineteenth century.

Whatever their actual rights and restrictions under the law, women remained primarily responsible for handling family budgets and did whatever was necessary to keep household members clothed and fed. They often used the services of the local pawnshop, hocking myriad forms of collateral. One of a number of coping strategies, pawning could be an act of independence, defiance, and even subversion. It allowed women to manage flimsy domestic economies and, at times, to work around obstinate or abusive husbands by drawing on a stock of household goods their men might not even notice were missing, thereby "exert[ing] considerable economic autonomy" as owners and managers of the family's property.[25] Indeed, wives used various strategies to keep their pawning a secret, including buying brass wedding rings (sold at the pawnshop) to replace the gold ones in hock and stashing their pawn tickets in locked tea caddies to conceal evidence of the loans.[26] Women continued these practices well into the twentieth century. For instance, in the late 1930s Margaret Winkle wrote to the Hands Loan Company in Stockton, California, desperate to get her collateral back. She explained,

> I had to leave for Home on very short notice so it was impossible to get my rings. So you will find enclosed a money order for $5.75 and I will expect my rings in the following mail as my husband did not know they were in Pawn and they are

not paid for. They belong to J. M. McEntee & Sons Jewelry in Tulsa. The wedding ring has Rays of Love & the Engagement ring is marked personally. I hope there will be no mix up or any trouble in getting them as it might cause serious trouble.[27]

It was also left to women to get their husbands' possessions out of hock—credit extended to him became her debt. In the mid-1870s "Old Darky Ford," for example, was spending all his money on alcohol at a local bar in May Port, east Florida. An itinerant fisherman wrote to his family back home that the man "Pawns his Violin there almost every week; and his Wife takes the money she earns Washing, and redeems it."[28]

Working-class women typically pawned and redeemed weekly. They often had no choice but to adhere to short and costly pawning cycles. A female house servant in 1830 earned between 75¢ and $1 a week. Her basic weekly expenses hovered around 50¢ for rent and 12½¢ for fuel. A seamstress earned a bit more, about $1.12½ weekly, but she was still left with "the sorry miserable pittance" of $23 for the entire year to cover food, clothing, and all other expenses.[29] As an economic strategy, pawning let women scrounge enough cash to cover their most pressing needs: rent and food.

Yet the practice, albeit necessary, also kept them mired in poverty. Julia McNair Wright's fictional work from 1869, *Our Chatham Street Uncle*, described just such a situation of a laundress for whom regular pawning was a normal part of life because people often delayed paying her. "This week," for instance, the laundress explained, "one of the ladies put in three dozen new collars; and of course, as she would not pay me extra for them, it put me out of pocket, doing so much starching." So she juggled and calculated, keeping income and expenses finely balanced. According to Wright, "The woman who had pawned the flat-irons seemed to think nothing of that kind of business: one day it would be her best bonnet and shawl, to get money for fuel; then the irons to be able to buy soap or starch for her laundry-work; then her best bed-quilt as soon as the irons were out."[30]

Staving off homelessness and hunger by perpetually borrowing cost women in the long run, though, since they still had to pay the full interest rate on their loans (usually calculated by the month) even if they redeemed their collateral within a week. Pawners certainly had the option of patronizing a rival pawnbroker in hopes of securing a higher loan. But this strategy could backfire: pawners could just as likely make a worse bargain with another pawnbroker and also risked jeopardizing any relationship with their usual lender. Indicative of the chronic economic hardships women faced, these short but high-interest loans kept them firmly situated in the lowest classes, just one pawnable possession away from destitution.

Often, women "put in" the family's Sunday best on Monday morning in order to cover the week's food and rent, redeeming the clothes Saturday night for the next day's church services.[31] One late-century pawnbroker referred to weekly pawning as "quite a different kind of trade," describing church clothes as "interchangeable property." He explained, "We do not value them in the usual way, but largely in proportion to the punctuality with which their owners take them out at the end of each week."[32] The outfits, embodiments of a person's credit history, thus held a stable value as collateral even though they were repeatedly worn and presumably became shabbier over time. Thus the loans were based not on the pawns' material worth but on the dependability with which pawners hocked and then redeemed them.

Many workers were paid on Saturday, making it convenient for families to redeem their good clothes the night before church. Even though Jewish-run pawnshops did not open until sundown on Saturday, redemptions far outnumbered those made on any other day of the week throughout the year. According to Provident Loan Society records from the late 1890s there were, on average, twice as many redemptions on Saturdays as on any other day.[33]

More than men, women knew the relative values of various domestic articles (including linens, clothing, and kitchen utensils) and often maintained less structured work schedules that accommodated regular visits to the pawnbroker. Female pawners in the Simpson ledger (including Julia Carpenter, Ann Conner, Celeste Livingston, Elizabeth McCarthy, and Mrs. Redford, to name a few) obtained loans on handkerchiefs, nightgowns, earrings, quilts, and like collateral. Any piece of property was potential cash. The Working Women's Protective Union, a philanthropic organization designed to shield working women from fraud and dishonest employers, gave out small "temporary loans" so their charges could "meet their immediate and pressing necessities." It wasn't much, "sometimes ten cents for a breakfast; sometimes two or three dollars with which to redeem articles pledged at the pawnbrokers," and sometimes more for investing in a sewing machine.[34]

Pawnbrokers served all economically disadvantaged groups. Often themselves victims of ethnic stereotyping, they saw no advantage in discriminating against their customers for any reason, unless they believed a pawner was bringing in stolen goods. And to that end, pawnbrokers *did* assess their customers, developing over time a keen ability to size up people and determine what kinds of things "belonged" with certain customers.[35] But if a personal possession appeared to be a pawner's legitimate property, a pawnbroker had no reason not

FIGURE 4.1. "Waiting for the Pawnshop to Open," *Harper's Weekly* 11, 558 (September 7, 1867): 561. Library Company of Philadelphia.

to accept it as collateral. It made good business sense to serve as many legitimate pawners as possible, regardless of gender, race, or ethnicity. An illustration from an 1867 issue of *Harper's Weekly* shows the typical pawners, waiting for the shop to open after sundown on Saturday, their bundled possessions looking like swaddled newborns or loaves of bread. Several women populate the tableau: a mother with her daughter in tow, a spinster, and an African American domestic (fig. 4.1). The text explains that these people are the face of "the basest poverty," whose wages do not cover the weekly expenses of food, and "too often," alcohol.[36] The scene was familiar in nineteenth-century lower-class urban American neighborhoods. For some, such as the two women chatting, a visit to the pawnbroker's could be a social occasion as well. (It is not inconceivable that neighbors Mrs. McKnight and Hanah Gold, who stood close to each other in line at Simpson's on August 15, 1838, and redeemed their collateral on the same day in December, accompanied each other on these excursions to the pawnshop.)[37]

Pawnshop customers did not come only from the lower and middling sorts. In addition to borrowing large sums at the upscale and exclusive "loan offices" described in the previous chapter, the rich frequented more pedestrian pawnships. They tended to rely on pawning much as we use ATMs today, to get quick cash to finance a night on the town or pay for petty luxuries. The 1855 book

The Winkles, or The Merry Monomaniacs contained depictions of this class of pawners, two well-to-do young men who, out "on a lark" one night, pay a visit to Laban the pawnbroker. The one explains to the other that he has to pawn his diamond pin because "I fear to forfeit the good opinion of my rich relatives by applying to them just at this particular time."[38] The caption of an 1857 cartoon from *Harper's Weekly* recorded the conversation of two middle-class women:

> VISITOR: "Won't you go to Saratoga this year, my dear?"
> LADY OF THE HOUSE: "Well, no, I hardly think we shall. I'm so tired of these crowded watering-places."
> LITTLE GIRL: "But you'll go, Mamma, won't you, if Pa gets a hundred dollars for your watch?"[39]

Members of the upper class most often obtained loans from pawnshops to avoid the embarrassment of approaching family members or their usual creditors. After the Civil War, New York City had at least three pawnshops known among the well-to-do, "where a lady could leave her diamonds for a short time without exciting any scandal."[40] Because among the elite credit was extended based on personal relationships and one's reputation, it could be risky to go to the bank for a loan, for it meant admitting financial duress to one's peers. Merchants, lawyers, and other men among the upwardly mobile found monetary relief at the pawnbroker's without inciting gossip that could very well ruin reputation and financial welfare. They especially needed the pawnbroker's services if their debts resulted from bad behavior. Men "of respectable connexions" pawned jewelry and fine pocket watches to fund drinking and gambling habits, allowing them to continue their "wild and dissolute" ways.[41]

To get to pawnshops, the upper classes typically crossed geographical boundaries into "bad" neighborhoods; this could be advantageous, granting these pawners the anonymity they needed. A midcentury cartoon from *Harper's Weekly* shows a "Lady from Fifth Avenue": stepping into a carriage, she exclaims to her liveried coachman, "And now, John, drive to the Pawnbrokers" (fig. 4.2). In addition to being shielded from the prying eyes of neighbors and business partners, upper-class pawners benefited from pawnbrokers' discretion, and many pawnshops were equipped with individual stalls to protect privacy. The discomfort of running into someone you knew was, in fact, the conceit of a song from the 1830s, titled "Who'd a Thought of Seeing You?" (fig. 4.3). The image on the cover of the sheet music shows a man installed in a privacy cubicle pawning a riding crop, stirrups, and a portrait miniature. He winces when an acquaintance, breaching etiquette, cranes his neck around the barrier to chat. The popular comic song, met "with great applause at the theatres," included this verse:

LADY FROM FIFTH AVENUE. "And now, John, drive to the Pawnbrokers."

FIGURE 4.2. "Lady from Fifth Avenue," *Harper's Weekly* 1, 50 (December 12, 1857): 800. Library Company of Philadelphia.

> The other day I pledged my watch
> (For being short what could I do)
> A friend popped from the other box
> "Why who'd a thought of seeing you?"[42]

The scene also illustrates the cubbyholes for storing collateral and shows a string of pawn tickets hanging on the wall, left with the pawnbroker for safekeeping. A similar scene showing the relative ineffectiveness of privacy cubicles appeared in the 1844 edition of Charles Dickens's *Martin Chuzzlewit* (fig. 4.4).

Uniting these disparate classes of pawners was their ownership of worthy collateral, whether diamond breastpins or linen handkerchiefs. Although anything of value could be pawned, certain goods retained more stable value over time, making them consistently sound collateral throughout the centuries. Public notices, newspaper advertisements, contemporary accounts, and the rare surviving business ledger indicate what pawners most often used as collateral and how these items changed over time with shifting consumer fashions and the effects of

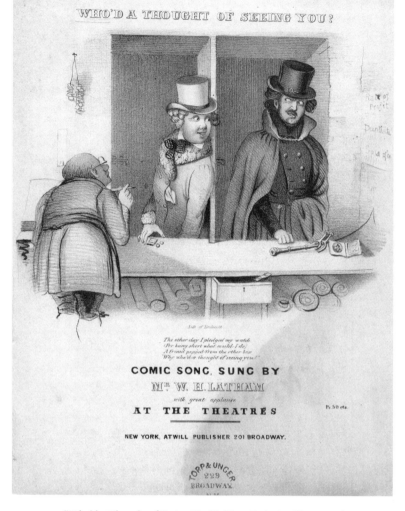

FIGURE 4.3. "Who'd a Thought of Seeing You?" (New York: Atwill, ca. 1830). Courtesy, American Antiquarian Society.

mass production. As Americans became increasingly materialistic, enmeshed in what would become a flourishing consumer culture during the nineteenth century, individual objects were less important as signifiers of status than the totality of one's possessions. Pawnshop dealings reveal the many roles goods played in people's lives—as abstract symbols, as repositories of personal sentiment, as tangible forms of monetary value.

Although people owned fewer personal possessions before nineteenth-century industrialization, the objects they did own were important because they had practical use and also marked one's status. The eighteenth-century consumer revolution was fueled by the material desires of colonists who wanted to be like their Continental counterparts. Consumer goods helped people "establish a meaningful and distinct sense of self through the exercise of individual choice."[43] Highly prized, most objects had a purpose; if people became attached to them at all, it was because they were useful—tools to earn their livelihoods and objects adding to physical comfort. T. H. Breen describes prerevolutionary Americans as being extremely attuned to European fashions, thirsting for the latest and most stylish consumer goods from across the Atlantic. People living in both the country and the city were being infused with the desire to consume. City residents had direct access to the latest goods through the many retail outlets dotting the streets, while people in the hinterlands were seduced by advertisements in country editions of newspapers, by traveling peddlers, and by what they saw on the shelves of well-stocked country stores.[44] Increasing imported goods, the rise of domestic manufactures, and more sophisticated transportation networks made goods of all

FIGURE 4.4. "Martin Meets an Acquaintance at the House of a Mutual Relation," Charles Dickens, *The Life and Adventures of Martin Chuzzlewit* (Philadelphia: Lea and Blanchard, 1844), facing 92. Library Company of Philadelphia.

kinds more accessible, turning America into a nation of consumers. They used their purchasing power to buy more things. Buying more (unnecessary) things left people with less cash. But conveniently, the things they had purchased could often be converted back into cash at the pawnshop.

Jewelry, tools, and articles of clothing have always been suitable collateral (and probably always will be). But the myriad other goods pawned through the centuries also reflect trends in material fashions and fads. Guns and saddles in the eighteenth century, multivolume book sets and cheap jewelry in the 1850s, phonographs in the 1920s, suitcases in the 1930s (one could go on—eight-track tape players in the 1970s, and yesterday's VCRs), mark shifting consumer preferences about what was considered viable collateral. People pawned everything imaginable. In 1828 the *National Advocate* published a week's worth of pledges compiled by the police, tallied from the eight pawnbrokers then operating in New York City. According the newspaper report, the 3,489 recorded pledges for the week included over 900 articles of women's dress; over 800 articles of men's clothing; 240 clocks, watches, and other timepieces; 45 gold watches; over 230 silver tablespoons and teaspoons; over 220 earrings, finger rings, chains, and brooches; 9 Bibles; and over 960 "other articles," which would have included bed linens, guns, books, shoes, tools, furniture, and kitchen utensils.[45]

The array of objects auctioned at sales of unredeemed collateral in the early decades of the nineteenth century suggests the incipient consumer revolution. A typical advertisement, published in an 1831 issue of the *Baltimore Patriot*, listed goods to be sold on behalf of pawnbroker Simon Eytinge that were of remarkable variety, quantity, and quality:

PAWNBROKER'S SALE.—Without reserve at our warehouse on Thursday, 22nd inst. at 10 o'clock, we shall sell a large lot of precious Jewelry, such as fine gold ear-rings; finger-rings, diamond, brilliant, garnet and pearl breast pins; watch chains; seals; keys &c. gold and silver watches, such as levers, l'epine, repeaters, &c. silver spectacles; pencil cases; knives and forks; carvers; rich plated castors; candlesticks; snuffers and trays; 1 portable writing desk; guns; pistols; swords; umbrellas; musical and other instruments, among which is a *Splendid Old Painting*, representing a wedding party at *Ovenback; in Germany*—in the Tower of the scene is fixed an excellent Clock, shewing the time precisely and strikes at the end of each quarter and at each full hour, in connexion with the same are Musical Works, which, after the striking of the clock, plays three different pleasing tunes, without any additional aid, the whole warranted in perfect order; 1 mahogany Sideboard; 2 knife Cases; 1 good second-hand Piano Forte; 2 excellent Violins, &c. brass Shovel and tongs; Andirons; Quilts; Blankets; Counterpanes, a large lot of men's and women's wearing apparel; Shawls; H[an]dk[erchie]fs; and other dry goods;

Carpeting, 1 pair elegant bronzed Astral Lamps; 1 d[itt]o plated d[itt]o; Looking Glasses; silver table and tea Spoons; cream Jugs &c.; mechanics Tools; a variety of fancy articles and other goods too numerous to particularise.[46]

The stock represented possessions of those at all income levels from the very poor to the very rich, who were pawning handkerchiefs, pieces of pottery, gem-encrusted jewelry, and fine oil paintings. Financial troubles seemingly plagued everyone. Auctioneers often found themselves with so many pieces of collateral that they divided their sales into genres. M. Thomas and Son of Philadelphia, for example, frequently ran clothing-, jewelry-, and linen-only sales, each featuring hundreds of items.[47]

A sample of loans made at Simpson's pawnshop in New York City in 1838 shows what different kinds of collateral were worth:

Apron	6¢
Two Bibles	12¢
Pants	18¾¢
Two belts	25½¢
Frock	31¢
Jacket	37½¢
Ring	50¢
Pair of boots	75¢
Blanket	$1.00
Three teaspoons	$1.50
Shawl	$2.00
Silver watch	$3.00
Coat	$4.00
Desk	$6.00
Gold chain	$10.00
Gold watch	$12.00
Two diamond rings	$20.00
Lathe and two dozen locks	$25.00
Gold lever watch	$30.00[48]

Because the pawnbroker could convert such disparate things into cash—the universal medium of exchange—pawnshops remained essential in the daily life of urban Americans, even after the widespread establishment of savings banks. The statistics of pawning business during the last week of 1828 for the eight licensed pawnshops in New York City are revealing. When extrapolated for the year, the figures amounted to 62 pledge transactions a day per pawnshop, or over

22,600 a year. Together the pawnshops handled roughly 181,000 transactions for the year, equaling nearly one pawn for every man, woman, and child then living in the city.[49]

The startling figures, published as an exposé in the *National Advocate*, shocked the public, igniting indignation on a par with the very first debates about licensing provisions. Within weeks of the story at least three other publications reprinted the report, including the *Saturday Evening Post* and the *Atlas*.[50] Mathew Carey even cited the statistics in his 1830 "Essays on the Public Charities of Philadelphia" about the economic straits of the poor in his own city.[51] If the estimates were at all accurate, they painted a sobering picture. The number of pawns recorded in the Simpson ledger ten years later was even more fantastic—over 27,000 in six months.[52] People were dispossessing themselves of hundreds of personal goods every day. Assuming a low average loan amount of $3 at a 25% annual interest rate, the newspaper estimated the total annual take in interest alone for these eight New York City pawnbrokers to be $135,000 "wrung from the sweat of the brows of the indigent!"[53] Referring to the shocking number of New York City pawns, Carey asked rhetorically, "Who can, without the deepest sympathy, contemplate the distress, the suffering, the anguish felt by those 71,000 persons before they resolved on such sacrifices" to pawn their most personal possessions?[54]

But how might these loans have truly figured into pawners' short-term economic strategies and affected their quality of life, for better or worse? We might start with two pawn tickets belonging to William McLean, illustrated in figure 4.5. In January 1835 McLean pawned two pocket watches, one silver and one gold, at Henry Holmes's Southwark, Philadelphia, pawnshop and received $15 on each one. It would have cost McLean $15.70 to redeem his watches in six months: the initial amount of the loan, plus 45¢ interest (at the 6% per annum allowed by the city, prorated), plus a 25¢ ticket writing fee. Our pawner might have been the William M'Clean listed in city directories as a wood sawyer. Or he could have been unlisted, one of the countless peripatetic "trampers" plying his trade in different towns, or among Philadelphia's disenfranchised with neither stable residence nor identifiable occupation.

Why might McLean have pawned the watches when he did? Thirty dollars was a significant amount of money; that he pawned two watches at the same time suggests a significant life event. The McLean household listed in the 1830 census records does not appear in 1840.[55] Perhaps the cash loan paid for medical expenses, covered funeral costs, or supplemented gaps in earnings created by nonproductive family members. It is also possible that McLean used the money to move out of Philadelphia—an investment in future prospects. (Spent over time,

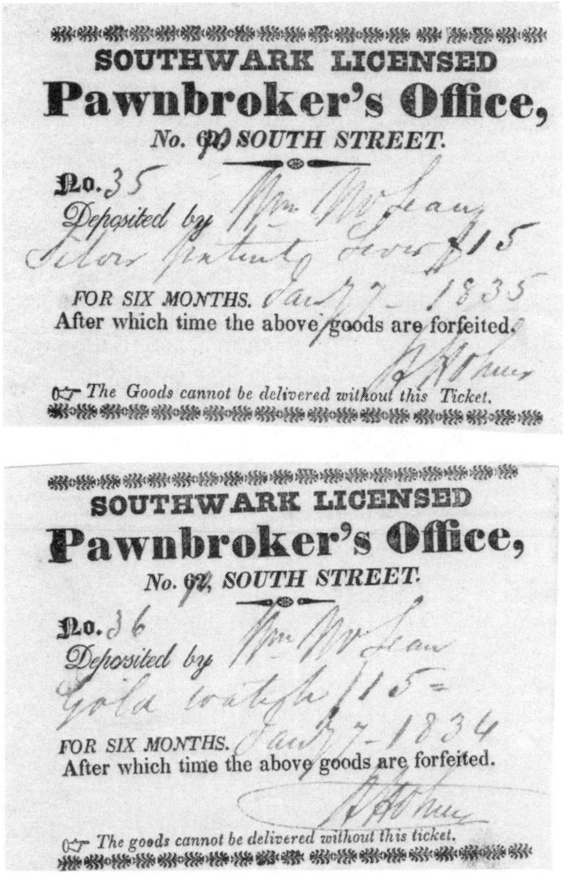

SOUTHWARK LICENSED
Pawnbroker's Office,
No. 92 SOUTH STREET.

No. 35
Deposited by Wm McLean
Silver plate[?] over $15

FOR SIX MONTHS. Jany 7 1835
After which time the above goods are forfeited.

☞ The Goods cannot be delivered without this Ticket.

SOUTHWARK LICENSED
Pawnbroker's Office,
No. 92, SOUTH STREET.

No. 36
Deposited by Wm McLean
Gold watch $15

FOR SIX MONTHS. Jany 7 1834
After which time the above goods are forfeited.

☞ The goods cannot be delivered without this ticket.

FIGURE 4.5. Pawn tickets issued by Henry Holmes of the Southwark, Philadelphia, Licensed Pawnbroker's Office, 1835. Historical Society of Pennsylvania.

$30 for the average family in the early 1830s would have covered a year's rent, more than enough fuel, or a quarter of the grocery expenses.)[56] Yet redeeming *each* watch would have required more than a month's salary earned at a well-paid occupation such as coachman. In a year's time McLean's watches, still unclaimed, were inevitably auctioned off at public sale.[57]

The income of unskilled laborers was so low that sickness, death, or even a slight increase in the cost of food or rent could break a family that lacked economic resources and social ties. A pawnbroker was often the only one who would extend them credit. Mathew Carey described the desperate circumstances of a number of families living in the Southwark area of Philadelphia in the 1830s (where McLean pawned his watches), including a married couple living rent-free "with a relation nearly as poor as themselves. The man had broke a blood vessel many months since, and was unable to work at his trade. His wife earned a paltry pittance by shoe binding. They had one child—and were obliged to limit themselves to two meals a day."[58] In circumstances like these, the pawnbroker was a costly yet necessary resource.

Developments in American manufacturing and increased consumption throughout the antebellum era multiplied the number and variety of goods available on the market that, once purchased, could be pawned, creating a synergy between pawning and industrial capitalism. By the time reporter George Foster wrote *New York in Slices* in 1849, the list of unredeemed pledges had grown to include minor luxuries and objects of comfort in addition to staple pawns. Public auctions of unredeemed collateral were "the most interesting part of the pawnbroking business," he observed, in large part because of the improbable variety of goods that found their way to the pawnshop:

> Andirons, ambergris, boot-jacks and baby-jumpers, calicoes, cullenders, crimping-irons, cradles, dust-pans and dictionaries, egg-spoons and electrical machines, fiddles and frying-pans, gaiters and go-carts, hampers and hunting-horns, inkstands and ipecac, jewsharps and joint-stools, kaleidoscopes, lamps and lavender-water, music, martingals and mattresses, necklaces and nine-pins, optical instruments and oboes, pie-pans and pin-cushions, quack medicines, quills, quicksilver, rings and rat-traps, saddles and shaving-boxes, tongs and tooth-brushes, urns, umbrellas, vandykes and vases, wigs and wicker-baskets, and so on.[59]

Pawning transformed consumer goods, giving them new life. These objects were not simply commodities to be exchanged in wholesale and retail spheres or possessions consigned to dusty corners of the home. One day part of a "gigantic rubbish heap," the next day they found new and unintended uses as loan collateral that eventually might be recirculated in resale markets.[60] An 1863 auction catalog for unredeemed goods to be sold by the semiphilanthropic Pawners' Bank of Boston listed a similarly wide variety of goods from the opulent to the pedestrian. High spots included a mahogany parlor set and two upright pianos (pushing the limits of "movable property"), perhaps belonging to downwardly mobile families. A tailor's pressing machine and shears might have come from a man with skills who could not find enough work or have been put up by a widow whose husband never returned from the war.[61]

Pawning continued to meet the needs of those who found themselves strapped for cash during the nineteenth century and also helped funnel tens of thousands of affordable consumer goods generated by the country's efficient factories into secondary and tertiary markets. In 1860 *Hunt's Merchants' Magazine* reported that New York City's East Side pawnbrokers handled over 1.7 million transactions in a year, lending more than $1.2 million. The city's pawnbroking statistics taken together (including an estimate of the West Side pawnbrokers) amounted to about 3.25 million pledges all told, with a total loan amount of over $2 million spread among the city's 813,700 inhabitants.[62] People continued to live on narrow margins: the average of each loan during this time was 62¢. What did that 62¢ mean in 1860? Most New York City workers earned between $1 and $2 a day, the typical range of unskilled to skilled labor, and women doing piecework or working as laundresses earned even less.[63] That 62¢ would have paid for four nights' lodging in a Philadelphia slum.[64]

And pawnshops remained essential to the general public at the end of the century; pawners drew on yet greater stores of material possessions made affordable and available by the Industrial Revolution. An 1894 study on borrowing in the Bowery speculated that "almost the entire population holds one or more pawn tickets at all times. The majority of families have a dozen or more in their rooms the greater part of the year."[65] The average amount loaned by New York's Provident Loan Society, which accepted only higher-end collateral, ranged from $18.16 in 1895 to $23.79 five years later.[66] The average loan granted by the First State Pawners Society of Chicago was a bit lower, perhaps because of the cities' different standards of living. The organization's loans averaged $15.02 during fiscal year 1899–1900 and $18.19 in 1900–1901.[67] Chicagoans living in the poorest neighborhoods were making between $5 and $10 a week as ditchdiggers, railroad workers, peddlers, and paupers. The "well-to-do" enjoyed weekly incomes over $20.[68]

Because most pawners belonged to the working poor, it is not surprising to find their meager belongings—broken pots, worn shoes, shawls—crammed onto pawnshop shelves. More remarkable are the numbers of pocket watches used as collateral, despite historians' claims that pocket watches did not become popular until much later.[69] Common pawns throughout the nineteenth century and into the twentieth, they exemplify the synergy between pawning and industrial capitalism. Pocket watches were part of the stock of the earliest auction sales of unredeemed collateral. About 14% of pawns in the Simpson ledger were pocket watches, ranging from the gold lever watch pawned for $35 to the secondhand silver model with broken glass and hands for $2.[70] They accounted for almost a quarter of the sales at the Pawners' Bank sale in 1863 and made up an even larger inventory at other sales. For example, in 1897 Cleveland gold watches outnumbered all other pledges; gold and silver watches together composed almost half (44%) of the total number of pawns in that city. The statistics for 1898 Chicago were similar: gold and silver pocket watches secured over one-third of pawnshop loans.[71]

In many ways the pocket watch was an ideal consumer good. Small and portable, it was a concentrated form of capital, valuable intact and as parts. A reliable timepiece was an extremely useful tool during the era of industrialization when factory work increasingly required laborers to obey the mechanized time kept by clocks rather than the cycles of the sun. Encased in precious metals and containing jeweled mechanisms, a pocket watch's component parts possessed calculable market value, quantifiable in karats and by weight. A pocket watch could be, and often was, personalized with inscriptions and monograms, rendering it unique—singular—to its owner.[72] Inherited, sold, resold, and pawned, pocket watches circulated promiscuously in retail, resale, and underground markets. Since they were easy to steal and convert into cash, pocket watches were a favorite quarry of George Appo, the hero of Timothy Gilfoyle's *Pickpocket's Tale:* after a particularly successful night at a fair near Toronto, he came away with $600 and twenty-two pocket watches.[73]

Like other desirable consumer goods, most pocket watches were imported from Europe in the antebellum years, manufactured chiefly in England and Switzerland. Domestic manufacturers gradually increased supply while reducing price, making pocket watches affordable and necessary to own—desired by the average consumer and well within reach. A contemporary writer estimated the value of watches imported into the United States from 1825 to 1858 to be almost $46 million.[74] In 1860 alone $2.8 million worth of watches were imported. Domestic manufactures added another $1.5 million in watches to the marketplace.[75] Following westward expansion and southern development, sellers and repairers of pocket watches appeared in towns as far-flung as Helena, Arkansas, and Athens, Georgia. In larger cities, hundreds of related professions also thrived, including importers, wholesalers, and suppliers of watches and watch parts, silver and gold platers, silversmiths and goldsmiths, engravers, and watchcase makers. The New York City firm of W. A. Hayward, for one, made watches, watch accessories, and "all kinds of JEWELRY, LOCKETS, BRACELETS, Coral, Lava, Mosaic, Gold Stone, and all kinds of Sets. All kinds of Fine Gold and cheap Rings, Studs and Buttons. Gent's Pins, Gold Chains, and a great variety of cheap Chains, Vest, Guard and Neck Chains."[76] Retailers offered affordable watches to the public by selling cheap imports and by taking advantage of emerging American manufacturing processes that mated machine-made cases with handmade internal workings. Though generally inferior, they were at least more affordable than watches made entirely by hand. In 1860 William M. Peters of Philadelphia advertised as follows:

> Manufacturer of the Celebrated PATENT WATCH CASES and importer of all kinds of English and Swiss Movements, has such arrangements as enable him to supply all kinds of American Movements at the manufacturer's prices. The trade can obtain Watches at one-third less than the usual prices, by purchasing the Cases made

by machinery. . . . The trade can always find a large and varied stock of English, Swiss and American Watches on hand to select from.[77]

Many watch retailers (including the seven in Oregon, the eight in Kansas, the eleven in Arkansas, and the thirty-six in Iowa in 1860) imported their goods from firms such as J. W. Benson of London, whose illustrated catalog contained over 160 examples of pocket watches alone, in addition to other pawnshop staples such as chains, fobs, and brooches. Ranging in price from 2 guineas (£2.10, or about $10) to 100 guineas, many styles could be acquired by the average wage earner, including "Everybody's Watch," a model that was durable, reliable, and "suitable for all classes" and whose least expensive version was considered affordable at 15 guineas (£15.75, or $76).[78] The nineteenth-century Philadelphia firm of John Fries and Son offered cheap watches "direct from the manufactories" and, like many other watch and jewelry sellers, also sold secondhand watches at "half their value."[79]

Pocket watches perhaps best illustrate the interdependence of industrial wage labor, rising consumption, and the utility of pawnbrokers. Earning about $2 a day, skilled laborers on the eve of the Civil War could afford some of the fancier pocket watch models. Workers in towns supporting large-scale production enterprises might conceivably be manufacturing the very things they would buy and then pawn, turning the Henry Ford philosophy of producing and consuming sideways.[80] Many of these watches were pawned by their owners at one time or another, realizing a quarter to a third of their retail value. Not only a timekeeper, a watch was also a reliable form of mobile capital carried in one's vest pocket. In fact watches, delicate and complex instruments, were often in need of repair and may have been more useful as collateral (and status symbols) than as practical timekeepers (see figs. 4.6 and 4.7).

Ulysses S. Grant was among the countless Americans who pawned a timepiece. Two days before Christmas in 1857, he took his gold hunting watch and chain to John S. Freligh's St. Louis pawnshop, perhaps availing himself of the shop's "private entrance from the alley in the rear," and received a $22 loan.[81] In his early thirties, Grant had returned to his family after a stint in the military to embark on "a new struggle for our support," as he called it, working tirelessly to establish a farmstead near St. Louis. Grant might well have used the money from his pawned watch to get his agricultural venture off the ground. "I managed to keep along very well until 1858," he explained in his autobiography, "when I was attacked by fever and ague." It was very bad timing: Grant fell ill during the aftermath of the Panic of 1857 and was ill for the better part of a year, crippling his farming operation. He finally gave it up in the fall of 1858, selling everything

[47]

DREW & COFFIN,

PHOTOGRAPH PUBLISHERS,

OFFICE	ROOMS
No. 270 Washington Street,	No. 365 Washington Street,
3d Door So. of Avon Place.	*3d Door No. of the Adams House.*
GEO. H. DREW.	A. K. COFFIN.

PHOTOGRAPHS, PLAIN OR COLORED.

Daguerreotypes on Plate or Glass, taken in the best manner.

☞ Particular attention given to copying Photographs, Daguerreotypes, Engravings, and Paintings. ☜

WILLIAM H. SMITH,

PREMIUM DIE SINKER,

STENCIL AND STEEL LETTER CUTTER,

Also, small Stencil Dies, Steel and Iron Stamps, Stencil Plates, Seals, and Embossing Presses, made to order.

☞ All Orders from City or Country promptly attended to. ☜

No. 89 Washington St....Up Stairs,

BOSTON.

MONEY TO LOAN.

G. K. GOODWIN,

MONEY AND EXCHANGE BROKER,

10 SALEM STREET, BOSTON.

On hand, a large lot of unredeemed Watches for sale at half the original cost.

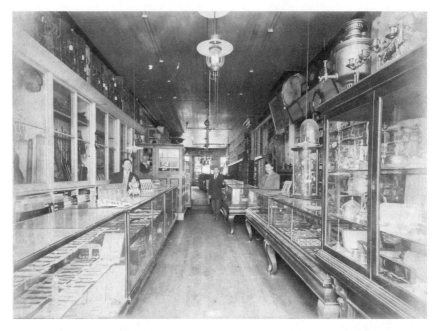

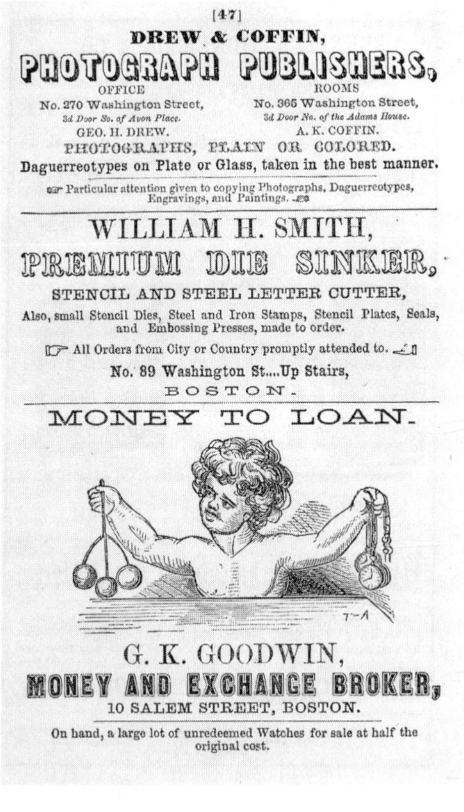

FIGURE 4.6. (*top*) Interior of I. D. Rubin's New York Pawnshop, Charleston, South Carolina, ca. 1910. Pocket watches, among other collateral, fill the showcases. Special Collections, College of Charleston Library.

FIGURE 4.7. (*left*) A pocket watch was a popular form of collateral. "Money to Loan," *History of Boston, from 1630 to 1856* (Boston: F. C. Moore, 1856), 47. University of Pennsylvania Library.

of value at auction, including tools and livestock.[82] That Grant's pawn ticket still exists suggests he was never able to redeem his watch—the future president was vulnerable, like so many others, to economic and physical downturns beyond his control.

Jewelry was also frequently hocked. Heirloom pieces connected present to past; serving as important memory objects, they were something people held on to and, when necessary, used as loan collateral. New pieces of jewelry flooded the nineteenth-century marketplace, purchased by consumers for whom public display and self-fashioning were becoming increasingly important. Like watches, jewelry underwent advances in manufacturing techniques that brought greater numbers and more affordable products to ordinary Americans. Further, improvements in plating and gilding enabled companies to manufacture cheap jewelry and watches that imitated models made of precious metals, masking the difference between chintzy and quality goods. Imitation gemstones, including artificial amethysts, emeralds, garnets, opals, and rubies, flooded the market, fooling even experienced jewelers and pawnbrokers, who had to keep abreast of these changes in order to make accurate appraisals. By the early 1860s jewelry of various qualities in addition to "solid" (18 karat) gold appeared in shops and at auction. "Massive jewelry," "filled-in," and "plated" were but a few.[83] In the pages of *Godey's Lady's Book* the fashion editor touted cheap breastpins, earrings, bracelets, necklaces, fob chains, and hair studs priced from $1.50 to $15.00, supplied by New England manufacturers. "The recent gold discoveries," Edgar Martin wrote of the California Gold Rush, "had given a fillip to the manufacture of solid and plated jewelry and brought its wares within the range of a greater number of people." In 1860 alone the country's 463 jewelry manufacturers reported a total output of $10.4 million.[84]

As both producers and consumers, Americans were becoming increasingly enmeshed in the system of industrial capitalism—dependent on the low-paying, low-skilled jobs that necessitated frequent visits to the pawnshop. Indeed, domestic manufactures were bringing more than pocket watches and jewelry to the market. On the eve of the Civil War most lower and middling folk could afford a few things beyond the basic comforts. The world of goods not only enabled but required Americans to become participants in the burgeoning consumer culture. Boldly, they displayed their citizenship as consumers, engaging in "a new culture, a market culture, in the form of objects."[85] Daily these consumer goods were bundled, tagged, and stored on pawnshop shelves. Interestingly, the family Bible, ostensibly the most precious of possessions, was the first thing to be pawned and was often abandoned. One pawnbroker observed, "When a family is hard up, the first thing they generally take to the loan office is the Bible, which is always a drag on the market, for in seven cases out of ten they are not called for, and they generally ornament the shelf for three or four years before they are disposed of."[86]

No matter what went in, all pawns eventually went out, redeemed by their owners or sold off at public auctions. In trickle-down fashion, auctions redistributed used consumer goods to even more people. By the end of the century so many unredeemed pawns were sold off that entrepreneurs established businesses dealing exclusively in these items, extending the channels of distribution deeper into secondary and tertiary markets. New York City dealer Robert Orr, for one, specialized in reselling all kinds of goods purchased at auction. He claimed to dedicate an entire floor of his four-story operation to men's clothing purchased at pawnbrokers' sales, seen to by a "small army" of workers that cleaned, inspected, and repaired the articles. Expert tailors remade the clothes to be better than new—certainly superior to "the shoddy 'racket' trash sold at cheap, new-made Clothing stores, the materials of which fade and grow threadbare, the buttons snap off, the lining tears and the pockets give way" (fig. 4.8).[87] Likewise, Orr's staff cleaned jewelry, reset gemstones, obliterated monograms on pocket watches through "dexterous effacing," and polished silver services until they shone.[88] Competitor Gold, Coleman and Company likewise specialized in used goods, selling overcoats, pants, and "odd vests" in its Pawnbrokers' Sanitary Second Hand Clothing Department.[89]

Secondhand goods enabled the poor of America's nineteenth-century cities to experience a few of the material comforts taken for granted by the middling. Although some of the destitute lived in filth in hovels or crowded tenements, they still found ways to enhance their surroundings. Reporters for the *New York Times* visited homes of the poor in 1859 to find out "how New Yorkers live." The cellar dwellers they described included an elderly man with rheumatism who lived with his wife and three children. In another one-room apartment they found a seventy-seven-year-old woman, toothless and hunched, occupying the space with six others. The reporters remarked that the tenants seemed to find happiness despite the "filthy, damp and dismal" quarters and strove to better their conditions. Reporters were surprised to find framed chromolithographs, a mantelpiece "crowded with plaster images" (although the dog was missing its leg and the cupids their wings), a Yankee clock, and a straw carpet.[90] Some of these things may have been picked out of refuse heaps or acquired at an auction of unredeemed pawns or bought from a secondhand dealer. The clock and carpet might very well have ended up in hock at some point: even people living on the margins owned something that could be pawned.

Wholesale Price List of Pawnbroker's Sanitary Clothing

The different prices stated below indicate different grades of quality, the higher prices meaning better quality. The clothing is all marked with a private cost mark which customer can easily understand.

MEN'S SACK COATS

$2.00	Light or dark
2.50	colors.
3.00	Light, medium
3.50	or
4.00	heavy weights.
5.00	

MEN'S SACK COATS AND VESTS

$2.50	Light or dark
3.00	colors.
3.50	Light, medium
4.00	or
5.00	heavy weights.
6.00	

MEN'S PANTS

$3.50	Light or dark colors.
4.00	Light, medium or
5.00	heavy weights.

FIGURE 4.8. Robert Orr, *A Great Business in the Heart of the Great Metropolis* ([New York], ca. 1890), 11. Collection of the author.

In addition to acquiring "new" secondhand goods, immigrants brought with them objects that not only linked them with their homeland and ancestors but were also readily convertible into cash. Many of these items, such as ceremonial chalices and embroidered textiles, helped them maintain religious and cultural traditions. Other possessions, including extra clothing and feather beds (which also, improbably, made transatlantic voyages), provided physical comforts. Among other items that ended up in the trash heaps of the so-called poor living in New York City's Five Points area were glass decanters and tumblers, specialized sets of tableware and serving dishes necessary in kosher households, tea sets, sewing kits, and even a water dish for a caged bird.[91] Some of New York City's pawnbrokers specialized in the transient trade, "particularly with Germans, who are accustomed to pledge a part of their goods as they pass through New-York to their Western homes, and redeem it out of their first earnings," according to one contemporary source.[92] In addition to and perhaps more important than "hope, enterprise, and courage," immigrants brought assets: "clothing, tools, and in most instances money."[93]

In order to survive, given the grim realities of their everyday circumstances, the economically disenfranchised—especially the working poor, new immigrants, and single women—had to make informed decisions about pawning strategies. Yet, tellingly, social commentators, whose opinions made it into newspapers, magazines, and official reports, paid much less attention to the economic role pawning played than to emotional and sentimental concerns about the pawns themselves. Because pawning alienated people from their possessions, it created problems regarding the role of goods and the role of consumers within the emergent consumer culture that increasingly defined American life. Producers encouraged Americans to spend, especially on domestically manufactured products, as a way to bolster the national economy and assert personal identity through material things. Yet critics also worried about the blurring of class distinctions, fearing that the lower sorts' purchasing wantonly or buying things above their station would result in social instability. While reformers and cultural commentators sought to control consumption in an age increasingly crowded with affordable and available material goods (as a way to maintain class boundaries through conspicuous consumption), consumers themselves were exercising a great deal of personal agency over what they bought and why.

The way public figures talked about pawns changed over time, reflecting the shifting place of material objects in nineteenth-century American life and growing concern over these value systems. During the first decades of the nineteenth century Americans desired consumer goods because they made the physical world more comfortable. For the poor and middling, it might have meant an extra shirt, a bit more food, or a restful place to sleep. For the rich, who already enjoyed material comforts, it meant even more comfort—the most fashionable wardrobes, spacious houses, more servants—and the ability to share that comfort with friends and family. Affordable consumer goods enabled purchasers to "share in the self-fashioning of new identities through the exchange of goods that facilitated the democratization of gentility and the fluidity of social identity."[94] When Mathew Carey published the statistics recording the incredible number of pawns in New York City pawnshops in 1828, he measured the value of pawns in economic terms, specifically, as the cost of one's labor. Possessions were obtained through hard work, wages converted into material property. To outsiders like Carey, pawnbrokers alienated laborers from the fruits of their labor.

By the late 1830s the discourse regarding pawns shifted from economic to social considerations. Popular print culture began defining and legitimating "proper" modes of consumption and the purpose of goods. The public used changing fashions of clothing, for example, as a barometer of economic and social status, creating among an otherwise undifferentiated mass of people "numerous artificial and arbitrary distinctions," according to Alexis de Tocqueville.[95] Widely distributed periodicals such as *Godey's Lady's Book, Harper's Weekly,* and *Graham's Illustrated Magazine,* in addition to countless advertising broadsides, newspaper advertisements, and works of prescriptive literature, created and diffused this information, thus forging an overarching popular culture. For the upwardly mobile, "fashion served both as a barrier which had to be surmounted . . . and as a standard which could be applied to the claims of those seeking admission from below," according to Karen Halttunen.[96] Auction houses, used goods shops, peddlers, and, surreptitiously, some retail stores recirculated used goods, thereby putting only slightly outdated styles within the reach of the lower and middling classes, democratizing consumer desire and material aspirations. (As businessmen, pawnbrokers too stayed up on the latest fashions, especially after the Civil War, and often loaned only on the value of the fabric a garment was made from—like scrutinizing precious metals and gemstones by considering the raw material only.)[97]

During his tour of America in 1831 and 1832 Alexis de Tocqueville noticed this nascent American materialism. In a democracy, when "the distinctions of rank are confounded together and privileges are destroyed," he observed, status as defined and marked by material possessions was always in play, and "the desire of acquiring the comforts of the world haunts the imagination of the poor, and the dread of losing them that of the rich."[98] The result was that people of all classes, living with the hope of upward mobility promised by the capitalist ethos, were not necessarily content with their social or material position and were perpetually striving for something more. Tocqueville wrote that people were "always straining to pursue or to retain gratifications so delightful, so imperfect, so fugitive," that they were never satisfied.[99]

The emergence of advertising and mass media, which began imbuing material goods with abstract properties (and associated them by proxy with owners), helped to fundamentally alter the role of goods in the culture. Notices such as J. Stickney's, which appeared in an 1820 issue of the *Kentucky Reporter* asking for the return of his stolen "pet watch," expressed the beginning of an era in which Americans were to become emotionally attached to the objects around them. Stickney's watch was nothing special, just "an old double cased gilt SILVER WATCH without any glass," yet it was dear enough that he offered $5 for its return.[100] The emergence of patent medicine advertising in the 1840s reinforced and legitimated

Americans' emotional attachment to goods, contributing to a "carnivalization of the psyche"—the belief that goods had the power to transform the individual.[101] Patent medicines promised to transmute sickness into health, torpor into vitality. Other products offered promises of a different sort (such as elevating one's social status or making one more attractive to the opposite sex). Simply adopting the correct style of dress or equipping a house with fashionable furniture could be transformative, elevating one's status through conspicuous consumption.

All of this was fine as long as people consumed in socially prescribed ways. But when consumers put goods to unintended use—repurposing them as loan collateral rather than using them up and buying again—it threatened the status quo. The Reverend William Ellery Channing offered a typical assessment of proper consumption and class mobility when in 1840 he lectured members of Boston's Mechanic Apprentice's Library Association about how to "elevate" manual laborers. "I wish them to rise," he insisted. But, he continued, "I have no wish to dress them from a Parisian tailor's shop, or to teach them manners from a dancing school. I have no desire to see them, at the end of the day, doff their working dress, that they may play a part in richly attired circles. I have no desire that they should be admitted to luxurious feasts, or should get a taste for gorgeous upholstery."[102] Channing and others urged the lower sorts to climb the economic ladder by working even harder. But they had no interest in seeing working folk ascend beyond their station to challenge the status of those at the top who *were* wearing French fashions and enjoying the luxuries of their well-appointed homes.

While outside observers such as Channing may have begrudged the middling and lower sorts their material aspirations, they projected their own bourgeois pretensions onto critiques of pawning by assuming that pawners assigned objects the same meanings that they themselves did. Additionally, they thought of these material things as inhabiting fixed, discrete states whose specific purposes were prescribed by producers and retailers. Anthropologist Igor Kopytoff has explained that a society's natural inclination is to arrange goods according to relative states of commoditization. Some goods are singular and inalienable, that is, one of a kind and separated from their owners or caretakers only under the direst conditions (such as a foreign country's gaining possession of the original Declaration of Independence). Other objects remain fixed as commodities, with clear exchange value. Most goods, however, can move among various spheres of exchange if allowed to enter the market to begin with.

Pawnbrokers, like most of their customers, regarded objects in the pawnshop as economic expedients. As good businessmen, pawnbrokers did not consider ethereal (and nonmarketable) factors such as the "sentimental" value of a pawn, causing detractors to see them as hard-hearted and greedy. Likewise, regular pawners familiar with the process made calculated decisions about what they would take to the pawnbroker, often having several items in hock at one time, perpetually pawning and redeeming. A gold locket, for example, might hold sentimental value for its owner. But pawned repeatedly, it also possessed a stable monetary equivalency at the pawnshop that could be reliably figured into the family budget. Popular commentators' critiques encapsulated their anxiety about these relatively fluid systems of value.[103] The pawned locket could inhabit two states simultaneously, possessing both a real economic value and a subjective sentimental value to the person who pawned it.

Although bourgeois commentators had plenty to say about the supposedly spendthrift ways of the classes beneath them, it is just as likely that the lower classes made purchases for rational economic reasons and not because they were unable to practice self-control. Easy convertibility into cash may have determined whether an object was purchased in the first place (and subsequently stored, and cared for, and transported from one place to another). Reformers either did not consider or conveniently ignored this simple fact, because it was easier to accuse the poor of inept money management than to acknowledge that many working people still could not make ends meet, even after making clearheaded financial decisions in sometimes desperate circumstances.

When commenting on pawnbroking, social critics focused almost exclusively on the abstract and symbolic properties of personal possessions-cum-pawns. This perspective gave them license to vilify pawnbrokers for supposedly stripping objects of their personal identity and holding hostage the historical and family connections they embodied. The mainstream business organ *Hunt's Merchants' Magazine*, for instance, described the household goods hanging in the pawnshop window, as "waving like the flag of wretchedness and misery." The "cherished relics" and "sacred possessions" had been "profaned," according to the writer's vivid imagination:

> There hangs the watch, the old chased repeater, that hung above the head of a dying parent when bestowing his trembling blessing on the poor outcast who parted with it for bread; the widow's wedding ring is there, the last and dearest of all her possessions; the trinket, the pledge of love of one now dead, the only relic of the heart's fondest memories; silver that graced the holiday feast; . . . the flute, the favorite of a dead son, surrendered by a starving mother to procure food for her remaining offspring; the locket that held a father's hair.[104]

If objects possessed transformative powers, an idea that people exposed to advertising claims increasingly bought into, then their appearance in pawnshop windows was a rejection of the bourgeois tenets of good taste and upward mobility on which American consumer culture was based.

In order to sell their products, business owners claimed that people could elevate themselves by accumulating goods. The role of pawning within this ethos of accumulation and desire, then, could only be troublesome. People had to divest themselves of their belongings because of the exigencies created by life within capitalism. Pawning opened up an alternative avenue for using goods that fell outside the legitimated realms of wholesale and retail commerce. As material objects filled more space in the homes and minds of genteel Americans, being dispossessed of these things carried greater symbolic significance. A character in the story *Undercurrents of Wall-Street* regrets having to pawn his pocket watch not because it is worth two hundred dollars, but because he is attached to it. As he hands it across the counter to the pawnbroker, he "looked at it. Never did it seem so much of a companion as at that moment." His friend chides, "You have been very foolish. Such a thing as a watch gets to be a part of yourself."[105] William James described the culmination of the consumer revolution in the final decade of the nineteenth century. Americans breathed life into the myriad baubles and trinkets they purchased, considering them extensions of the self. James wrote that "*a man's Self is the sum total of all that he* CAN *call his,* not only his body and his psychic powers, but his clothes and his house, his wife and children, his ancestors and friends, his reputation and works, his lands and horses, and yacht and bank-account. All these things give him the same emotions. If they wax and prosper, he feels triumphant; if they dwindle and die away, he feels cast down."[106] To the bourgeois, the biography of the things one owned, then, was inextricably linked to a consumer's personal biography: the fate of one's possessions equaled one's own fate. And the totality of one's possessions demarcated one's personal empire and reflected one's ability to control the surrounding material world.

James was writing in the 1890s, after the second Industrial Revolution and at a time when affordable goods were ubiquitous. People who owned many things could categorize them and compartmentalize their use: some objects served as repositories of sentimental value, while others were functional. Objects might both connote status and have use (for example, an elaborate tea set). But the sentimental objects owned by the wealthy remained in a wholly separate category from the practical and the functional. In contrast, people who owned fewer possessions relied on them to serve many purposes. A pocket watch handed down from one's father, for example, was at various times a useful timekeeper, a fashionable item, and a cash-generating piece of collateral. Yet social commentators, reformers, and the like tended to sensationalize the objects traveling to pawnshops: if possessions embodied a man's self, as James asserted, then pawning meant losing one's self, one piece at a time.

Mass consumption increasingly shaped the physical and psychological universe of all classes of Americans during the nineteenth century. After the Civil War both urban and rural dwellers had their pick of thousands upon thousands of affordable consumer items to decorate and order their external world. Mail-order catalogs such as Montgomery Ward (beginning in 1872) and Sears, Roebuck (1886), "department stores in a book," enabled the far-flung to purchase a vast array of mass-produced goods.[107] Chromolithographs, needlework samplers, rocking chairs, hall stands, pocketknives, and of course clothing all came in different shapes, sizes, and styles to suit the tastes and supposed needs of each individual. The actual use of an item was often less important than its efficacy in "acting out social strategies."[108] That is, using goods to create impressions of oneself in relation to others.

In addition to mail-order catalogs and advertisements in mass-distributed magazines and newspapers, department stores also helped thrust consumer culture into the landscapes of American cities and small towns. These were "grand depots" faced with plate-glass windows, filled with sprawling showcases and mazes of specialty areas selling everything from oriental rugs to pianos, clothing to jewelry. Department stores brought consumers into immediate and intimate contact with new goods. They turned shopping into an "emotional experience," one in which "acquisition and consumption [were] the means of achieving happiness."[109]

Thorstein Veblen, perhaps the most astute observer of "conspicuous consumption," theorized that Americans living at the time of the second Industrial Revolution consumed to acquire status symbols they could show off to others. "The possession of wealth," he wrote, "confers honor."[110] Purchasing luxury goods demonstrated one's economic prowess, and through proper display people could ascend the social ranks. In Veblen's view, the pursuit of goods drove the consumer revolution; for many, it was their reason for being. Performing good deeds no longer mattered, nor did being adept at a trade. Instead, making the right purchases proved one's worth, indicating economic status and also reflecting character. Veblen observed, "So soon as the possession of property becomes the basis of popular esteem, therefore, it becomes also a requisite to that complacency we call self-respect."[111]

Pawning was anathema to this cultural ethos. If goods defined the core of the individual self, according to William James, or asserted membership in a specific class of late nineteenth-century American culture, as Thorstein Veblen theorized, then taking possessions to the pawnshop diminished not only one's self but also one's status as a full-fledged American. Although pawners did not necessarily see things that way, their critics certainly did. In 1892 Jonathan Gilmer Speed wrote favorably of semiphilanthropic pawnshops, describing their work in lending money as "a strictly business transaction to which no reproach should be attached." Yet "for obvious reasons," he noted, going to a private pawnshop "pretty nearly always lowers the self-respect of the borrower."[112] Another Progressive Era writer described pawning in terms of addiction, referring to the "pawning habit" among women: "once fixed upon them" it was "difficult to overcome."[113] And Louis L. Freligh, the owner of Ulysses Grant's pawn ticket (and likely the pawnbroker's son) waited over fifty years to sell it, "because so many people consider it a disgrace to patronize 'mine uncle,' & I did not wish to give offense to the renowned general's family, by exposing the matter. If you don't want to buy the valuable paper," he requested of a manuscript dealer, "kindly keep quiet."[114]

Today's pawnbrokers call their loyal customers the "in-and-outers," referring to the reliability with which they pawn and redeem goods. A hundred years ago, people with the "pawning habit" likewise relied on credit to make ends meet. Yet what so many reformers did not understand or acknowledge was that pawners figured regular loans into domestic budgets to manage chronic disparities between earnings and expenses. Possessions were deployed as collateral to meet unexpected financial crises brought about by unemployment, sickness, and death.

To assert that people exercised agency when going to the pawnbrokers, however, is not to suggest that pawning was a casual act or that the collateral held no meaning for the pawners. In fact, because nineteenth-century Americans experienced such a profound shift in the role and meaning of goods in their lives, they had to be even more mindful of what they bought, what they saved, what they cherished as inalienable, and what they pawned. What was more, consumers were offered an ever-expanding array of goods in specialty retail shops, mail-order catalogs, and department stores. From among these items they had to choose what necessities and luxuries they could afford and compare the relative quality of seemingly similar items. Decisions were influenced by advertising rhetoric, and consumers had to educate themselves. The marketplace offered new opportunities for members of all classes to be consumers, enabling them to enjoy physical comforts and the freedom of self-fashioning through the world of goods. But this freedom came at a price: Americans had become inextricably enmeshed in the structures of industrial capitalism; more informal economies had become much less accessible. Consumer choice—brought about by the solidifying of industrialization that relied on low-paying, menial labor—was both liberating and burdensome.

Like consumers, pawnbrokers also had to educate themselves about the varied goods for sale in the marketplace, and by the early twentieth century many were beginning to specialize. The sheer number of goods being produced, imported, and circulated in various markets precluded even the most skilled pawnbroker from accurately appraising every piece. It became exceedingly difficult to calculate the true value of all goods at all times, especially if we consider that pawners brought not only fake jewelry but also inferior pocket watches ("shedders" covered in flimsy electroplated coatings), cheap musical instruments, and textiles colored with fugitive dyes. Pawners themselves were often deceived about these goods, learning their true worth only when pawnbrokers would not lend anything on them. Not long after opening its doors in 1890, the Lynchburg, Virginia, pawnshop of L. Oppleman began trading primarily in musical instruments. By the twentieth century, William Simpson earned a reputation for accepting luxury goods and exotic one of a kind objects that average pawnbrokers might turn away because they were too difficult to appraise and to sell if unredeemed. They included "the fabulous Hope Diamond . . . a Stradivarius . . . prayer rugs . . . manuscripts illuminated by the loving brush of a fifteenth-century monk . . . Old Masters, of course, and etchings, drawings and rare old prints beyond counting . . . an Oriental dancing girl made of gilded teakwood . . . [and] the two-handed beheading sword of a Chinese Mandarin."[115]

Perhaps the most compelling evidence that pawners exercised agency and managed their daily economies as best they could can be seen in redemption rates—the percentage of loans paid off, with the pawns returned to their owners. Regardless of whether a pawn was a useful object, a status symbol, or a sentimental possession, it had a good chance of being redeemed. Rather than trapping most pawners in an endless cycle of poverty, as was the common perception, pawning was instead a viable strategy enabling ordinary people to endure financial shortfalls. An article in *Hunt's Merchants' Magazine* in 1860 estimated redemption rates in New York City at between 85% and 90%. The *Hunt's* article noted that "the pawnbroker exerts an influence that is rather conducive to the comfort of the poor than to their ruin. The articles they receive form a fund to provide against an emergency somewhat like the deposit in a savings bank, and the hope of regaining them unquestionably acts as powerful stimulus to exertion."[116] During the many severe downturns that plagued nineteenth-century economic life, pawners, like everyone else, had a more difficult time paying their debts. In 1837, 1857, the Civil War years, 1876, and 1893 redemption rates dipped, but not by that much.[117] Data from the Simpson ledger recording pawning in the aftermath of the Panic of 1837 indicate redemption rates of over 90%.[118]

During years of stable economic activity, redemption rates remained surprisingly high. A pawnbroker working in Milwaukee in the early 1880s estimated his redemption rates at 80%, noting that some goods were redeemed after five years of being in hock (meaning that these pawners made regular interest payments and faithfully renewed their loans).[119] The Provident Loan Society's redemption rates from 1896 to 1898 ranged between 97.5% and 98.5%, evidence "that the aid furnished by this Society is effective in most instances" by getting people back on their feet.[120] The experience of the First State Pawners Society of Chicago was virtually the same: redemption rates from 1899 and 1917 averaged 94%.[121]

People assumed that pawners never saw their things again once they went "up the spout," and critics used this misperception as yet another reason to vilify pawnbrokers. But what we know about high redemption rates indicates that most pawners *did* redeem their goods. The great number of pawns ending up in resale markets simply illustrates the tremendous volume of pawnbrokers' business, if hundreds of unredeemed pawns per pawnbroker per year constituted only about 10% of the total number of loans. This was borrowing on a grand scale, suggesting that many more Americans, especially those living in cities, relied on ready access to credit as early as the antebellum era.

Yet reports of high redemption rates did not fit social critics' preferred narrative, which demonized pawnbrokers for depriving the most vulnerable members of society of their meager goods and amassing inflated profits. The narrative also portrayed the poor as profligate and indolent spendthrifts who did not know how to manage their money. In truth, using personal goods as collateral required pawners to make considered decisions about what they would pawn and when. Pawning cycles were based on various factors such as which items were expendable at that moment, which would generate the highest loans, and which might feasibly be redeemed by the expiration of the loan. Sometimes more humble goods such as nightgowns and petticoats put up for a fraction of a dollar could be paid off more easily, thereby becoming more viable collateral. Other things such as coats and tools secured higher loans and could be pawned seasonally.

Using personal possessions gave pawners a greater incentive to get them out of hock. And those who were more economically disenfranchised tended to have better credit histories. Directors of the Pawners' Bank of Boston remarked that "borrowers of small sums, and on what would ordinarily be considered the poorest class of property, are the most prompt to redeem their pledges." They contrasted the good habits of those pawning the "poorest class of property" with those hocking better collateral for higher loans, who nonetheless "take the longest period of the credit allowed them."[122] Founders of Boston's Emergency Loan Fund learned the hard way about the efficacy of securing loans with physical collateral. They hoped to circumvent pawnbrokers by matching people in need with individual benefactors who would personally see to their financial welfare. Organizers of the Loan Fund assumed that if borrowers knew their lenders personally they would feel more obligated to make good on their debts than if they frequented pawnshops. Mary C. Jackson, one of the fund's organizers, recalled, "From 1880 to 1890 the money went out in small sums; for the most part to the very poor, and was secured by people of the same class, thinking the incentive to pay the note would be greater were a personal friend to suffer. This theory is good," she wrote, "but the borrower and guarantor too often went to the wall together; and more notes were counted as lost than the entire number sacrificed during the next two decades."[123]

The interpersonal relationships that secured and fostered transactions based on credit in the past (and only for the elite) had by the end of the nineteenth century been rendered largely irrelevant. Rather than feeling the burden of obligation to their fellowmen, pawners were more likely to feel obligated to their *things*, having a greater incentive to repay a debt secured by their own collateral than by a third party. Commentators insisted that pawnshop transactions, necessitating a physical surrender of goods, diminished pawners by separating them from parts of themselves. In truth, the physical nature of the loan collateral provided a powerful incentive for people to get their stuff back. Whether the family Bible or a gold pocket watch, pawns concretized to varying degrees tradition, sentiment, utility, material aspirations, and real value. Being aware of these many aspects of physical goods proved crucial to making both wise purchases and wise pawning decisions. The economically disenfranchised had to be at least as astute about and engaged with the evolving consumer culture as the middle and upper classes, for whom the economies of daily life were not persistent concerns.

CHAPTER FIVE

PAWNBROKING AND CRIMINAL ACTIVITY

Pawning enabled average Americans to make ends meet—to pursue honest work when, as often happened, that work did not pay enough to cover even basic expenses. As industrial capitalism became more solidified and inflexible, more people made their way to the neighborhood pawnshop. Pawnbroking, too, opened up new entrepreneurial avenues for those ingenious and motivated enough to operate within gray and black market economies. Like secondhand goods dealers and junk sellers, pawnbrokers helped circulate and recirculate consumer goods and commodities at various stages of their life cycles, from the brand new or slightly used to the utterly disintegrated and used up. And they dealt closely with people from all walks of life, especially the desperate and disenfranchised.

While ordinary wage workers and day laborers often felt the crushing pressure of long days at meager wages, there were also opportunities for those willing and able to work at or beyond the margins of the legitimate economy. It is undeniable that some pawnbrokers engaged directly in criminal dealings and gained reputations as trusty fences for stolen goods. Some merely abetted criminals—for example, by selling forged pawn tickets. More often, pawnbrokers took part in criminal acts unwittingly or were themselves the victims of violent crimes and confidence schemes. They frequently entered into cooperative arrangements with police, providing information about dubious goods and pawners in exchange for less surveillance.

Because of the nature of their occupation, pawnbrokers constantly negotiated white, gray, and black markets, dealing with authorities, honest pawners, and crooks alike. Like most other businessmen, pawnbrokers were enterprising people who were rewarded for their ability to work the system to their own advantage. They followed the rules of legitimate business practice when it was prudent and profitable and transgressed the boundaries when that proved more remunerative. Yet the intersections of criminal activity and pawnbroking, as opposed to "mainstream" business operations, perhaps best reveal the fractured economic and social relationships that characterized everyday experience in many nineteenth- and early twentieth-century cities. Pawnbrokers stood at the nexus of these fractured relationships, their businesses emerging out of—and dependent on—the large-scale shifts in American life and culture detailed in the previous chapters.

Tracking the goods that went into and out of pawnshops over time, through licit and illicit channels, shows how various economies worked, forged and experienced by real individuals, sometimes in concert with transactions considered "legitimate" and sometimes in opposition. Personal possessions were (and continue to be) physical and emotional anchors that moved about extensively. They traveled with their owners: as jewelry and clothing worn every day; as household furnishings loaded into carts when it was time to move; as objects relinquished and abandoned, subsequently to be circulated among others. The movement of goods reflected the behaviors of people in various circumstances and shows the entrepreneurial opportunities within the more flexible underground economies, especially in recirculating stolen goods.

Notices asking for the return of lost and stolen goods began appearing regularly in eighteenth-century newspapers, and many made reference to pawning. Watches, jewelry, cigarette boxes, and other personal effects, evidence of a nascent consumer culture, were both theft-worthy and pawnable. Francis Blake's announcement in a 1764 issue of the Georgia Gazette is representative of the genre: "LOST OR STOLEN, A SILVER TEA SPOON, marked F.ᴮM. Whoever brings it to the subscriber shall be rewarded; and if offered to be pawned or sold it's desired it may be stopt."[1] Thieves also coveted guns, which had even more practical and monetary value than teaspoons: "Stolen or Taken away" in 1784 was "A SILVER Mounted Pistol, with a screw barrel and stock lock, made in England, maker's name on it R. W. Wilson." The owner beseeched, "If offered to be pawned or sold pray stop it."[2] Even before the establishment of formal pawnshops, Americans assumed that valuable property might be used as loan collateral. Advertisements for lost and stolen goods sought the return of a variety of things, including wigs, toothpick holders, pocket watches, spectacles, snuff boxes, razor cases, petticoats, candlesticks, silver tankards, and Bibles.[3] Portable and often fashioned of valuable materials (ivory, gold, silver, and pewter), these desirable items were easily convertible into cash through middlemen, complicit and unwitting alike. To be effective, underground entrepreneurs had to know their markets and remain abreast of the latest consumer fads. "Like established storekeepers," they would "closely monitor evolving popular tastes in material culture." To decide what was theft-worthy and determine how to unload it, thieves "develop[ed] a keen eye for quality and authenticity."[4]

That valuable goods circulated so liberally was just cause for anxiety among owners, who worried that their valued and valuable personal possessions would be stolen. In addition, people worried about how money generated from collateral loans would be used, and those who took things in pawn (even legitimately) were often accused of contributing to moral turpitude by giving borrowers money to use for gambling and drinking. The first known reference to pawning in America, as it happens, is a complaint that pawnbrokers enabled alcohol abuse and dates from the mid-seventeenth century. The *Minutes of the Court of Burgomasters and Schepens,* regarding Dutch settlers in 1657, documented concerns brought to the magistrates of the New Netherland colony "against the many tapsters and tavernkeepers." The problem was not just that they were selling spirituous liquors but also that they allowed patrons to continue drinking after all their money (which they should have taken home) had run out. By accepting goods as pawns, including furniture and clothing, proprietors enabled customers to "obtain the means of continuing their usual drinking bouts." (Officials took these concerns seriously, fining tavern keepers for the first offense, doubling the fine and shutting the business for six weeks for the second infraction, and closing the place for good on the third.)[5]

Informal loan transactions of the seventeenth and eighteenth centuries often occurred at the local bar. Tavern keepers and innkeepers operated as casual pawnbrokers before the maturation of a distinct lending profession. People still needed ready cash, and proprietors of "ordinaries" saw a constant stream of both new and familiar faces carrying property that could be exchanged for drinks or used as collateral for short-term loans. Proprietors often accepted personal property in lieu of cash for a night's lodging, food, and drinks. For example, in 1790 Charleston's justice of the peace recovered a London-made silver watch apparently stolen "by a Spaniard, who says his name is John Lopez, and pawned, *as it is said,* in a dram shop for the value of Twelve Shillings." The owner of the dram shop turned the watch in to authorities, but not before Lopez had gotten a few drinks out of the deal.[6]

Even the most respectable taverns of the eighteenth century were seedy places patronized by rough customers, which did nothing to burnish the reputation of the collateral loan process. The "enforced intimacy" of taverns impelled strangers to interact with each other in very close quarters. And the constant flow of people through their doors allowed tavern keepers to capitalize on more than just serving drinks and the occasional meal. Local taverns and inns, often functioning as the town hub, were active places overseen by proprietors who offered myriad services to their many customers. "They kept packages, delivered messages, loaned small sums of money, or rented horses."[7] One Philadelphia tavern keeper sold sundries, stored items (including a parrot in a cage), and returned lost property.[8]

Goods circulated casually and promiscuously, taking on various roles as they moved within layers of informal economies. For example, a presentation saber— gold-plated, embellished with military emblems, and engraved with George Washington's name—finally made its way to the president after taking a circuitous route. A mystified Washington wrote at the time, "A gentleman with whom I have no acquaintance, coming from and going to I know not where, at a tavern I never could get information of, came across this sword . . . pawned for thirty dollars, which he paid, left it in Alexandria, nine miles from my house, in Virginia, with a person who refunded him the money and sent the sword to me." It apparently had been brought over from Amsterdam, to be presented to Washington, by the maker's son Daniel Alte, who a year later could not be tracked down. Washington surmised that the object "got into such loose hands, the sword was either stolen from Alte or pawned by him, ending up being pawned in a tavern somewhere for $30."[9] A proprietor's ability to "hustle up business and make a penny where it could be made," on humble and spectacular items alike, not only enabled him to keep his doors open but also greatly expanded his connections in the informal economies.[10]

By the end of the eighteenth century Americans began to make more critical connections between pawning and nefarious dealings, including both the trafficking of stolen goods and pawning's supposed contribution to intemperance. People were observing with mounting concern the living conditions in cities on the other side of the Atlantic. In addition to scanning newspaper and magazine accounts, Americans were reading books such as Patrick Colquhoun's *Treatise on the Police of London*, published in Philadelphia in 1798. The author, a police magistrate and reformer, estimated that some 115,000 criminals lived in London. Included in his "shocking catalogue of human depravity" were spendthrifts and rakes, "Swindlers, Cheats, and low Gamblers," "Fraudulent and dissolute Publicans," ruffians and bear baiters, and 4,000 he categorized as "Receivers of Stolen Goods, from petty Pilferers at Old Iron Shops, Store Shops, Rag and Thrum Shops, and Shops for second-hand Apparel, including some fraudulent Hostlers, small Butchers, and Pawnbrokers."[11]

Americans feared that the ills of such cities as Birmingham, Dublin, and London foretold what might be in store for citizens if Boston, Philadelphia, New

York, and other growing cities were inadequately policed. Stifling pollution, grinding poverty, and rampant crime were bound to plague new cities if they followed Europe's path. Reformers seized on Colquhoun's sensational statistics while overlooking his larger point, that pawnshops, gambling parlors, and lottery agencies were symptoms rather than causes of poverty, vice, and crime and that these pressing social issues emerged because of rapid industrialization and the widespread exploitation of factory workers. "The moral principle is totally destroyed among a vast body of the lower ranks of the people," wrote Colquhoun, "for wherever prodigality, dissipation, or gaming, whether in the Lottery or otherwise, occasions a want of money, they avail themselves of every opportunity to purloin public or private property . . . and to raise money at the pawnbrokers, or the old iron or rag shops."[12]

Despite the best efforts of reform-minded citizens, social and economic problems did visit themselves on American cities well before the eighteenth century turned to the nineteenth, exacerbated over time by capitalism's creeping influence. The problems themselves proved intractable, endemic to the economic system. But reformers, earnest and desperate to do *something*, sought out clear causes of crime and poverty that they could address. Neither economic inequity, the influx of unskilled immigrants, nor racism was responsible for the country's social and economic problems, many contended. Pawnbrokers—who provided credit to patrons primarily belonging to the working poor—critics determined, were a collective source of most vice. They believed that eliminating pawnbrokers would miraculously eliminate most crime and discourage bad habits.

Working on the widely held assumption that pawnbroking was a corrosive institution, government agencies began addressing the "problem" in the first years of the new century, with the New York City Common Council first taking up the issue in 1805 and establishing the country's first pawnbroking regulations in 1812. Common Council members took it for granted that pawnbrokers were receivers of stolen goods and hoped regulatory efforts would curb trade in illicit goods and protect pawners against high interest rates and illegal fees. To obtain a license, a pawnbroker had to back up his proof of "good character" with a $500 bond placed with the mayor to cover any claims brought against him. Authorities also required pawnbrokers to maintain detailed ledgers recording the particulars of each loan and to make their books available to city officials on request. Regulations also forbade pawnbrokers to accept collateral "from any minor, apprentice, servant or slave . . . under the penalty of *One Hundred Dollars*, for each offence," because such goods were likely to be stolen.[13]

Like New Yorkers, reformers in other cities of the early republic worried about how pawnbroking might be contributing to crime, vice, and poverty in their own neighborhoods. The Pennsylvania Society for the Promotion of Public Economy, a philanthropic organization founded in 1817, admitted in one of its first reports to having "very little information" about pawnbroking yet concluded that "the effects of pawn-brokers cannot from their nature be otherwise than pernicious, and in but few instances are the poor, we presume, able to redeem their goods."[14] Organizers of New York's Society for the Prevention of Pauperism agreed, asserting that "the facilities which they afford to the commission of theft, and the encouragement they give to a dependence on stratagem and cunning, rather than on the profits of honest industry," could not be tolerated.[15] The latter argument—that pawning encouraged sloth and deception—was particularly persuasive at a time when hard work was considered an essential republican virtue and crucial to building a strong, healthy nation. A pawnbroker defended his profession by arguing that loans were made to adults whose mental facilities were presumably intact and who were therefore able to make decisions for themselves. He wrote, "Intemperance and dissipation do not arise from the fair use of the Pawnbroker's shop, but from the abuse of its benefits. . . . Surely it cannot be expected," he continued, "that [a pawnbroker] should go with his customers to see that they lay out the money prudently."[16]

Much early local policy, in fact, came as a response to reformers' vocal attempts to control both the money and the property of the lower classes. In 1820 the New York City Society for the Prevention of Pauperism reported, "The managers are led to believe, that the laws and regulations on this source of pauperism, are salutary and duly enforced."[17] Owing to pressure from the Pennsylvania Society for the Promotion of Public Economy, Philadelphia passed its first pawnbroking ordinances in 1823. Its unintended consequence was to drive many pawnbrokers to the city's southern fringes in the Southwark area, just outside the reach of the law.[18] A newspaper columnist at the time "regretted" that the "very excellent ordinance passed" had "been rendered nugatory" because so many pawnbrokers had moved beyond city limits.[19] This cat-and-mouse game between authorities and pawnbrokers, exacerbated by constant pressure from reformers and officials, continued throughout the century.

Only a few years after the first ordinances passed, officials and reformers alike continued to blame pawnbrokers not only for receiving stolen goods, but for encouraging theft by their mere existence. The reports parroted one another. A New York City grand jury concluded in 1833, "The facilities afforded by pawnbrokers to persons who subsist by petty depredations, may well excite alarm."[20] And a Philadelphia grand jury two years later determined that pawnbrokers, in addition to scrap dealers and proprietors of tippling houses, "from the various cases which have been brought in review . . . give great facility to the perpetration of almost every species of petty crime" and "induce as powerfully to the commission of crime, as the temptation which the golden trinket itself presents."[21] The *Saturday Evening Post* remarked at the time that "there is nothing which tends more to the encouragement of roguery, than the petty Pawnbroker's shops, with which our city is so plentifully supplied," adding that pawnshops provided the "light-fingered gentry" with a convenient place to unload their goods, no questions asked.[22]

When Philadelphia physician and reformer James Mease pushed the city to establish a nonprofit pawnshop in 1836, he claimed that a beneficial result of access to low-interest loans would be "the prevention of numerous petty thefts by those who are in absolute want of food or clothing, and by others who are enabled to procure either for pledges, except at such a sacrifice, as leads to the temptation of stealing, in preference to obtaining a loan by pawns."[23] Mease was one of the few people who acknowledged the interconnection of poverty and crime; lack of work (and hence lack of food and clothing) *did* force many to steal. The Boston Society on Pauperism and Crime also recognized the complex dynamic between poverty and illegal activity, but the organization failed to look beyond "second-hand clothes-dealers, junk shops, and pawn brokers' offices, as among the most prolific sources of crime" and propose a workable solution.[24] So ingrained was the belief that pawnshops promoted crime that in 1856 a bill was introduced to the New York City Common Council to suppress *all* pawnshops "and other receptacles of stolen property."[25]

Tamping down the growth of informal and unregulated practices proved impossible, regardless of reformers' efforts and the legislation enacted on their behalf. In fact, the emergence of industrial capitalism spurred business in underground markets as enterprising sorts found opportunities created by the needs of the working poor. Illegal moneylending outlets based on traditional taverns and inns continued to serve people in need of drinking money. The Southwark area of Philadelphia in the 1830s, for example, was lined with grog shops doubling as pawnshops. Hiding behind the legitimacy of their licenses, pawnbrokers reportedly accepted goods in payment for alcohol: "Three golden balls over the door, stuck out upon three prongs, indicate a Pawnbroker's establishment, while the rubicund bottle in the window, and the slinking look of the customers, indicate [that] both liquor is sold, and encouragement given to theft," according to one contemporary account.[26]

The popular press articulated the myriad concerns regarding pawnshops again and again throughout the century, insisting on characterizing pawnbrokers as major fences (and purveyors of alcohol) while ignoring or making only glancing references to the true movers of stolen goods, the junk and scrap dealers. In 1866, for example, the *New York Times* identified pawnshops as "a very fruitful source of crime," essentially excusing the conduct of other known receivers because criminals operated in a different world and their nefarious activities remained largely invisible to law-abiding citizens. What was more, pawnbrokers allegedly encouraged would-be criminals by making it easy for people to do bad things. Pawnshops provided an outlet for "the tempted person who would steal if he knew what to do with the stealings." The *New York Times* referred to the local pawnshop as a "constant invitation to the commission of crime." According to the prevailing logic, without pawnbrokers to accept stolen goods, there would be no theft at all. "Any loafer or rowdy can take to him valuable articles, the possession of which is almost *prima facie* evidence of theft" under the pretense that the stolen goods are collateral but assumed "on both sides" to be an outright sale. By then unloading the unredeemed collateral at auction to be circulated in tertiary markets, pawnbrokers moved these goods into ever wider circles, making any links to their original owners so tenuous as to render them beyond recovery.[27]

Social critics accused pawnbrokers of being active fences, but most in fact were not. At the beginning of the century pawnbrokers were more inclined to reunite personal items with their owners as an act of goodwill. A Philadelphia businessman who advanced money "Upon Watches, Plate, Jewels, Household Furniture, and other valuable articles" kept ledgers for the sole purpose of recording lost and stolen goods so that he could return them to their owners. Offering the service free, he announced in an 1809 advertisement that "any persons being defrauded, or having lost, or had property stolen, are requested to leave a particular description of the same in writing . . . that the property may [be] detained if brought, and the parties secured."[28] By taking the side of honest business, pawnbrokers were also able to ingratiate themselves with the authorities. If they asked for reward money, they could earn a tidy profit by returning lost or stolen property and perhaps identify a suspected thief.

It was important for pawnbrokers to build good relations with the police who surveilled them. While fencing goods was a lucrative side business for a minority of pawnbrokers, it was an occupational hazard for even the most honest businessman (who risked losing his license—and hence his livelihood—if found with stolen goods on his shelves). By the 1830s the average pawnbroker was completing hundreds of transactions a day and dealing with thousands of customers each year. Accepting collateral that pawners had not come by honestly was unavoidable. Later in the century one observer of "our criminal population" concluded that "any pawn-broker or junk-dealer is liable to, and very often does, become innocently a receiver of stolen goods; but the amount of property that can be worked off through them is inconsiderable."[29]

Wisely, most tried to stay out of the stolen goods business altogether. But where once pawnbrokers might have reunited owners with lost or stolen items free, they now saw yet another way to make a bit of extra money. Local ordinances prohibited pawnbrokers from "knowingly" taking in stolen goods, putting them on notice yet leaving room for plausible denial. Pawnbrokers were also required to surrender to police any articles that matched printed descriptions of stolen items. Public notices describing stolen property often appeared next to ads for dealers in used goods to attract the attention of the people most likely to come in contact with stolen property. John Brock, who promoted his Cheap Store for American and English Fine Gold Jewelry in the *National Police Gazette,* probably scanned the lost and stolen goods listings adjacent to his own ad. Brock's store, on Chatham Street in the heart of New York City's used goods district, sold gold and silver items of all kinds—spectacles, watches, forks and knives, thimbles, and more. In addition to repairing watches and jewelry, he bought them and took them in trade. The $10 reward ad for a stolen pocket watch, just above his own, would have caught his attention:

> $10 REWARD.—Stolen from the premises No. 3 Chambers street, on the 23d Nov., a lever watch, G. W. Robinson, Liverpool, maker, No. 6977, and having attached to it a gold-washed guard chain. The above reward will be paid to any person who shall return said watch and establishment to Mr. David Vane, No. 26 Elm st. Pawnbrokers and others are requested to give notice if the above article is offered to them.[30]

Pawnbrokers and jewelers could thus earn money on the side by paying close attention to such announcements and collecting reward money.

But it wasn't quite as simple as that. Operating at the intersections of many conflicting interest groups, exchange spheres, and personal motivations, pawnbrokers constantly negotiated between degrees of legal and illegal transactions. Surely the pawnbrokers who accepted silver watches and pitchers from a gang of boys roving the New York City streets in 1821 figured the items were stolen. In fact, they were breaking the law simply by dealing with the minors. But this particular group of boys, running in packs of as many as two hundred, were terrorizing the city and were blamed for "many depredations of late." The five boys who were at last apprehended confessed to snatching valuable goods from people's houses and selling them "for trifling amounts, to the pawnbrokers." It is possible that the pawnbrokers felt coerced into accepting the goods from the menacing gangs, although they did not turn the boys in to police.[31]

In printed robbery reports, the press frequently branded pawnbrokers as "known receivers," reinforcing the commonly held perception that they were routinely involved in criminal behavior. In 1846, for example, dry goods clerk James Byers took "large quantities" of silk, velvet, and other expensive fabrics he had stolen from his employers to six pawnshops around the city. When apprehended, he accused pawnbroker Aaron Adolphus of taking some of the fabrics in pawn and purchasing others outright. Rather than placing the blame on the thieving clerk, newspapers pointed to "the infamous practices of the pawnbrokers of this city who have become, almost in a body, known establishments for the purchase of stolen goods."[32]

Sometimes pawnbrokers deserved their bad press. And large busts garnered still larger headlines, like the "TABLES COVERED WITH WATCHES" that could be seen at headquarters after the police raided William Hallissy's New York City pawnshop in 1879 and confiscated his inventory. The pawnbroker and his assistant had been receiving substantial numbers of stolen watches, many recorded as legitimate collateral in the pawnshop's books. "On one table," the *New York Times* reported, "were exposed 146 silver watches. On another 90 gold watches were placed in rows, with scrupulous regard to their size. Finger-rings of every description, and gold chains and necklaces occupied still another table." Men "streamed" into the place to reclaim their property, which was sometimes intact. Many watches, however, were found "bereft of their cases."[33]

Fences fronting as pawnbrokers understandably kept police investigators at arm's length. But even the most upstanding pawnbrokers resented police intrusion into their operations. Except for junk, scrap, and secondhand goods dealers, pawnbrokers were the only businessmen dealing in material property who had to be licensed. Unlike wholesale merchants and retailers, they operated under constant police scrutiny and were required to open their books to any official who asked. It did not mean they always did so willingly, however. New York City police inspector William Bell, who was assigned to the pawn and junkshop detail in the early 1850s, documented the recalcitrance he encountered during regular inspections. For example, one afternoon he visited Henry Regan's pawnshop attempting to track down a stolen pocket watch and chain that had been hocked a few hours before. He noted, "A young Lady was tending the shop she refused to give us any information." Bell and his partner were forced to return to the station house and obtain an official order compelling the woman to open the books, and when she did, they found that "their was [*sic*] no entries later than the 2nd inst. She said the watch had not been Booked."[34] Even though the people in Regan's shop had nothing to hide, they refused to cooperate with police voluntarily.

Often frustrating and antagonistic, Bell's experiences typified those of people working in law enforcement before the establishment of professional and effective police forces. The police had only as much power as people were willing to grant them, and people chose to cooperate or resist according to what suited their own interests at the time. Bell clearly knew his way around the fringe neighborhoods he patrolled, yet he was thwarted more often than not. As peers and authority figures simultaneously, Inspector Bell and his colleagues were recruited from the neighborhoods they patrolled and drew on an individual rather than an institutional authority that "rest[ed] on closeness to the citizens and their informal expectations of his power instead of formal bureaucratic or legal standards."[35] Until 1853 Bell did not wear a uniform, and he and his fellow officers were armed only with nightsticks. It was not until the 1860s that they began routinely carrying pistols.[36]

Requiring pawnbrokers and other dealers in secondhand goods to apply for licenses annually and to meticulously document their transactions was a way for authorities to compensate for lack of effective surveillance. Although even licensed pawnbrokers had plenty of opportunity to accept things off the books, most in truth tried to run clean businesses and draw as little attention to themselves as possible. More elusive were the small operators who, even if licensed, might yet be making money through side businesses while neglecting to keep records for any of them. On the hunt for a stolen coat, Inspector Bell stopped at Charles Cudlipp's pawnshop, where "he is carrying on the Business of Second Hand Dealer in the same Building. I asked to see his Book that the Law requires S.H.D. to keep. He told me he kept none, he was offering goods for sale while I was there."[37] Cudlipp's business profited from and exemplified the fluidity of nineteenth-century economic activity. Although a licensed pawnbroker, Cudlipp was also brazenly selling secondhand goods outright in front of a police officer. Failing to keep any ledgers, he was in violation for both businesses yet seemed unfazed by Bell's presence.

Still other businesses were not licensed at all and were known to the underclass and underworld through word of mouth. Operating on the fringes out of small storefronts and basements or in more respectable areas, they challenged and often confounded police officers, especially the unlicensed brokers catering to the upper classes. "The daily papers teem with the advertisements of these men," noted *Harper's New Monthly Magazine* in 1869. "Their offices may be found, at frequent intervals, throughout all the business portion of the city. They are keepers of 'loan offices,' diamond brokers, auctioneers, lawyers who have on hand funds to dispose of for their clients; and they even nestle among the more aristocratic neighborhoods without any external 'sign' of their calling."[38] Entrepreneurial criminals capitalized on the police's inability to track the tens of thousands of people and goods that increasingly traversed the urban landscape. The most illustrious fence of the nineteenth century, Fredericka Mandelbaum, may have gotten her start in the business through her husband's pawnshop. She ran her wildly successful fencing operation out of a seemingly legitimate dry goods store and reputedly amassed $1 million by the 1880s.[39]

Because they were some of the most visible and most stable institutions, pawnshops could be easily fingered for much of the crime occurring at this time. Inevitably, pawnbrokers *did,* in fact, function as active yet often unwitting conduits for stolen goods. Even regular customers, with whom pawnbrokers had built long-standing relationships, could not be completely trusted. Trying to maintain its reputation as an upstanding business, Simpson and Company wrote a letter to the editor of the *New York Daily Tribune* in 1853, a rare instance of a pawnbroker's defending himself in public. It came in response to an allegation that the pawnshop was colluding with a pawner—someone's servant accused of theft who had been arrested with a number of Simpson's pawn tickets on her. Understandably defensive, the owners wanted to clear the record, and the letter bears quoting at length:

> To the Editor of the N.Y. Daily Tribune—As the statement in your widely-circulated journal of this date might have a tendency to impress the great many of your readers that we do not conduct our business of Pawnbroking in as fair and legitimate a manner as circumstances will generally permit, we beg, in justice to ourselves, to state, with reference to the colored woman, Wilson (who had so many of our tickets in her possession when arrested) that we hav[e h]ad dealings with her since the year 1847, when she commenced business, and up to the time of her being arrested; and our books will prove all along that she was regularly redeeming her pledges in the usual way, leading us consequently to infer that she was entitled to receive loans at our hands. It is usual for colored [servants? persons?] to be entrusted with the goods of their white employers to pledge, especially on account of those who have a repugnance to do their own business in person, and they (unfortunately for themselves, perhaps) form the most numerous class in this City. Whatever view may be taken by the Legal Authorities in this case, we feel [?]ed that we have acted from no improper motive by receiving the goods in question, and that we had no suspicion of their having been feloniously attained.[40]

Proprietors of Simpson's pawnshop argued that they saw no reason to distrust this woman. It was common for "colored people" to pawn items for themselves and on behalf of their employers, so her appearance in itself was not enough to arouse suspicion. In addition, the pawnshop had been dealing with pawner Wilson for some six years, and they believed they could trust her, since she "was regularly redeeming her pledges in the usual way." If anything, the pawnbrokers themselves were the victims, not only losing the money they had loaned on the stolen collateral but also suffering a tarnished reputation from the negative publicity.

Undoubtedly, a fair number of the thousands of pieces of unredeemed collateral auctioned off at public sale were in fact stolen. As a result, pawnbrokers played a role, however unintentional, in laundering thieves' booty by channeling it back into legitimate markets. Yet thieves went to the pawnbroker only if they were content to settle for less than full underground market value and did so reluctantly. When they did, criminals used a variety of tactics to evade detection by police and to escape scrutiny by the pawnbrokers they were using, since pawnbrokers, watched closely by the authorities, did not want to face charges of receiving or abetting. Toward the end of the century Ellen Linn leveraged her lowly position as a "migratory domestic servant" to steal from a string of employers. She distributed the goods among several pawnshops in the area so as not to arouse suspicion: Mrs. McLean's gold earrings, bracelets, breastpin, and topaz ring ended up at Newman's pawnshop; Mrs. Clausen's gold locket, chains, cross, earrings, sleeve buttons, breastpin, and shirt studs ended up at Heaney's. At Clickner's and Selig's pawnshops the thief unloaded a cloth sacque, a pair of gaiters, monogrammed plates and spoons, a wool dress, two rings, and a neck pin whose owners had not been identified when the report hit the newspapers.[41] Linn's ability to target a number of houses and dispose of her booty at several pawnshops suggests, too, the mobility and anonymity of urban life. People taking various temporary jobs and living essentially as transients in rented quarters epitomized extreme social dislocation. But alienation also presented entrepreneurial opportunities within thriving gray and black markets.

That stolen goods were often reported as found at pawnshops understandably reinforced the common perception that pawnbrokers actively encouraged theft and were members of the criminal underworld. It was more likely, though, that pawnbrokers were victims' best allies. Theft was an undeniable part of nineteenth-century urban life, and stolen goods that ended up in pawnshops stood a much greater chance of recovery than if they were funneled anywhere else. Straddling the criminal and commercial worlds, pawnbrokers were in a unique position to help police solve both serious and petty crimes and to help owners recover their property. Mostly they helped passively, by opening their ledgers, however reluctantly, and allowing authorities to scrutinize entries and inspect collateral. For instance, in 1852 Simpson's turned over "a lot of valuable wearing apparel" identified by two victims of William Owens, who had stolen the garments from their lodging house right down the street.[42]

When pawnbrokers helped return collateral to rightful owners, they often split reward money with police officers, so that they all shared a material incentive for chasing certain goods. The relative autonomy of individual police officers allowed them some latitude to mete out street justice and negotiate informal agreements among aggrieved parties. This "discretionary authority" also created an opportunity for some to take advantage of lax oversight and flexible, vague rules.[43] Reward money, for instance, might help grease the wheels of justice. "Every article of silver, amounting to a very large sum," was stolen from a New York City house in 1830. The owner posted a $200 reward, and within a few hours "the whole was returned uninjured" by the pawnbroker who had accepted the pieces as collateral.[44] The *National Police Gazette*, presumably no friend of the pawnbroker, published this announcement in an 1845 issue:

STOPPED.

BY PAWNBROKERS AND OTHERS.

Supposed to have been stolen.

Four heavy silver soup spoons, marked "N.R."

A gold watch, No. "2082, Geneva," with the words "A.U." engraved
on the inside of the case.

A piece of satinet, about 35 yds, iron grey, no marks.

A silver watch, number "2731," French make, French face.

A pair of gold spectacles, heavy, square sides—valuable.[45]

Pawnbrokers, who were required to maintain detailed records of pawner and pawned, could often provide the only physical evidence linking criminals to their crimes. Their books were so potentially useful to authorities that Brooklyn tried to enact "open ledger" legislation in 1870 to assist police in tracking stolen goods by making pawnshops' records more immediately accessible to the authorities. Pawnbrokers had valuable information that other presumed receivers did not. The *New York Times* remarked in 1876, "Great difficulty is experienced in obtaining the conviction of a receiver of stolen goods, and a chief obstacle in the way of discovering the authors of robberies is presented by the difficulty to be encountered in tracing the property after it has reached the hands of the receiver."[46]

Local police worked under challenging circumstances because goods circulated far and wide and in various ways through both underground and legitimate avenues. The diamond rings, gold watch, and other jewelry stolen from Mary Ann Archer in 1868 took typically circuitous routes. Alleged thief James Campbell spent the night of the robbery with Annie Morris, who, with accomplice Thomas Hanley (alias "Shang"), stole the goods from Campbell the next day. Morris, who "was quite bold," attended a ball wearing the watch and chain she had stolen from her fellow crook, knowing Campbell, being complicit, could not file a complaint against her. At the very same event *another* crook known as Goose stole the watch and chain from Morris. One of the diamond rings ended up in a pawnshop, pledged one day by Morris and redeemed the next by her partner Hanley. Although none of the jewelry had been recovered, records of the pawned diamond ring provided information that helped identify the suspects. They were finally apprehended over 160 miles away. A few years later, a man named Grimes sold stolen ribbon to one John Burney. Burney sold it to Benjamin Witkowski, who sold three boxes to Soloman Sulzberger and two to a man named Peyser; he pawned two and a half boxes at Alexander's pawnshop.[47] Beyond traveling blocks from where they were pilfered, stolen goods, as unfettered as their new "owners," often wound up in other cities entirely.

Pawnbrokers also played a role in solving more serious crimes. Pawnbroker Aaron Adolphus, whom police inspector William Bell suspected of working as an active receiver, proved instrumental in solving the "Staten Island Murders"—the lurid killing of a woman and her child that captivated New Yorkers in 1844. A person resembling the suspect had pawned a valuable watch reportedly taken during the crime. When called in to headquarters Adolphus confirmed the woman's identity, thus providing the only piece of concrete evidence linking the suspect to the crime. When asked about the pawned watch, Adolphus, the newspaper reported, "*at once identified her as the person who had left it.*"[48] He later confirmed that he "was positive in regard to her identity, as before," sealing her fate.[49]

The proprietor of a small pawnshop on Chatham Street helped police trace the perpetrator of a robbery and murder. Mr. Noe, a rich elderly gentleman, had been mugged by a man he caught stealing lead pipes from his building. The criminal knocked Mr. Noe out with a length of the pipe, took his gold watch and chain and a unique silver monkey head that embellished the man's cane. Noe regained consciousness only long enough to describe the articles taken from him; he died about a week later. Detectives scoured pawnshops for the watch, chain, and monkey head with no success. Eventually a pawnbroker came forward with what he believed to be Noe's stolen possessions. The recovery of the watch and chain, and the eventual discovery of the silver monkey head, led to the criminal, who would not have been arrested otherwise.[50] New York City police circulated descriptions of stolen jewelry to authorities in all major East Coast cities hoping to solve the robbery and murder of a Mrs. Hull. Until a pawnbroker recognized the articles and provided relevant information to the authorities, Mrs. Hull's husband had been the prime suspect. Although "not very good," a pawnbroker's description of the pawner eventually pointed police to a former servant who had been casing the Hull residence for over a year. The newspaper article reporting the case concluded, "This arrest entirely absolves Dr. Hull from all suspicion that has been directed against him from every quarter."[51] By tracking the goods, often with the assistance of the very people thought to be receivers, police were able to track those committing crimes.

Trails of physical evidence proved much more elusive if stolen goods ended up somewhere other than the pawnshop, and there were countless petty entrepreneurs eager to carry on lucrative fencing operations. What was more, because pawnbrokers had so much to lose by colluding with criminals, they were more apt to cooperate with police when pressed. Those who refused might themselves wind up ensnared in the judicial system. For example, a New York court in 1901 convicted a pawnbroker of receiving stolen goods based on testimony from the burglar who brought them in. Similarly, in a Minnesota supreme court case from 1909 charging a pawnbroker and his clerk with receiving stolen goods, the thief who had stolen the clothes and sold them to the pawnbroker testified against the defendant.[52]

But especially when dealing with established pawnbrokers, criminals typically did not have the upper hand. Thieves knew that legitimate pawnbrokers likely would cooperate rather than jeopardize the business, that collateral they held could become evidence as easily as cash, and that ledger entries documented transactions. One contemporary observer noted that by fencing goods at a pawnshop, "the thief incurs a risk he will not take until all other expedients fail."[53] An exposé in *Harper's Weekly* featuring detectives who worked the stolen goods beat praised the pawnbroker's ability to recall nearly every pawner and what was pawned.[54] Indeed, reputable pawnbrokers whose businesses had been years and often generations in the making did everything they could to keep from jeopardizing their own and their families' financial well-being, especially for such relatively small gains (fig. 5.1).

Police in serious pursuit of stolen goods knew to concentrate on the major offenders—the scrap and junk dealers. In their hands a stolen table service or piece of jewelry was expeditiously melted down, forever lost to its original owners. Other receivers included jewelers, watchmakers, and many operators trading within secondary markets. In 1846 Francis Armand, proprietor of a porterhouse, was arrested for receiving a gold watch and chain worth $236.[55] That same year, used clothing dealers David Pestkl and Louis Slotorisky were locked up for receiving stolen clothes, and scrap dealer Anne Norton was taken in for receiving, among other things, stolen railroad iron, a coil of rope, and a bag of wedges.[56] In 1847 Philadelphia jeweler John Vantine was arrested and sentenced to three years of solitary confinement and hard labor for being a fence for "the most notorious thieves of the country."[57] Later in the century the *New York Times* estimated that only a fraction of all stolen goods ended up with a pawnbroker. The writer

FIGURE 5.1. "Detectives Recovering Stolen Goods," *Harper's Weekly* 32, 1650 (August 4, 1888): 569. Library Company of Philadelphia.

claimed that "about one-fifth of all the business done by the pawnbrokers is in advancing money upon stolen property." "We are not," he insisted, "prepared to say that this is done knowingly."[58]

Frustrated attempts to nab "known" or "suspected" receivers were common refrains in Inspector Bell's diary. While he located his fair share of stolen goods at the local pawnshops on his beat, the junk shops and scrap metal dealers invited his most intense scrutiny. Bell spent an entire day in November 1850 cycling through myriad junk shops looking for stolen goods. He got nothing but the runaround:

> Special Deputy Sherriff called upon me and stated that some 2 months since Patrick Cooney Keeper of Junk Shop No. 10 Governer Slip had in his possession a lot of Africian [African?] Wool which he offered for sale. *The wool was stolen.* We went and saw Cooney (who was very abusive + impudent) and questioned him concerning the wool[.] He said he did not know who he bought it from or who he had sold it to as he kept no books for that purpose. While I was in there I saw him buy a Bottle from a Boy about 6 years old for one cent, we next went to a Junk Shop in the Cellar of No. 92 Montgomery St. Kept & owned by Wm. Mullins (as

so stated by Michael Hargin who was then in charge of the shop)—I saw 3 small Boys there who were recognised as Theives by Officer Van Hoesen. They had just sold some old rope to Hargin. On going down South St. I met a gang of small dock Theives. One of them had a bag full of short peices of old rope & Iron. He told me he was in the habit of selling his stuff to Mullins.[59]

"On my way down to the office," Bell wrote on August 30, 1851, "I called in at Dickson's Second Hand Dealer No. 8 3rd Avenue. The person in charge of the store said they had no Carpenters' tools [which had been reported stolen]. This store is considered by the officers of the 17th Dist. as a *Fence*."[60] Another entry reads, "Charley Judd told me that the Jewelers Store in Canal near Church It was a fence & also a little rum hole."[61]

Receivers, like other entrepreneurs, had their hierarchies—a food chain of illicit dealing. "There are the millionaires whose traffic in stolen securities is well known, but whose operations are too acutely conducted for the hand of justice to lay hold of them. There are the dealers in cheap jewelry, the melters down of plate, the purchasers of clothing stock, and so on, down even to the blear-eyed wretch who buys from children the pilfered trifles which come within their reach," observed one reporter. Members of the criminal underworld, these characters formed their nefarious alliances "by birth and association."[62] Despite their legal standing as legitimate businessmen, pawnbrokers could not shake their association with this rogues' gallery. An illustration in James McCabe's 1868 *Secrets of the Great City,* a sensational exposé of postwar New York, shows rough customers gathered in an illegal dramshop exchanging goods and information (fig. 5.2). The pawnbroker is easy to spot—he is the hunched, bearded figure in the center of the tableau, transfixed by a watch chain. (The caption, "The Thieve's [sic] Exchange—a Drinking Saloon Where Pawnbrokers Go to Buy Stolen Goods," is illogical. Illicit goods came to pawnbrokers; they did not have to seek them out.)

Stolen goods stood the best chance of recovery if they ended up in hock, because they were whole, they were identifiable, and they could often be tracked back to the pawner-criminal and eventually, with the help of the police, to their owners. Most of the items stolen in October 1860 by Anna Baunan, a one-woman crime wave, were recovered at various New York City pawnshops and found their way back to their rightful places: Miss Haggett's cloth cloak, Mathew Ryan's frock coat, James McQuade's silver watch and two gold chains (valued at $35), Officer (!) Riley's $15 gold chain, and Dr. Carpenter's case of pistols.[63] Descriptions of some $6,000 worth of jewelry stolen by Libby O'Brien in 1877 appeared in the newspaper, along with clues to possible owners and the pawnshops

FIGURE 5.2. Gray and black markets thrived in the nineteenth-century city. "The Thieve's [*sic*] Exchange," from James McCabe, *Secrets of the Great City: A Work Descriptive of the Virtues and the Vices, the Mysteries, Miseries and Crimes of New York City* (Philadelphia: National, [1868]). Library Company of Philadelphia.

where their possessions ended up. Because so many pawnbrokers came forward with collateral from their vaults matching descriptions, police were still holding twelve unclaimed packages when the newspaper article appeared in print. With the help of pawnbrokers Miss Asher was able to reclaim her trinkets and gold watch valued at $150, Mrs. Hamilton recovered her diamond earrings and finger rings worth $200, and ten others were able to do the same.[64]

Stealing did not occur exclusively among strangers. Acquaintances, lovers, and family members of all classes also stole from one another. Parents of delinquent and sometimes desperate children first checked their local pawnshop when household goods went missing. They hoped, in fact, that their heirloom dishware, jewelry, and Bibles had found their way to the pawnshop, where they could be easily recovered. In 1846 an "interesting but wayward and misled young girl" stole her mother's dress and pawned it for 50¢. During the same year the sexton's son pawned the carpets from St. Luke's Church in New York.[65] An 1868 issue of *The Detective's Manual* reported a case involving a "man of considerable wealth and influence" who filed a police report on behalf of his son, whose diamond breastpin had been stolen. The pin not only was valuable but was also "a much prized family relic." Perceptive investigators noticed the son's discomfiture and asked the father about the young man's financial circumstances. The youth, it turned out, had recently been cut off and banished from the house. Investigators followed the son to a pawnshop, where he pawned his pocket watch. They made inquiries, recovered the "prized" diamond pin, and extracted a confession from the son (who was "very fast" and "had bad associates" and "low tastes"), who had actually stolen it himself. Worth at least three times the $900 the pawnbroker loaned on it, the pin generated funds for the son to "roam around, dissipating freely and gambling."[66] Similarly, "fast youth" Henry "Nasty" Heffernan, "an outcast from his father's house," stole a sealskin sacque and muff worth $200 from his parents, which he pawned for $5. He was arrested in a brothel, after having considerately left the pawn ticket behind so his parents could recover their property.[67]

Con artists were particularly adept at schemes involving emotionally vulnerable lovers who were willing to believe more than they should have. For example, in 1849 apothecary and physician Augustus Rencke was arrested for defrauding Mina Wachet. Having "recently seduced" the woman, he promised to marry her but kept putting off the engagement because he could not afford "increasing his expenses just then." Rencke convinced the young Miss Wachet to pawn "her best clothing and jewelry" so he could pay his rent. He asked her to pawn yet more of her belongings to post $1,000 bond on the fraud charge itself (she refused, and he was remanded).[68] Also victimized by a suitor was Fay Dalton, who in 1881 brought a complaint against George Johnson for theft. One night she showed Johnson her pawn tickets for various pieces of jewelry, including a locket, two rings, and a gold watch. Johnson then stole them and redeemed the collateral. Realizing her goods had already been claimed, Dalton reported Johnson to the police. When apprehended, he still had one of the stolen tickets on him.

Scheming women, too, used their position as the presumed weaker sex to their advantage. Their credibility as pawners made it simple to reel in men and take their money. Commentators expressed little sympathy for the gents who were duped, implying that they deserved what they got for being so foolish. The *National Police Gazette* provided details of one case in which an attractive young woman seduced a rich older man. He gave her valuable pieces of jewelry, which she then converted into cash at the pawnshop. The magazine tersely commented, "There's no fool like an old fool."[69] Likewise, in his autobiography William Simpson told of a young woman working the "sucker circuit." She first appeared in Simpson's New York City pawnshop one Monday, "unusually pretty and dressed in the best of taste," and was given a $400 loan on a diamond and emerald bracelet. Simpson noted that "the only remarkable thing about the transaction [was] that the young lady knew to the penny how much she could borrow on her bracelet." At the end of the week the woman returned with an older gentleman on her arm, who presented the pawn ticket and $410—more than enough to cover the loan and interest. "When the clerk handed him the change and the bracelet," Simpson noticed that "he took the jewelry and carefully fastened the clasp about the young lady's wrist. She began to weep a little and then hugged him tightly for the moment." The woman came in the next week too and pawned the same bracelet, again for $400. "On Saturday she reappeared, this time on the arm of a slender, well-preserved man of sixty who looked like a Wall Streeter." He forfeited the pawn ticket and $408. "Touching his arm as though he were too wonderful to be true," Simpson wrote, "she whispered, 'Oh, you are so good to me.'" The woman worked her lucrative scheme for months on different men. Simpson, whose profession had made him wise to nearly every kind of racket, was impressed. "We could hardly believe she could keep this string of suckers coming," he remarked.[70]

Women, especially attractive ones, proved very adept as scam artists. They took advantage of their new roles as consumers to frequent retail spaces and used their sex appeal to distract proprietors. In *A Nation of Counterfeiters* Stephen Mihm describes female "shovers" who were able to pass counterfeit bills by "adopting the outward trappings of respectability" and used their gender to "cultivate trust in settings where appearances mattered."[71] Pawnbrokers were not such easy marks. In *Secrets of the Great City* James McCabe related the tale of a female jewel thief who tried to put one over on a New York City diamond broker by using her feminine wiles. "Remarkably handsome and elegantly attired," she entered the broker's shop under the pretense of finding out about a loan on some jewels. During the conversation the woman glanced casually at a number of the broker's gemstones on display, "merely with a natural feminine curiosity." As she got up to leave, telling the broker she would return the next day with her diamonds, the proprietor noticed that a pearl was missing. Possessing a "quick eye" and, no doubt, enough cynicism from years in the business, he accused the woman of stealing the pearl. Under protest she consented to be searched. Although the pearl did not surface, the broker was undeterred: he let her choose between drinking an emetic and answering to the police. The broker "recovered" his pearl in due course, and the woman left the city.[72]

Pawnbrokers had to stay abreast of not only their own immediate business concerns but also ever-evolving swindles. Their customers were not exactly trustworthy, and increasingly the goods they pawned were not either. Technological developments in manufacturing made it much more difficult to tell real from bogus goods, and pawnbrokers' appraisal skills were constantly being tested by sophisticated fakes. In 1854 a Philadelphia pawnbroker loaned $36 on seventy-two bottles of champagne that were actually filled with "pure Schuylkill"—water from the notoriously polluted local river. The pawner, "losing sight of the established usage of 'honor among rogues,'" took off with the cash without paying the bottler his cut. The pawnbroker would have been out his money if not for the "virtuous indignation" of "rogue number two," who admitted what happened and provided information leading to the pawner's arrest.[73]

Scientific and technological developments, encouraged by growing consumer appetites, abetted the manufacture of all kinds of spurious goods.[74] Improvements in plating and gilding techniques, for example, enabled companies to manufacture cheap jewelry and watches imitating those made of precious metals. Electroplating produced convincing imitation gold and silver skins for candlesticks, pocket watches, and everything in between.[75] Imitation amethysts, emeralds, garnets, opals, and rubies flooded the market as well. *Godey's Lady's Book* proclaimed in 1854, "The art of making artificial pearls has been brought to such perfection in Paris, that even jewellers and pawnbrokers have occasionally had a difficulty in deciding between the artificial and the real."[76] And by the early 1860s pawnbrokers had to judge the qualities of various grades of metal used to make jewelry, including several kinds of gold, from the precious to the nearly worthless.[77]

By the end of the Civil War technological innovations and scientific discoveries made it possible to manufacture these simulated gemstones and fake precious metals on grand scales, making it even more difficult for pawnbrokers and other professionals to separate real from imitation. Boiling gemstones in solutions of sulfuric acid, copper, or nickel could heighten or change their color. Heating made fire opals more vibrant, and chlorine disguised blemishes in diamonds. Coating the backs of poorly colored stones with paint, foil, or colored glass also improved their appearance. The newly discovered mineral zircon, if properly heated, faceted, and placed in a quality mount, passed for a diamond: "It is set in a massive ring of good gold and pawned for several times the value of the metal," a writer for *Harper's* explained. "The ignorant pawnbroker has mistaken the stone for an inferior but large diamond. Of course, as the jargoon [zircon] has little commercial value, though of high scientific interest, the ring is never redeemed."[78] Pawnbrokers remained ignorant about new developments in manufacturing processes at their peril, and they risked being victimized even by people with whom they had long-standing relationships. A Cleveland pawnbroker recalled repeatedly lending $50 to an "in-and-outer" on a diamond ring. The pawner "came so often that the ring was quite a familiar object" to the pawnbroker. One evening at dusk, the same man brought in the same ring, casually placing it on the counter. "I, without examining it, was about to give him the usual $50," the pawnbroker recalled, "when I accidentally noticed that the sparkle of the diamond was rather peculiar." It turned out to be paste—utterly worthless.[79]

Goods—new, used, authentic, fake, legitimate, stolen—circulated freely in the nineteenth century, presenting economic opportunities for people working in all commercial spheres, whether wholesale and retail, secondary and tertiary, or gray and black markets. Fringe entrepreneurs also identified yet another ingenious entrepreneurial opportunity with pawnbroking—trafficking in the pawn tickets themselves. For each piece of collateral a pawner received a pawn ticket, a receipt for the transaction. Pawn tickets were forms printed on small pieces of paper (slightly larger than a contemporary lottery ticket) on which a pawnbroker scribbled a number, a brief description, the loan amount, the due date, and the pawner's name and address. A pawn ticket was the only physical proof that a piece of collateral belonged to the person claiming it; with few exceptions requiring police intervention, one had to present a pawn ticket to redeem collateral. Small and ephemeral, pawn tickets were easily lost. More to the point, they were transferable: they were like pieces of currency that could be traded and sold. Pawners often kept them under lock and key (for losing a ticket meant losing one's collateral). And they were often stolen.

For police, pawn tickets provided important evidence in criminal cases. Suspected thieves left paper trails of their crimes if caught holding pawn tickets for goods later determined to have been stolen. The pawn tickets not only linked criminals to crimes but also connected objects to specific pawnshops where they could eventually be recovered. Circumstances leading to James Williams's arrest in 1844 were typical. Williams, although "rather fashionably attired," was accused of stealing a lady's gold watch and breastpin from a boarder at the Fulton Hotel. The pawn ticket that police found on his person provided "conclusive" evidence "as to the commission of the offence," and he was remanded for trial.[80] In 1849 Charles Smith, "a respectable looking man," was charged with theft for allegedly stealing $400 worth of jewelry from his employer. When New York City police searched his premises, they found not the goods but pawn tickets issued by shops in Philadelphia.[81] Similarly, a man caught trying to pawn a stolen watch in New York City had lifted it a month earlier from a woman in Owego, an upstate town almost two hundred miles away.[82]

Pawners, who often had more than one item in hock at a time, locked their pawn tickets in tea caddies, hid them under mattresses, and sometimes left them at the pawnbroker's for safekeeping (shown in fig. 4.3). They did not carry them on their persons. Therefore simply being caught with a wad of pawn tickets suggested something fishy. For example, in 1850 Ann Graham, "of very dubious demeanor," was arrested on suspicion because she was carrying *forty-seven* pawn tickets. Although she "could give no good account" of herself, she was released ("in the absence of proof") on condition that she leave Brooklyn immediately and never come back.[83] House sitter Silas C. Ryer was charged with grand larceny in 1878 for stealing items from his employer while she was on a two-month vacation in Saratoga. At the time of his arrest Ryer had twenty-eight pawn tickets on him.[84] When approached by police in 1879, Ellen Lonrigan, an "'artist' at her trade," swallowed an entire roll of pawn tickets to destroy the "evidences" of her criminal acts.[85]

Pawn tickets, beyond suggesting theft, invited other kinds of crime. Because pawn tickets were transferable, they held value for the person who possessed them. The only way to redeem a pledge was to present the pawn ticket, and anyone presenting the ticket, whether the original pawner or not, could redeem the collateral by paying the loan amount and accrued interest. Some pawners, realizing they did not have enough money to repay a loan before its term expired, cut their losses by selling a pawn ticket for less than the amount required for redemption. (For example, a pawnbroker might lend $50 at 36% annual interest on a pocket watch with a market value of $200. As the six-month expiration of the loan approached and the pawner realized he could not come up with the requisite $59, he might decide to sell the pawn ticket to a third party for, say, $20. That person could then redeem the watch and resell it, possibly making $121 on the deal.) This was a tricky business, though, because the person purchasing the pawn ticket had to be sure a piece of collateral, sight unseen, offered a reliable return on investment. Yet for people well connected to secondary and tertiary markets, buying pawn tickets was a viable, if marginal, way to make a living.

That pawn tickets were transferable meant they had street value and often circulated like currency. In 1845 the *Brooklyn Eagle* reported the arrest of two men involved in a counterfeiting ring who in addition to bogus currency carried forged pawn tickets.[86] In 1858 the *Broadway Dandy* cautioned readers about responding to ads such as this one: "1,000 PAWN TICKETS WANTED, FOR WHICH FAIR prices will be paid; those on watches and jewelry preferred." The paper editorialized: "Having in the first place parted with their property for one quarter its value, they will receive a mere trifle for the ticket which would enable them to redeem it, and so lose it altogether. The buyer of these tickets makes, without any trouble worth mentioning, about fifty per cent. on his investment."[87] Pawn tickets were sometimes the last shreds of capital for people so poor they could not redeem their pawns. Scam artists found room to operate within even this truly marginal market. As the *Broadway Dandy* noted, "The necessities of one class of people form the stepping stone of others to achieve fortunes."[88] The capitalist ethos suffused even the most obscure transactions.

Some people made money by reselling pawn tickets. Like goods that traveled from wholesale to retail and were incrementally marked up from one market to the next, pawn tickets created their own economic hierarchies, and people capitalized on any economic opportunity that presented itself. For instance, the *Brooklyn Eagle* reported in 1847 that a person "who has been endeavoring to dispose at a price much below the real value, of a number of pawn tickets—the representative of several valuable articles" had been arrested and suspected "of having dishonestly come into the possession thereof." The pawns, including two gold watches, a gold curb chain, two bracelets, and a ring, were tracked to particular shops via the tickets and recovered by police.[89]

Pawnbrokers sometimes worked in cahoots with pawn ticket dealers. People who ultimately bought these tickets might get lucky by purchasing the right to redeem a fine piece of collateral on the cheap. Seeing the collateral minimized the risk, and it was within a person's rights to inspect collateral stored at a pawnshop (because the pawnbroker did not legally own it but was rather the "bailee"). But many pawnbrokers illegally charged prospective ticket purchasers an "inspection fee" for previewing the pawned items, which they split with the ticket sellers. The "dropped ticket" trick was a variation of this scam. Fraudulent pawn tickets written out for $1 to $5 on supposedly fine jewelry would be randomly scattered on the ground as if they had fallen out of someone's pocket. People who picked them up might decide to take a chance on the collateral and consent to pay the pawnbroker's 25¢ inspection fee. If they realized they were being shown cheap, plated goods, they could walk away minus the quarter. Or, seduced by the convincing if worthless goods, they might take a gamble by paying good money to get the collateral out of hock. Or they might be even more entrepreneurial, selling the errant ticket outright, ending up with more money than they started with and impelling someone else toward the pawnshop door to be victimized. Pawn ticket dealers and crooked pawnbrokers stood to gain almost any way the scenario unfolded.[90]

Making out fake pawn tickets with inflated loan values to sell to gullible people was yet another variation. In the mid-1870s pawnbroker Patrick McHugh and his accomplice Lorenzo Burdo were each sentenced to six months in jail for "obtaining money by false pretenses." Burdo had in his possession a pawn ticket from McHugh for a $35 loan on a gold watch supposedly worth $90. The pawner approached John Carrigan and claimed that owing to "destitute circumstances" he would sell the ticket for $2, "a trifle, because he did not have money to redeem it himself. Carrigan bought the ticket and paid pawnbroker McHugh $38.50, the amount outstanding on the loan. He discovered he had paid $38.50 for a watch that was "almost worthless." Burdo and McHugh had gulled at least four others the same way.[91]

Criminals were still working this angle two decades later. The bait might be a newspaper advertisement along the lines of "Diamond necklace, cost $1500 Tiffany's. Circumstances compelled me to pawn it at ———'s for $500. Ticket sacrificed." Respondents who seemed gullible enough were told "a tale of woe," setting the hook. Then they were reeled in:

> The price of the ticket should be two hundred and fifty dollars, for the brilliants are most valuable; but the final price will be partly left to you: only please examine the gems at once, because the holder is in desperate straits. You examine the pledge at the pawnbroker's, paying fifty cents for the privilege. The diamonds are certainly diamonds, although of a shape and quality known to the trade as rose diamonds; and, rather than expend five or ten dollars to compensate an expert for going with you, you conclude that it is safe for you to advance ten per cent. upon the ticket and make it your own. The holder refuses at first, but finally yields, and departs with fifty dollars of your wealth, and leaves you the owner of the property, subject to the pawnbroker's lien thereon.
>
> You then redeem it, which costs you from five hundred and fifty dollars to five hundred and seventy-five more; and on taking your prize to a dealer in diamonds you learn that the entire piece of jewelry is really worth, and would be salable at, the sum of two hundred and fifty dollars!
>
> Did the skilful and well-informed pawnbrokers, then, really lend five hundred dollars on a collection of stones and fourteen-karat gold worth only two hundred and fifty dollars? Not at all. They probably advanced one hundred and fifty dollars, perhaps two hundred dollars, and made out a ticket for five hundred dollars, agreeing with the borrower to divide the profits on the redemption of the ticket by a third party.[92]

It might be easy (and self-satisfying) to wonder how people could have been so gullible. Yet then as now, Americans were living in a complex and changing world. The world of consumer goods was seductive and enticing. People wanted to feel like equal participants in a society that increasingly valued good purchasing decisions and emphasized the ability to show off those wise purchases. What was more, perpetrators of these schemes needed to make money just like everyone else, seizing opportunities where they could.

Although common, pawn ticket scams occurred close to the ground, worked on individuals who rarely filed police reports. Other kinds of crime in the pawnbroking milieu had a much higher visibility and were used to reinforce the age-old stereotypes about the profession. Arson in particular garnered a great deal of press and, like receiving, was considered a crime committed primarily by pawn-brokers and other businessmen dealing in used goods. Setting one's own building on fire was supposedly a common tactic to get insurance money. It was also a crime with pointedly ethnic associations, and by the turn of the century every-one knew such arson as "Jewish lightning." Cartoons in illustrated magazines caricatured the misdeeds of Misters Burnheimer, Burnstein, Smokenstein, Bla-zenheimer, and Burnupsky. There was some foundation to the characterization. Among Jews, property crimes were much more common than crimes against people, "for reasons of skill, opportunity, and temptation."[93] Indeed, in 1880 po-lice arrested New York pawnbroker Morris Levy for setting fire to his pawnshop. The circumstances were suspicious. Levy had just relocated to the new shop and was renting the building's first three floors for the storefront, living quarters for his wife and six children, and storage for collateral. According to accounts, he had closed the shop an hour early the night of the fire. His family left the building shortly before the flames appeared, and neighbors saw the pawnbroker watching the scene from nearby. Although there were no casualties—remarkable consid-ering a large family lived on the fourth floor and the building was attached to a tenement that housed some fifty families—the fire gutted the structure, causing $5,000 in damage to the building alone. Levy's son Henry, who helped evacuate tenants just as the fire started, was arrested as his father's accomplice.[94]

Pawnbrokers were more often victims than perpetrators of crime, however. Owing to the nature of their business, they sometimes faced direct threats of violence, since criminals knew they could find both cash and valuable collateral at pawnshops. Offenders might be among the desperate—personally and finan-cially stressed and perhaps under the influence of alcohol or narcotics. Pawn-shops were often conveniently located on the outskirts of cities or in "vice" dis-tricts also home to brothels, illegal saloons, and gambling dens, making them even more opportunistic targets. In response, pawnbrokers often kept firearms at hand and prepared to meet violence with violence. In 1874 George Pratt at-tempted to shoot an employee in McAleenan's pawnshop before aiming his gun at a police officer trying to arrest him. He had "a number of pawn tickets in his possession," and police had "every reason to believe that Pratt was a thief."[95] A watchman was on the regular payroll of McGarry's pawnshop in Philadelphia by the final quarter of the nineteenth century, earning 50¢ a week to protect the store; in 1876 proprietors spent $1 to buy him a pistol.[96] An early trade organi-zation, the Associated Pawnbrokers of Pennsylvania, established a plate glass window fund to collect money for replacing windows broken by robbers and vandals, incidents that had become fairly common by the end of the nineteenth century. The New York Times reported just such an occurrence in 1880, when a belligerent James Branigan entered Daniel Lamey's pawnshop and was summarily ejected. Branigan reportedly "became very abusive, and, picking up a piece of crockery, hurled it at the show-window of the store, smashing a valuable glass, and damaging several watches and other articles of jewelry."[97]

Also to protect their investments, pawnbrokers equipped shops with hefty storage vaults to house the most valuable collateral—gemstones, jewelry, and silverware. But cash was all around. Simpson's well-regarded shop in the Bowery was robbed in 1846. "While the attention of the clerks was drawn to another part of the store," the report stated, the thief "slipped behind the counter and stole a lot of pennies, amounting to $44, and made good his escape."[98] Safes were only as secure as their locks, and locks only as sound as their owners' stewardship; pawnbrokers who left their vaults unlocked during business hours often paid dearly. While sitting on the front stoop of his shop with his family one day, pawnbroker Solomon Westhome was being robbed by "sneak thieves" who entered from the rear. "The safe was not locked, and the thieves ransacked the receptacle and stole a number of gold and silver watches and a quantity of jewelry," noted the newspaper report.[99] This was a devastating financial blow to Westhome, because the thieves were able to make off with $2,000 worth of collateral for which he would somehow have to reimburse his pawners.[100] Yet Westhome's losses were nothing compared with the Philadelphia business Friedenberg and Brothers, robbed in 1879. Thieves broke into the pawnshop from the roof and took from the safe some $40,000 worth of unredeemed pledges including gemstones and jewelry.[101] McGarry's invested in state-of-the-art electrified vaults that would automatically signal the security company if opened without authorization.

As businessmen whose occupation made them particularly vulnerable to crimes against property and person, pawnbrokers did what they could to protect themselves and use their situation as brokers—middlemen of sorts—to negotiate the worlds of goods and people. A common and essential survival strategy was to build good relationships with the police charged with investigating their shops. Pawnbrokers could not help but take in stolen goods from time to time and could themselves be victims of crimes. They needed police both to exercise leniency and to protect them.

Cooperative arrangements with the authorities helped personal items find their way back to their owners and provided an added economic benefit for both pawnbrokers and police. Regardless of how collateral came into pawners' possession, pawnbrokers were acutely aware that they would lose any money they loaned on goods they had to forfeit. They were understandably reluctant to freely hand over property determined to be stolen and expected something in return to defray expenses. Pawnbrokers typically did not disabuse people of the misapprehension that owners had to pay to get their things back, and police did little to clarify the issue. Upon his arrest, a serial bedding thief who stole from many of Philadelphia's innkeepers in 1824 confessed to pawning many of the linens at a local pawnshop. "Thither the suffering innkeepers repaired," reported the newspaper, "and, ignorant that they had a right to take their own property wherever they found it, paid the sums for which the sheets had been pledged, and marched home with their property."[102] The vagaries of the law frustrated everyone. In 1846 the *National Police Gazette* reported on a Baltimore watchmaker who was pawning watches that customers had left for repair and pocketing the money. The watches, eventually tracked down, were returned only if the owners paid up, "compelled to replevin them to satisfy the demands of the pawnbroker." The *Gazette*, disgusted, editorialized, "He should have been compelled to deliver them up without any such legal proceeding, or been held to answer for receiving them with a fraudulent intent."[103] By midcentury collusion between pawnbrokers and authorities had become commonplace; detectives freely accepted reward money, often unsolicited, and split their take with the pawnbrokers who assisted them.[104] The New York City Police Department crafted a regulation at the end of the century prohibiting officers from accepting rewards except those granted by the department itself (but this may have been honored more in theory than in practice). A person writing to the *Morning Oregonian* in Portland wondered whether pawnbrokers were entitled to receive reward money for returning stolen property. The response described common practice, not the law: "Often pawnbrokers assist detectives to apprehend thieves, and detectives of course desire to have their co-operation. It has been the habit of Portland detectives to try to get pawn-brokers reimbursed for money advanced upon stolen goods, so that in future the brokers will not attempt to conceal stolen articles."[105]

Pawnbrokers exercised their power behind the counter circumspectly, at times standing firm against authorities and at other times assisting them. That pawnbrokers sometimes worked with police did not mean they always did so willingly. They cooperated when they felt it was necessary and in their own interest; police in turn treated helpful pawnbrokers leniently when they discovered stolen goods in the shop. Following up on a complaint lodged by a pawner in 1851, Inspector William Bell stopped in at Jackson's New York City pawnshop and met with the proprietor's brother: "Upon stating my business to him he insulted me and ordered me to leave his place." Bell then redoubled his efforts, taking the complainant's statement and filing charges against the pawnbroker. Pawnbroker Jackson appeared as ordered, contrite. According to Bell, he was "very sorry for what his Brother had done and made an apology & promised to deliver the articles belonging to Miss Doneley. Upon those considerations he was let off."[106]

When Thomas Wilson was arrested in 1871 for stealing a watch, he claimed he had sold it to pawnbroker Elias Tannerhotz. Police suspected collusion between the two men, and when they brought Tannerhotz in for questioning, he claimed he didn't know the watch was stolen (a common defense of the pawnbroker). Police released him, "upon the promise to return [the watch] to the owner." If authorities were unable to arrest Tannerhotz for receiving the stolen watch, at least they could compel him to return it to its owner. Although everyone knew the watch had been stolen, they also knew it would be difficult to prove in court. Because Tannerhotz never did return the watch, breaking his gentleman's agreement with authorities, he was arrested and held for trial.[107]

A brief passage in detective Allan Pinkerton's slightly fictionalized *Claude Melnotte* alluded to the "understanding" between police and pawnbrokers, which often involved bribes and promises of reward money. Assigned to investigate a case involving jewelry stolen from a prominent Chicago family, Pinkerton was urged by the patriarch to scour pawnshops and interrogate other suspected fences. Certain that the jewelry remained in the hands of the thief's mistress, Pinkerton decided not to waste his time inquiring at pawnshops and secondhand stores. "I knew perfectly well," he remarked, "that even an offer to compromise for money would be ineffectual, since none of the professional thieves or 'fences' had possession of the stolen articles."[108]

An 1888 article from *Harper's Weekly* described the tenuous cooperation between pawnbroker and police officer and the subtle shifts in balance of power:

> [The pawnbroker] may, if he pleases, tell the detectives that he has entirely forgotten the circumstances attending the pledging of this lot, but the detectives will not believe him. If he insists on pleading a poor memory, he will be rightly held in suspicion, and to be under police surveillance would be detrimental to his business. The detectives have a right to be inquisitorial. There has been a burglary, and a lot of silver has been made away with. . . . The man of the pawn-shop when under the screws sometimes finds that his memory is suddenly refreshed, and he gives a minute description of the person who pledges the silver-ware.[109]

The accompanying illustration (fig. 5.1, above) shows detectives examining the pawnbroker's ledger and inspecting a lot of pawned silver. The pawnbroker has to decide the degree of his selective amnesia, especially when "under the screws."

Even after local ordinances codified procedures for recovering stolen goods from pawnshops, police took it upon themselves to act as intermediaries when negotiating settlements. They often pocketed part of the reward money and in this way were like so many others (including those they apprehended) who took their cut by legitimate and illegitimate means. American society during this time was not as "well regulated" as some have claimed. Indeed, the "plethora of laws, ordinances, and regulations," if they existed at all, were not in fact "effective and enforced," as we have seen, but rather left much wiggle room for people to take advantage, especially those who were particular wily and enterprising.[110] Historian William Novak argues that "the notion of a well-regulated society secured by a state police power was an essential part of the American governmental tradition."[111] Yet clearly police power, even after the Civil War, was not effective at enforcing laws, and society was anything but well ordered. (Although one could argue that underworld society was actually well ordered in that there were clear codes of conduct, collectively enforced, and transgressors were justly punished.) Hardworking police inspectors like William Bell did their best to surveil pawnbrokers, junk shops, and suspect petty enterprises, but they operated at a disadvantage because civilians (especially of the criminal sort) so outnumbered officers. Authorities often had no choice but to work with suspected offenders and could find it advantageous to arrive at agreeable compromises to keep the peace and make some extra money.

Because of the nature of their business, pawnbrokers were at the heart of urban activities, crucial intermediaries between goods and people, the authorities and the underworld, legitimate and underground exchange. Sometimes they were active participants in the criminal economy, other times they were its victims. Through pawnbrokers' doors came all manner of objects and people who traveled in respectable and criminal circles alike.

Crimes of opportunity occurred all the time. Pawnbrokers were very often on the receiving end, fooled by imitation goods, taken in by scams, the victims of theft, eyed by the police, and threatened with violence. They also occasionally gave in to the lure of easy money, acting as reliable fences for a faithful criminal customer base, abetting pawn ticket scams, and on occasion even burning down their own shops. Most pawnbrokers, however, were like so many other proprietors who worked long hours and devoted many years to building up respectable businesses and had no interest in becoming ensnared in others' problems. This proved impossible to avoid, because pawnbrokers, unlike almost all other professionals, operated across class, ethnic, and economic divides.

"Respectable" pawnbrokers were acutely aware of their reputation as receivers and attempted to rehabilitate the profession by associating it with seemingly "legitimate" enterprises. In an effort to rid the city of smaller and shadier pawning operations, the New York Common Council in 1881 pushed to raise pawnbrokers' license fees 2,000% (from $50 to $1,000) and their bond tenfold (from $1,000 to $10,000). Tellingly, established pawnbrokers supported the proposal, which would eliminate unwanted competition and create a more favorable image of the profession as a whole. They pointed fingers, accusing small-scale pawnbrokers of "swindling the public by overcharging" and taking in pieces of collateral "knowing them to be stolen." Of course the smaller pawnbrokers retaliated, criticizing the more prosperous for trying "to build up a big monopoly . . . and enable a few large firms to crush out their smaller competitors."[112] Pawnbrokers, traditionally among the most maligned of professionals, were trying to go legit even if it meant turning against each other. But counteracting nearly one hundred years' bad press proved impossible. A new and improved reputation as honest businessmen was one thing pawnbrokers could not acquire, no matter how hard they tried, through legitimate or illegitimate means.

CHAPTER SIX

LOAN SOCIETIES AND THE LEGITIMATION OF PAWNBROKING

In the very first decades of the nineteenth century some Americans were already seeing a need for organized operations that would provide small collateral loans to the working poor on reasonable terms. But it would not be until nearly a century later that anything resembling a pawnshop would attain the status of a legitimate institution. While perhaps novel to Americans, nonprofit pawnshops had been successful in Europe for centuries. Yet so hostile were reformers to the very idea of pawnshops that they resisted establishing their own loan societies until the mid-nineteenth century. Refusing to come to terms with the true neediness of many families, philanthropists and local governments continued to oppose efforts to establish nonprofit pawnshops. When a group of reformers and businessmen at last established a successful philanthropic pawnshop in the final decade of the century, their efforts were motivated as much by a drive to make money as by a wish to create a much-needed benevolent institution. Pawnshops—and only those of a certain form—gained legitimacy when investors decided they could generate healthy and reliable profits.

In 1810 Philadelphia physician James Mease began urging the Common Council to establish a municipal pawnshop—a nonprofit pawnshop run by the government. Well known in Philadelphia for his efforts on behalf of the urban poor, Mease dedicated his life to remedying the physical and economic woes of his city's inhabitants. He proposed that pawnshops modeled after time-honored European examples be located in every urban area "by public authority, for the relief, at legal interest, of those whose necessities oblige them to apply for small pecuniary loans."[1] Referring specifically to the municipal pawnshops and savings banks in France, Mease wrote, "I do not pretend to the entire originality of this plan." But he remained confident it could be adapted to suit the country's needs.

Because the doctor believed that economic health created social stability, he also proposed the innovative "Chest of Savings," city-run savings banks offering the poor and middling a place to stash their earnings and providing the impetus to do so. As much mechanisms of social control as philanthropic gestures, the two proposed institutions together would, ideally, curb crime and vice. By encouraging people to deposit extra money, the Chest of Savings would minimize wasteful (and sinful) expenditures on "tippling, gambling, and other modes of dissipation and idleness."[2] Similarly, in addition to alleviating much of the grinding poverty and alienation already endemic in the early nineteenth-century city, municipal pawnshops would prevent "numerous petty thefts by those who are in absolute want of food or clothing." Thwarting criminal activity would in turn improve a city's general moral character by creating a law-abiding citizenry with fewer ex-convicts. Another important benefit of municipal pawnshops was that offering loans at below market interest would drive out private pawnbrokers—those notorious receivers of stolen goods. Finally, Mease argued that the proceeds from interest on the loans and from the sale of unredeemed pledges could be used to run the business itself, with surplus funds put toward poor relief. Eliminating a large part of the underclass would relieve cities of great financial burdens and alleviate many social problems.[3] Although the proposals went unheeded for decades, the social and moral agendas underpinning them resonated throughout the century.

Mease's efforts were frustrated for decades as authorities resisted appearing to sanction pawnbroking, even though many European countries had been supporting public, nonprofit pawnshops since the mid-1500s. It was a tradition Mease cited often.[4] In his proposal for a public loan office, the physician named the Mont-de-Piété and the Lombard Bank as his models. Monts-de-piété had been operating relatively independently in various French states since the early seventeenth century.[5] In the early nineteenth century they were reorganized and placed under government control. In the years immediately following the French Revolution, the monts-de-piété helped reduce interest rates from 30% to 18% per annum. Proceeds from interest paid on loans and the sale of unredeemed pledges, in addition to funds from investors and supplements from the government, created fairly self-supporting institutions. Relatively simple operations, they required little public capital for start-up, and they not only generated enough money to cover expenses but amassed a surplus that went toward poor relief. The success of municipal pawnshops had also been demonstrated in many other European countries including Italy, Germany, and the Netherlands. It was exactly the kind of institution that Mease proposed to the Philadelphia Common Council. Mease concluded that council members did not know what they were talking about when they called municipal savings banks "unnecessary" and twice (in 1810 and again in 1836) rejected his plan for a city-run pawnshop. He wrote bitterly, "Had they sought for knowledge on those subjects, their report might have been different."[6]

Unlike most of his contemporaries, Mease knew that pawnshops or comparable loan institutions were essential to the survival of those living in cities during the early nineteenth century. Gold and silver specie was scarce, and in an economy run largely on credit, new immigrants had little access to economic and social networks that would help them make ends meet. They could not turn to banks. The savings banks organized beginning in the 1810s were designed as repositories for extra earnings, to be drawn on only in exceptional circumstances such as sickness and death. Often acting as philanthropists, early bank organizers hoped the institutions would educate common laborers about saving money. One way to alleviate poverty, they believed, was to encourage the middling and working poor to be more frugal with their earnings. People were poor because they spent too much and saved too little, not because their incomes did not meet their expenses.

For example, the Philadelphia Saving Fund Society (PSFS) opened its doors in 1817 "to promote economy and the practice of saving amongst the poor and labouring classes of the community; to assist them in the accumulation of property, that they may possess the means of support during sickness or old age, and to render them in a great degree independent of the bounty of others."[7] Early banks like the PSFS were savings, not lending, institutions designed to rein in the profligacy of the middling sorts who had neither the wits nor the self-control to save for themselves. Officers of the Bank for Savings in the City of New-York blamed workers' "vanity" and "desire of accumulation" for too much spending and so little prosperity. And some people were considered just too stupid to manage their money properly: "Seamen are, proverbially, improvident," the report declared, "not so much perhaps from a love of waste, as from a total ignorance how to dispose of their money."[8] The Provident Institution for Savings report stated even more bluntly that if money was not placed in savings accounts, it "would otherwise be spent in fine clothes, or useless amusements," such as "in grog shops, those common pests to our country."[9] Describing the Sixpenny Savings Bank established in New York City, *Hunt's Merchants' Magazine* remarked, "One great cause of continued poverty is the want of such a habit [of economy], for in this country no person need be indigent long, unless they are thriftless spendthrifts." Look no further than the wealthiest of the wealthy, the article encouraged, to see the ennobling effects of poverty: "Our richest men have generally started in life poor boys. . . . It is for its beneficial influences on the character that the savings bank is so valuable to poor lads. By depositing their little earnings in such an institution, they obtain a practice of economy which not only enriches them at the time, but contributes to the formation of their future character."[10]

Ultimately, savings banks failed to substitute for pawnshops not only because were they relatively inaccessible, but also because they did not grant immediate short-term cash loans, which were what the country's urban poor truly needed. The PSFS, for example, opened its doors for only two hours on only two days a week. Monday mornings it accepted deposits, and Thursday mornings it allowed withdrawals. And the Provident Institution for Savings in Boston noted curtly, "*No business can be done at the office but on* WEDNESDAY *from nine o'clock to one.*"[11] In addition, institutions placed heavy restrictions on withdrawals, as did the PSFS, which required two weeks' notice and set the minimum at $5.[12] Similarly, the Provident Institution for Savings in Boston, while encouraging deposits, retained the right to award withdrawals in bank stock rather than cash, of little use to someone trying to pay the weekly rent or buy a loaf of bread. In addition, initially withdrawals could be made only semiannually, a policy relaxed to allow quarterly withdrawals, but even then only with one week's notice.

Undoubtedly, savings banks *did* encourage and enable saving by people who otherwise would not have saved. Many middling people with modest but steady incomes amassed substantial nest eggs over a lifetime of disciplined work and saving.[13] Notorious spendthrifts, seamen would have benefited from socking their money away in savings banks rather than spending it all on alcohol and prostitutes when in port (consumption habits that firmly entrenched them in poverty and often bound them to shipmasters for years). But for many reasons people remained suspicious of banks. The American Seamen's Friend Society remarked in 1830 that its savings bank had done as well "as could have been reasonably expected" and that "the prejudice and distrust with which seamen at first seemed to regard this most benevolent and disinterested institution, appear to be wearing away."[14]

Yet whatever their benefits, savings banks could still not help people in immediate financial need, especially the urban poor. Of the ten savings banks operating in the country by 1820, only four were outside New England. Philadelphia itself supported six pawnbrokers by 1817. By midcentury the number of pawnbrokers continued to dwarf the number of savings and loan institutions in the same regions.

The dearth of alternative sources of personal credit made pawnshops inevitable. Most civic leaders so reviled them, however, that they continually resisted efforts to establish philanthropic nonprofit models that they themselves could oversee, even if these new institutions might drive independent pawnbrokers out of business while generating public revenue. By 1836, when James Mease published his proposals in a pamphlet titled *On the Utility of Public Loan Offices and Savings Funds*, pawnshops had become familiar fixtures in the urban landscape. Because pawnbrokers continued to be dogged by accusations that their loans abetted crime, encouraged vice, contributed to poverty, and led to idleness, government officials could not align themselves with pawnbroking in any way, even if a nonprofit institution might contribute to the public good. Members of various benevolent organizations (pawnbroking's most outspoken critics) wanted to outlaw pawnshops altogether, certain that if they did, crime, poverty, and slothfulness would disappear along with them. Pawnshops, they claimed, "have afforded great facilities for the concealment of stolen property" and were places "in which other gross abuses have been practiced."[15] The New-York City Temperance Society blamed alcoholism on the easy cash made available by pawning. "How much of this owes its necessity to intemperance?" their 1829 report asked about the numbers of goods pawned at local pawnshops.[16] And the notion that people could obtain money without working contradicted the Jeffersonian ideal that hard work built a strong and noble country. Addressing members of Boston's Mechanic Apprentice's Library Association in 1840, the Reverend William Ellery Channing exalted labor as having "a far higher function, which is to give force to the will, efficiency, courage, the capacity of endurance and of persevering devotion to far-reaching plans. Alas, for the man who has not learned to work! He is a poor creature. . . . He depends on others, with no capacity of making returns for the support they give."[17]

An early private nonprofit pawnshop (organized and run by a group of investors rather than the government) was the New York Lombard Association. It was granted a state charter in 1824 through the efforts of Benjamin Judah, "an old and respectable merchant" who, like Mease, was inspired by seeing Europe's nonprofit pawnshops. Ideally, the institution was to establish branches throughout the city, "so that the whole system of pawnbrokerage would have been done away with and a responsible public institution furnished in its place." The New York Lombard Association enjoyed great initial support from investors who realized how profitable it could be. Three times as many people wanted to purchase subscriptions as it had to offer. Yet ironically the association failed, a victim of the board members' overreaching. Instead of reinvesting capital in the organization and concentrating on the needs of the poor, officers "considered that they might as well be borrowers as lenders" and put the money toward ill-fated lottery schemes and "large pledges to mercantile men."[18] A newspaper article referred to the New York model in proposing a similar institution in Philadelphia, but it never got off the ground. In 1838 Philadelphians petitioned the Pennsylvania state legislature to establish a Lombard Association for the city. These seventeen men knew that small loans on movable property could make a world of difference. Of the "necessitous poor" they wrote, "The relief which is thus afforded them is frequently of the most valuable kind, enabling them in Seasons of difficulty to provide funds for their immediate Support and in many instances preserving themselves and families from utter ruin."[19] Yet sympathetic reformers could not convince enough people with the power and money to establish such a venture that they should have anything to do with pawnshops.

During a particularly intense era of philanthropy before the Civil War, Americans once again considered the merits of municipal pawnshops and public savings banks to meet the needs of the poor in various cities. In the late 1840s Brooklyn's city fathers proposed a government-run nonprofit pawnshop to be overseen by "retired merchants or practical business men in whom the public can have perfect confidence"—unlike private pawnbrokers, they implied.[20] Advocates pointed to tried and tested European models. Dr. John Corson commented that the system of municipal pawnshops in France "impressed me very strongly" and that "the confidence of the public in these institutions is unbounded."[21] Unredeemed pledges were resold and circulated in new markets and, to Corson's surprise, showed up even in "respectable" resale shops. Boosters also claimed that European customers felt more comfortable in municipal pawnshops: "Multitudes who would, from strong prejudice, never enter a private pawnbroker's shop, hesitate not to take advantage of their facilities. No one ever suspects them of unfairness."[22] Yet elite Americans remained generally unwilling to fund such operations themselves or to lobby for government institutions. Like the earlier efforts of James Mease in Philadelphia, John Corson's proposal to establish the Benevolent Loan Institution for the City of Brooklyn, endorsed by the local newspaper in 1848, did not gain traction.[23]

By the time lawyer, iron merchant, and philanthropist Stephen Colwell incorporated Philadelphia's Chattel Loan Company in 1855, reformers had largely given up thinking they could eliminate pawnshops altogether. Instead they acknowledged that pawning, as "banking for the poor," fulfilled an important role in the urban economy. Colwell's circular to potential investors described the Chattel Loan's purpose in sentimental terms—"to save the *Family Relics:* the Father's Watch, the Mother's Breast Pin, the Mechanic's Chest of Tools, the Bed and the Table. These articles, once pawned at heavy rates of interest, are almost exclusively soon lost to the owner."[24] A significant shift in thinking from just twenty years earlier, borrowing and lending came to be seen as part of normal and acceptable economic activity for rich and poor alike.

Indeed, more than providing affordable short-term loans, nonprofit pawnshops might teach the poor how to handle their money, reinforcing the didactic work of savings banks. In 1849 *Hunt's Merchants' Magazine*, the standard record of contemporary commercial activity, acknowledged the importance of pawnshops and did not begrudge "some very respectable members of the Jewish persuasion" their "prosperity." But the magazine criticized the practices of most independent pawnbrokers, who allegedly took advantage of the most vulnerable, "the neediest of the needy, the wretchedest of the wretched."[25] The magazine advocated the establishment of nonprofit pawnshops to "increase the power of the poor to help themselves."[26]

Investing in pawnshops became an increasingly appealing proposition among the elite, who embraced the idea that institutions run under their guidance might have a salutary influence on the behavior and morals of pawners. What was more, founders and investors stood to make a lot of money. The circular for Philadelphia's Chattel Loan Company (CLC) in 1855 touted the organization's lofty goals: "This Company hopes, by a very low rate of interest . . . to encourage borrowers to attempt the redemption of the articles pledged, to encourage them in all meritorious efforts, by receiving small payments on account, and by advice and pecuniary assistance, to save much valuable property from inevitable loss, and its owners from destitution."[27] In true philanthropic tradition, the group was interested only in the "worthy" poor and proposed lending solely "to meritorious and necessitous applicants."[28] Sweetening the pot, CLC founders promised potential investors a 6% annual return, a profit beyond the hopes of all but the most prosperous independent pawnbrokers.

By midcentury supporters of institutional pawnshops no longer claimed that *all* pawnshops were corrosive—only independent ones. Boosters also stopped blaming people's need for quick cash solely on profligacy, as earlier philanthropists had done. Indeed, champions of domestic manufactures urged people to buy novel—and unnecessary—goods as a way to contribute to the growth and health of the maturing American economy. Men like Daniel Webster believed that capitalism and democracy could be united as one force and "saw no contradiction between commercial and industrial development and moral elevation."[29] *DeBow's Review* published an article in 1855 arguing for the establishment of more savings banks affiliated with municipal pawnshops. The writer insisted that excess consumption was a good thing, arguing that if all men practiced the precepts of "Poor Richard" society would not advance, since the consumption of all the vast variety of unnecessary commodities would cease. . . . In a similar manner, those who practice and experience self-denial in order to save money, although they confer a benefit on society by accumulating capital that is loaned to productive industry . . . do not directly cause a demand for mechanical labor, as in the case of those who lay out their money in furniture and other articles of family comfort.[30]

In other words, consumption sustained production; contrary to Benjamin Franklin's maxims, frugality was not going to help improve the country's economic fortunes. The *DeBow's* article also acknowledged that in addition to ephemeral financial instruments, material possessions had value: "The law seeks to secure the money saved, but takes no notice of capital saved in the shape of goods."[31] Regular pawners already appreciated, and took advantage of, the latent value of goods as movable collateral. Economic experts and social reformers had at last realized this as well—a significant shift in thinking.

The Chattel Loan Company, however, did not last long. While the operation may have been favorable to investors, its terms remained unattractive to potential customers. They didn't know what the interest rate was, and neither, apparently, did the organizers, who could only say that it was "a very low rate of interest—certainly not *one fourth* of that charged by the Pawn Broker, and frequently not *one-tenth*," according to incorporation documents.[32] Pawners were deterred by other factors as well. A significant drawback was that the CLC prohibited loan extensions beyond eighteen months and reserved the right to auction off collateral if a loan went beyond six months, even if a pawner had made payments toward the balance. The act of incorporation showed just how rigidly the CLC intended to operate: "Payments on account shall be received and credited to the borrowers, which payments, if not in full, shall not postpone or defeat the forfeiture or right to sell."[33] The inability to renew loans indefinitely and pay over longer periods proved untenable to would-be pawners, who were subject to the market's boom and bust fluctuations and greatly relied on the flexibility of pawnshop loans.

The Pawners' Bank of Boston (incorporated under the name Collateral Loan Company in 1859 and opened for business in 1860) was the first successful "semiphilanthropic" pawnshop.[34] Like their predecessors, organizers of the Pawners' Bank validated their efforts by citing the success of municipal pawnshops in Europe and dissociating their work from independent pawnshops. The organizing committee was "convinced that such loans are needed to a large extent," but that existing pawnshops "are entirely unworthy of our city, and of her well-earned character." Philanthropists now frequently condoned pawning if it occurred through controlled and legitimate institutions: places organized and overseen by the philanthropists themselves. Organizers equated services offered by the Pawners' Bank with what their own lending institutions provided, and "stand[ing] in the same relation to the day laborer that the banking-house does to the merchant."[35] Pawners' Bank founders insisted they were not setting up a pawnshop but were creating a benevolent institution that, under their wise and proper guidance, would provide an essential service for the city's underclass.

They were actually doing a bit of both, joining in a profit-making venture that would help people who needed money. Although purportedly modeled on European examples, the Pawners' Bank was significantly different, controlled not by the government but by a group of private individuals. In addition, it (and the other semiphilanthropic pawnshops that would follow at the end of the century) was not subject to the municipal regulations that controlled independent pawnbrokers. The Pawners' Bank did charge lower rates than its independent competitors, yet it cannot strictly be considered "nonprofit" because the operation was quite lucrative for investors. Pawners' Bank founders included the well-known Boston minister Charles F. Barnard and prosperous merchant Jacob Sleeper (who later in life helped charter Boston University)—a mixture of the philanthropically minded and business-minded who saw 8% annual returns on their investments. The institution offered reasonable interest rates for pawners—1.5% per month (18% annually)—and established uniform appraisal standards: four-fifths the value of gold and silver and two-thirds the market value on everything else. Its listing in the 1863 *Boston Directory* succinctly described services to potential customers and advantages for investors: "Loans made on all kinds of goods every day. Dividends in January and July."[36] In 1871 the directors were "happy to record another year of steady and remunerative business, with out any unusual loss or disappointment" for investors. The annual reports resembled those of other organizations at the time, filled with income and expenditure tables. Accounts of actual pawning transactions seemed almost an afterthought, appearing beneath the subheading "Interesting Statistics connected with the Company."[37]

Those organizing and investing in semiphilanthropic pawnshops such as the Pawners' Bank distanced themselves from independent pawnbrokers, whom they referred to as "unscrupulous parties, who have no sympathy for distress."[38] The "charitable" pawnshops legitimated their brand of pawnbroking by connecting it to mainstream business enterprise and philanthropic efforts. Supervised by the right kind of people—"upstanding" members of the community—pawnbroking provided a necessary service and was a public benefit. "We have had the pleasure," remarked one officer, "of helping parties to means to take their property from other hands, where it was pledged at ruinous rates of interest."[39] And as investors in semiphilanthropic pawnshops saw their returns go up, they became more convinced that independent pawnbrokers—the competition—should be eliminated. Miss Cornelia Bradford opened her Jersey City benevolent pawnshop, she said, "to antagonize the professional pawnbrokers," into lowering their interest rates to 4% to match hers.[40] A contemporary writer noted that "the pawnbroker cannot afford to do business on the basis of six per cent. per annum [the going rate of banks] for the use of money."[41]

Proponents of the Pawners' Bank drew on what had become familiar stereotypes to distance the organization from private pawnbrokers and imbue their own actions with an enlightened sense of purpose. "There is no degradation in dealing with it, nor anything more humiliating in proposing a loan to it, than there is in offering a note for discount to any regular bank," wrote one Pawners' Bank booster. "Its business is utterly removed from the degrading associations connected with pawnbroking and with the wholly vile character of the persons engaged in it."[42] Sanitized, co-opted, and controlled by the business elite, pawnbroking was just like any other legitimate business. "While the Pawners' Bank was started originally as a charity," recalled founder Charles Barnard, "it is really a business concern, conducted on business principles and," he hastened to add, "is reported to pay regular dividends to its stockholders."[43]

The 1893 crash spurred reformers in other cities to establish semiphilanthropic pawning institutions similar to the Pawners' Bank (which trundled along over the decades thanks to regular capital infusions from investors). Some aimed to generate revenue for poor relief; others unapologetically sought returns for investors. All, however, were united in their desire to put independent pawnbrokers out of business. The most successful benevolent pawnshop was the Provident Loan Society (PLS) of New York City, founded in the year of the crash. Described at the time as "one of the most perfectly organized societies," the PLS adapted the factory system of the second Industrial Revolution as a business model, organizing operations by vertical integration, taking advantage of economies of scale, benefiting from regular infusions of investor capital, and exploiting an unskilled workforce.[44]

The genesis of the PLS occurred during an era of renewed philanthropic enterprise, characterized as "scientific philanthropy," when principles of streamlining and efficiency were brought to poor relief in the decades following the Civil War. The efforts were in large part meant to tamp down social unrest in the turbulent Reconstruction era, meant as "an instrument of urban social control for the conservative middle class."[45] Those with economic and social power were hard-pressed (and often disinclined) to solve the problems of urban poverty by addressing its root causes, because they themselves were the beneficiaries and often the owners of manufacturing companies using low-paid wage labor that they drew from a pool of idle workers. Indeed, according to Alexander Keyssar, "Unemployment was one expression of the power of ownership and the dependence of employees in a market economy."[46] By generating a chronically needy pool of laborers and then overseeing them where they earned, spent, and borrowed, businessmen-philanthropists could control—and profit from—every aspect of workers' economic lives. This arrangement was very much part of a larger tradition of American paternalism witnessed, for example, at the Pennsylvania mill town of Rockdale. Anthony F. C. Wallace has written of manufacturers' "moral dilemma" of feeling responsible for their workers' improvement yet at the same time creating "noxious working conditions." "The solution," Wallace notes, was not for these men to implement better working conditions but to "urge reform . . . of the community."[47]

The success celebrated in the PLS's first annual report proved emphatically *"that aid can be given on a strictly business basis,"* although the organization tellingly did not mention to whom the aid was given.[48] Rationalization, streamlining, and vertical integration were managerial techniques quite familiar to the brokers, industrialists, and railroad magnates who were the PLS's founders and investors. It was perfectly logical that they would apply their time-tested practices of "trustification and amalgamation in business" to charitable endeavors.[49] Describing its operating philosophy, the PLS deployed the phrases "business basis" and "business management" five times in its first annual report.

Inevitably, philanthropists modeled reform efforts on their personal ideas of who qualified as respectable (and deserving), guided by their own moral, ethical, religious, and cultural principles. In post–Civil War America those "deserving" of philanthropy were people who worked. Workers were better than idlers, and reformers were convinced that direct monetary aid only made people disinclined to work. They were more concerned about "building character rather than relieving need."[50] The wealthiest of the wealthy, Gilded Age philanthropists put their money behind projects that they believed would have a civilizing influence, molding the underclass into model citizens in the elite's collective self-image. To that end, "philanthropy was less the handmaid of social reform than a substitute for it," according to historian Robert Bremner.[51]

Organizers of semiphilanthropic enterprises such as the PLS took credit for their role in social reform. By taking on and then settling a debt, a pawner learned discipline by borrowing and repaying, eventually becoming a true and enlightened participant in the modern economy. Ideally, pawners entering the doors of the PLS took away this valuable lesson. "They have almost all belonged to a self-respecting class anxious to preserve their self-respect by borrowing on a business basis rather than by applying for charity, and undoubtedly the self-respect of many has been preserved by the aid thus extended to them," noted the first annual report.[52] Cynically, as David Wagner writes, this kind of Progressive Era philanthropy could be seen as a money-laundering scheme for the rich, "the conversion of vast amounts of wealth accumulated during America's 'Gilded Age' by conservative, anti-labor, laissez-faire businessmen into 'clean money.'"[53] Conveniently, scientific philanthropy also kept benefactors (investors) at a safe distance from beneficiaries (pawners) so that the wealthy could say they were involved with charitable efforts without having to cope with the gritty realities and shabby possessions of people in need.[54]

Some of the era's most prominent men and women worked together as officers, members, and investors to make the PLS run smoothly. The wealthiest bankers and investment brokers contributed money and, no doubt, offered advice about making the PLS into an operation that consistently generated returns. The list of contributors read like a Who's Who of contemporary merchant princes. One founder was wealthy banker James Speyer, one of the leading financiers of the late nineteenth and early twentieth centuries, involved in the railroad bond market and international trade. Through his estate, Cornelius Vanderbilt, one of the initial founders and largest contributors, continued to provide financial support after his death. Magnate J. Pierpont Morgan also put tens of thousands of dollars behind the PLS. Other major contributors included Solomon Loeb, one of the original partners in the prominent banking house Kuhn, Loeb and Company, and his son-in-law Jacob Schiff, who took over the firm when Loeb retired. Harris C. Fahnestock, described as an "adept financier," was a partner in the powerful firm of Jay Cooke and Company. George F. Baker was a founder of the First National Bank in New York City. William E. Dodge cofounded Phelps, Dodge and Company, one of the largest mining companies in the country at the time. Railroad financier John Stewart Kennedy, one of the richest men in the United States when he died, was also director of the Bank of the Manhattan Company in addition to being involved with the National Bank of Commerce, the New York Life Insurance Company, the United States Trust Company of New York, and other high-profile financial institutions.[55] While not a money man by trade, John Sloane, of the firm W. and J. Sloane, also numbered among the PLS's supporters. Circulating among New York City's elite and making his fortune as a prominent dealer in furniture and oriental rugs, Sloane catered to and shaped the tastes of the upper crust at the turn of the century. He used his money to build Wyndhurst, the largest of the "Berkshire Cottages" (whose landscaping was designed by Frederick Law Olmstead) and later in life became a trustee of the Mutual Life Insurance Company. One of Sloane's clients likely was Mary Clark Thompson, who lived on Madison Avenue and contributed $7,500 to the PLS in one year. The daughter of a governor of New York and wife of Frederick Ferris Thompson, a founder of the First National Bank (to become Citibank), she too was well connected.

Other PLS supporters, also the wealthiest of the wealthy, were more personally involved in philanthropic efforts. Robert W. de Forest, one of the most generous PLS benefactors (he contributed $30,000 in 1901 alone), also coauthored the 1903 book *The Tenement House Problem* and served as president of the Charity Organization Society of the City of New York. Likewise, banker D. O. Mills took a hands-on approach to poor relief in New York and was best known for building the Mills Houses, hotel-like quarters able to accommodate over 2,100 of the worthy poor. For 50¢ a night (a more expensive yet nicer alternative to Bowery flophouses), a man got nourishing meals, a clean if small room, and access to laundry facilities, a library, and recreation. Determined to see his lodgers out "hustling" for jobs, Mills locked them out of their rooms from 9:00 a.m. until 5:00 p.m. every day. Like the PLS, the Mills Houses provided a form of poor relief with strings attached. It was also, like the PLS, profitable philanthropy, and Mills was said to be generating up to 5% returns on his $1.5 million investment in building the Mills Houses.

Savvy entrepreneurs, organizers determined to expand the PLS soon after setting up the first outlet. Neighborhood branches extended the reach of the PLS into more areas of the city. "Distance has proved a serious obstacle to the use of the Society by the poorer classes, who most need its aid," noted the PLS's first annual report. Therefore "the next step in the Society's progress would seem to be the establishment of a branch office in the crowded east side tenement district of the city."[56] This was a wise business strategy: having several PLS branches would allow for economies of scale, enable streamlined operations, and open up new customer bases. "The future policy of the Society," noted the second annual report, "should be one of gradual extension. It is increasingly evident that its benevolent purposes can only be fully accomplished as branches are established in the immediate neighborhood of the poor."[57] Being able to cater equally to the workman, the small merchant, and the "Park Avenue matron" by establishing branches in all kinds of neighborhoods, the PLS benefited from reaching out to the largest population possible: "The Times Square, Fourth Avenue, East 60th Street, and City Hall offices make comparatively large loans and their customers are generally well dressed and prosperous looking. The Grand Street, Eldridge Street, and Brownsville offices make smaller loans on poorer grades of security."[58]

By 1898 PLS officers were boasting of their new branch office in the University Settlement Society's building on the Lower East Side, outfitted with fire-proof safes and a basement for storage. "The people of . . . perhaps the most densely populated square mile of any city in the world—have already begun to avail themselves of the opportunities we offer those in temporary distress," the president remarked.[59] The next year, the PLS noted that Branch A was meeting expectations. Loans were much smaller here, but PLS officers could finally say they were reaching the institution's target population.

Twelve PLS branches dotted New York City by 1919. Proceeds from the ever-growing surplus fund enabled the PLS to buy two more buildings outright and build nine others from the ground up. Being so well capitalized, the organization was able to establish branches in strategic locations and design the buildings to its own specifications with vaults, storage rooms, office space, and customized facades. The organization thrived. With the exception of 1908 and 1909 (years following the Panic of 1907, when the PLS temporarily capped loans at $50), the total amounts loaned annually increased sharply, from a relatively modest $229,000 in 1894 to almost $23 million in 1918.[60] More loans paid out meant more interest collected and more money generated from the sale of unredeemed collateral. By 1919 the PLS had a surplus of $4.2 million.[61]

Supporters consistently saw good returns on their investments. What was more, philanthropy made them look good. At the end of the nineteenth century, the *Brooklyn Daily Eagle* sardonically remarked, "The backers of the Provident Loan Society of New York have had the blessed pacification of their consciences for some time, and they are not displeased now to discover that the stale bread of charity which they cast on the waters is coming back in the form of cake, quite fresh and inviting. In plain speech, they win back a 6 per cent. interest on what they suddenly learn was an investment."[62] A contemporary book on the American charities movement likened charity work to other elite pastimes, such as "balls, entertainments, [and] oyster suppers." The authors stated that "after religious influence" came "social influence" as a reason to engage in philanthropy, and it was, they stated, "one of the means by which social advancement is secured."[63]

Organized and run by industrial magnates of the day, the PLS benefited from a significant infusion of capital to maintain its stability once the enterprise got off the ground. Because it was not run by the government, it also profited from a fluid and flexible movement of funds. Although an economic depression in 1895 prevented the East Side branch from opening on schedule, the PLS was nevertheless able to pay investors dividends of 6%, a rate of return they "may confidently expect to receive" in the future.[64] The PLS also benefited from the men's collective business acumen, which included making prudent investments in the bond market on the PLS's behalf.[65] In addition, officers with ready access to credit were able to steer the organization through financially rocky years, an economic advantage independent pawnbrokers did not have. Further, the PLS's branch system enabled it to redistribute funds, shifting surplus money from some outlets to those with deficits.[66] The fifth annual report from 1899 reported sanguinely that it "has a sound foundation in the financial results attained." The total earnings from interest collected and sales of unredeemed pledges covered not only all operating expenses but also all dividend payments, with $16,000 left for the reserve fund.[67]

Experienced investor-organizers were good at what they did from a high-end business perspective. But they also found themselves modifying the way pawnshops traditionally did business, thus changing the nature of the operations. A pawnbroker's success hinged on his ability to make prudent loans. He did this by making fair and accurate appraisals on a wide variety of goods. Appraising was as much an art as a skill, best learned over many years of working in a pawnshop. Assigning monetary value to material goods to be used as loan collateral was more complicated than it might seem. Many factors, from the pawner's creditworthiness to an object's resale value, had to be considered during appraisals. Since pawnbrokers kept unredeemed collateral for a year on average after initially making a loan, they also had to speculate on its future worth, whether it was more likely to appreciate or depreciate. A pawnbroker had to assess his customers' reliability and trustworthiness, predicting whether they would make good on the loan, and consider whether the collateral might be stolen. Pawnbrokers also had to anticipate the financial calculations pawners themselves might make down the road. They loaned enough to secure the transaction but not so much that the loan was not paid off when it came due because the debt was too great or the collateral could be replaced for less than was owed on it.

In all, appraising was a nuanced procedure involving both economic and psychological calculations. It seemed nearly impossible that charitable pawnshops could keep their doors open without experienced professionals. For this reason Champion Bissell called the new charity pawnshops "ridiculous and impracticable" because appraisals could not be systematized. He wrote, "Every transaction over the lender's counter involves a careful appraisement, and only individual prudence can be relied on for this."[68] As they added new branches and handled more kinds of collateral, PLS officers gradually realized this simple yet crucial fact. Far from a mom-and-pop operation, the expanding institution more closely resembled a complex factory requiring sophisticated managerial oversight. Initially the PLS hired a "practical pawnbroker" plucked from his own shop to manage the branches and make appraisals. After ten years of service officers replaced him with a cadre of professionals, including "a man of greater capacity and wider knowledge of social and financial matters" who would hire and supervise "a group of technically trained executives in charge of its departments of appraisal, finance, law, audit and personnel . . . and a system of operation and control which leaves little to be desired."[69]

Independent pawnbrokers oversaw every aspect of their shops' business from appraisals and ledger keeping to storage and upkeep. In contrast, the PLS divided these responsibilities into discrete tasks performed by different employees whose skills were limited in scope and who, with few exceptions, had no prospects of moving up. Rather than having the expertise to make appraisals, balance the books, deal with customers, handle inquiries from authorities, and oversee storage and retrieval, as independent pawnbrokers did, PLS employees had to know only the one task assigned to them. Professional compartmentalization engendered efficiency and security and allowed few people direct access to the cash and collateral. Cashiers only handled money and pawn tickets; vaultmen worked the combinations to the safes, storing and retrieving collateral.[70] Only a few who began in menial positions worked their way up to appraising; most remained unskilled, which was part of the overall business strategy. And everyone was replaceable.

Trustees brought to the PLS an ordered, vertically integrated system that typified Progressive Era rationalization. At first they were able to apply the strategy to all functions except appraising, which, as a skill attained through years of personal experience, defied systematization. Yet, remarkably, PLS organizers *did* devise a way to streamline and rationalize appraising, deconstructing the skill that, until then, had formed the bedrock of a pawnbroker's business. The PLS's "training plan . . . could, in a relatively short period of time, create its own diamond appraisers out of nothing but willing and deserving applicants with good eyesight!" exclaimed Peter Schwed, a former PLS employee.[71] By adopting such a system, the PLS removed the element of expertise—born of hard work, tradition, experience, and lineage—that linked generations of the most successful family-operated pawnshops.

The PLS's appraisal system was inspired by a larger interest in what would come to be known as scientific management. Time-and-motion studies carefully scrutinized factory workers' movements, breaking jobs down into component parts that could be measured, quantified, and made more efficient by changing the choreography of man and machine. Applied to appraising, rationalization meant dividing the valuation process into discrete components. That the system worked only on limited kinds of collateral—precious metals and gemstones whose weight and quality could be quantified—posed a seemingly insurmountable problem. Yet the PLS was content to limit accepted collateral to these items at all but the branches serving the poorest customers. The PLS could therefore expand its labor pool as necessary, and practically on demand. While "diamond men" relied on their "professional experience, knowledge, and 'feel,' or instinct," observed Schwed, "a Provident appraiser is taught merely how to look keenly, note, and then find the answer in a book." Hence the PLS "brew[ed] Instant Appraisers" rather than using "the traditional percolated brand."[72]

Then as now, appraisers considered a diamond's size, color, flaws, and cut when assessing value. Carat weight was determined simply by putting a stone on a scale (or, if mounted, by taking measurements with calipers and using those dimensions to calculate total weight). Evaluating other qualities was more subjective. The color and clarity of a diamond, for instance, required a value judgment, and perception varied depending on lighting and time of day. Minimizing the element of subjectivity, the PLS created "test sticks" for all its appraisal departments. Each stick was composed of six one-carat diamonds in colors ranging from the clearest and best at the top to the poorest at the bottom. A coding system corresponded to each of seven color qualities from FW (Fine White) to VSO (Very Slightly Off) to BW (Biwater, of poor color). A PLS appraiser simply had to match his diamond against one of the examples on the stick and assign it the appropriate predetermined PLS color rating.

Similarly, the organization devised a system to evaluate diamond flaws by drawing on the collective knowledge of its established appraisers. They were asked to examine hundreds of diamonds and rate values based on various flaws. The appraisers, working from nickel-sized line drawings of the tops and profiles of the stones, then conferred to decide the flaws' effect on value. Like the colors, the flaws were then given ratings, from o for flawless to 5 for highly flawed. Schematic charts showing detailed top and side views of flawed diamonds and their corresponding evaluation numbers were distributed to the branches and became an essential tool for employees "that no professional diamond dealer had ever come across in his life" (fig. 6.1).[73]

After a year of obtaining measurements from tens of thousands of diamonds using a magnifying device designed especially for the purpose, the PLS also determined the "ideal" cut of a diamond. Deviations from the ideal were also quantified. For example, according to the system, a diamond weighing almost 3.75 carats of fine but not perfect color, with a medium flaw and fairly poor cut translated into the language of PLS appraisals as 3.70 W 2–30. They used a logarithmic formula to calculate the market value for each diamond category (because the worth of diamonds grows geometrically as they increase in size).

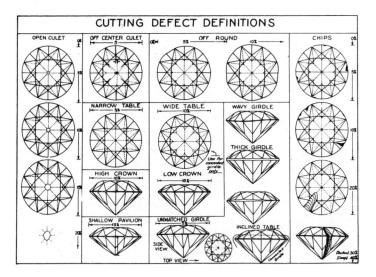

FIGURE 6.1. The appraisal process made into a science. Peter Schwed, *God Bless Pawnbrokers* (New York: Dodd, Mead, 1975), 108. Courtesy, the heirs of Peter Schwed.

Charts plotted these several information points and listed corresponding loan amounts (fig. 6.2). From these graphs the PLS prepared books of tables covering every size and category of diamond. Now all an employee had to do was consult the charts mapping color, cut, and flaws, find the matching diamond in the book of tables, and write down that loan amount. This allowed no wiggle room, no negotiation, and no mistakes. A PLS worker needed no formal skills because a rigid system of charts and graphs had supplanted traditional appraising based on an individual's expertise. The employee "just took out his little book, ran his finger down the appropriate page until he found the weight (or size) of the diamond, and then read across in cold print that he should lend, let us say, $265 on this particular stone. Not $270 and not $260. $265."[74]

The PLS also applied its strategy of rationalization to the architecture of its buildings, which reflected the institutional detachment pawners would find inside. Branches looked nothing like the familiar neighborhood pawnshops, typically dark places fronted by picture windows filled with pawns and prominently marked with the sign of the three balls. The PLS main branch first operated out of the United Charities Building, an imposing structure dominating the entire block of Fourth Avenue at Twenty-second Street (fig. 6.3). When it took up permanent residence just down the street, organizers chose an even more intimidating structure—the Church Missions House, with an ornate Gothic cathedral—

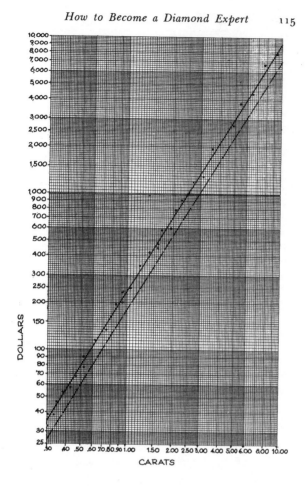

FIGURE 6.2. Rating numbers on a chart corresponding to dollar value. Peter Schwed, *God Bless Pawnbrokers* (New York: Dodd, Mead, 1975), 115. Courtesy, the heirs of Peter Schwed.

like archway one had to pass under to reach the PLS's door. Except for two existing structures that it modified, the PLS custom-built all additional branches. The buildings, substantial and nondescript, possessed a bank's solidity and a post office's no-nonsense practicality that organizers described as "commodious, dignified public space for its clientele of both sexes"[75] (fig. 6.4).

In all respects the PLS strove both to differentiate itself from independent pawnshops and to situate itself above them, asserting superiority through everything from architecture to annual reports. Rejecting the stereotypical grimy, cramped quarters of typical pawnshops, the PLS constructed spacious, comfortable quarters for customers to conduct their business. The PLS's systematic appraisal system eliminated the vagaries of loan amounts. And it charged reason-

FIGURE 6.3. The monolithic face of semiphilanthropic pawnbroking. "The New Building for the United Charities of New York City," Hughson Hawley, illus., *Harper's Weekly* 35, 1814 (September 26, 1891): 736. Library of Congress.

FIGURE 6.4. PLS branch offices had the facelessness typical of large institutions. "Bronx Office," *The Provident Loan Society of New York: Twenty-fifth Anniversary, 1894–1919* (New York: Provident Loan Society, 1919), facing 23. Library of Congress.

able, affordable interest.[76] By establishing a presence in many of the city's most neglected neighborhoods, the PLS not only offered economic relief to some of New York's poorest people but also educated them about legal lending practices, hoping to dissuade them from patronizing unlicensed pawnbrokers or dealing with loan sharks. In offering favorable terms below legal interest rates, the PLS also informed people what those legal rates and fees were. Even if customers opted to go elsewhere, they came away from PLS branches with a better understanding of their legal rights as pawners, empowering them when dealing with independent pawnbrokers.

Undeniably, the PLS offered significant material relief to hundreds of thousands of city dwellers who otherwise would not have been able to make ends meet. In 1931 alone, at the beginning of the Great Depression, the PLS loaned over $36 million to more than half a million people, averaging two hundred transactions a day at each of the seventeen branches open at the time.[77] By then the PLS's firm financial foundation and economic muscle served it (and its customers) well. At a time when independent pawnbrokers were going bankrupt, the PLS, "run on a strictly business basis," survived. What was more, its success inspired elites in other cities to establish similar lending institutions. By 1932 there were twenty-seven remedial loan societies scattered across the country, from San Francisco and Dallas to Sioux City, Iowa, and Duluth, Minnesota. The First State Pawners Society of Chicago, for example, was founded by the Merchants Club in 1899. Board members and officers included John V. Farwell, a leading dry goods merchant in the city, and Edwin G. Foreman, head of one of Chicago's largest banks at the time.[78]

It was essential that these organizers differentiate their operations from independent pawnshops. While championing a new collateral loan society in Brooklyn, a writer for the *New York Times* in 1888 referred to the city's pawnbrokers as extortionists and receivers of stolen goods. He added, not quite convincingly, that "the honest pawnbrokers, who have suffered from the excesses of the unscrupulous persons of their craft, are said to be in favor of the new company."[79] The main priorities of semiphilanthropic pawnshops were providing reasonable short-term loans for the needy and earning money for their investors. In addition, they sought to drive down the interest rates charged by independent pawnbrokers and ideally to eliminate them altogether.

But the enduring success of the Provident Loan Society in New York and smaller operations in other cities did not, in fact, lead to the extinction of private pawnbrokers, no matter how hard their organizers tried. "The philanthropy that would do away with the pawnbroker is a spurious philanthropy, since the city can no more dispense with the pawnbroker than it can with the baker or the milkman," observed Champion Bissell at the end of the nineteenth century.[80] If these large institutions granted loans on more favorable terms, why did the public continue to patronize independent shops? Boosters of the charitable institutions chalked it up to pawners' fear and irrationality. No matter, for instance, that it took almost half a century and "repeated amendments to its charter" to keep the Pawners' Bank of Boston afloat, until "the public grew up to it."[81] Another commentator inexplicably concluded that pawners had become so "accustomed to the extortions of the regular pawnbrokers" that they "at first refused to trust the new municipal pawnshops."[82]

But the converse was just as likely: that charitable lenders did not trust their customers. Independent pawnbrokers did not question the moral character of the pawners coming through their doors (except when they suspected stolen goods). Being judged as a good or bad person, worthy or unworthy, a new immigrant or longtime resident, of one ethnicity or another did not affect the terms of the loan. While he much preferred collateral to be redeemed, the pawnbroker loaned on so slight a percentage of its market value that it did not make much difference whether the goods came from a degenerate gambler or a society dame or what circumstances impelled the pawner to seek the sign of the three balls. In contrast, institutions such as the Workingmen's Loan Association (established in 1888 in Boston), which provided small loans to people of moderate means on collateral of domestic goods, assessed the worthiness of potential customers before lending: "It must and does discriminate carefully between the safe and reliable borrower and the thriftless and improvident. The association will not loan to persons who frequently change their residence and are of disreputable character or to certain nationalities among immigrants, races that have not yet evolved a sense of honor, and to persons who have recently become residents of the city."[83] Organizers of Boston's Emergency Loan Fund required borrowers to submit to a personal interview giving "full confession" of their need. If found worthy, they went through an intermediary to secure the loan and then submitted to periodic follow-up visits from officials. It was not an equal-opportunity lending agency, however. The Emergency Loan Fund did not lend "for the chronic backward rent, or to people living on the lowest round of the social ladder"—in other words, to the truly needy—because members had determined that their "ambition is dormant and . . . [they] are unaccustomed to thinking of the larger responsibilities in life."[84]

Other than detecting criminals bringing in obviously stolen goods, the private pawnbroker did not care one bit about his customers' race, residence, nationality, or how they might use the money. He considered everyone a "worthy" borrower who could generate a profit for him. Charitable institutions, however, unapologetically discriminated among those entering their doors: "This society was organized to relieve the distress only of the worthy; not to make an easy way to get a drink," the *Brooklyn Daily Eagle* wrote of the PLS in 1896.[85]

Greeted with layers of bureaucracy, people seeking loans from benevolent institutions had to fill out intrusive and complicated paperwork. The Workingmen's Loan Association explained that "each applicant is questioned with great care and fills out a blank application, giving present residence, previous residence, and business references, and deposits thirty-five cents" for the privilege of getting a loan.[86] The process—formal, exacting, and protracted—was like getting a bank loan, only borrowers still had to put up their personal property as collateral. Often they did not have time to fill out forms and wait for them to be reviewed and evaluated. "The managers may make it so difficult for a needy person to get aid or assistance," noted a writer for *Harper's Weekly*, "that the beautiful bloom is entirely taken off the kindly deed of charity, and that the lack of timeliness may defeat the very end that is sought in the first place."[87] (D. W. Griffith even took up this issue in his 1908 screenplay *Old Isaacs the Pawnbroker*, the story of a little girl who is forced to hock her doll at the pawnshop because she cannot navigate the red tape of "Amalgamated Association of Charities.")[88] Semiphilanthropic institutions had it both ways, enjoying the veneer of charitable work while functioning with the cool rationality of big business.

Pawners also enjoyed a sense of familiarity with "their" neighborhood pawnbrokers that was lacking in the larger institutions. While pawners did not necessarily have to *like* "my uncle" and may have resented going to him time and again, they did feel comfortable negotiating loan terms and knew what to expect. In contrast, municipal pawnshops, by design, resembled other monolithic and alienating institutions. "For generations," PLS historian Rolf Nugent wrote, "the word 'pawnshop' has brought to mind a gallery of vivid pictures, sordid, depressing or ludicrous according to one's own experience—Shylock demanding his pound of flesh; the three-ball sign of the Medici family; ramshackle, dirty shops; sharp-practiced shopkeepers; despondent, down-and-out borrowers."[89]

The PLS and other semiphilanthropic pawnshops strove to sanitize pawning while distancing themselves from it by obliterating history. And so they did away with the pawnshops' symbolic three balls—a sign recognizable to everyone and especially important to non-English-speaking immigrants and the illiterate. Refashioning and destigmatizing the pawnshop also entailed situating branches in rich as well as poor neighborhoods, limiting "acceptable" collateral to precious metals and gemstones, and hiring employees of Anglo-European origin to present the public face of the institution. They even preferred the vaguer term "pledge" to "pawn." In his late-century treatise on the law of bailments, law professor James Schouler noted this strategic shift in verbiage: "Now that the pledge may be made of great things as well as small, of mercantile as well as household articles, . . . and while the pawnbroker still plies, under license, the individual trade with misery and humble stations, a corporation, organized for a wider reach of the same business, *nominally sinks the pawn*, and is styled a 'Collateral Loan Company.'"[90]

The staff of the PLS branches appeared as faceless as the buildings, reflecting the organization's bureaucratic shift. During the first years after its founding the PLS hired skilled independent pawnbrokers to oversee all appraising. These men brought their long experience dealing with a variety of pawners and could accurately judge the likelihood that a pawner would redeem his collateral. Knowing the personal history of regular pawners—whether a man was a skilled gambler, whether a woman was temporarily unemployed as an actress—factored into the amount of the loan extended and the likelihood that it would be paid off (but not whether a loan would be granted at all). Although essential to the survival of independent pawnshops, at the PLS personalized service increasingly counted as a liability, an inconvenience.

When the PLS adopted a "scientific and implacable lending schedule," it in effect eliminated the social aspects of making appraisals that created relationships between pawner and pawnbroker and might eventually lead to more forgiving loan terms. The president of the PLS acknowledged at the time that "people who patronize commercial pawnshops again and again—have always been responsible for more than half of all the loans they make."[91] Yet officers actively thwarted the formation of personal relationships between pawners and pawnbrokers by rotating appraisers among the various branches. Clerks no longer worked at one branch long enough to cultivate "favorites" or have "regulars," and that was the way PLS overseers preferred it. However, "the policy did have its drawbacks from a public relations standpoint," according to Peter Schwed. "Very often screams of protest arose from the faithful pledgers, who objected to the removal from their locality of someone they had turned to as Father confessor, psychiatrist, and even . . . physician."[92] As a result, pawners sometimes followed favorite appraisers to their new assignments, which could be across town, an hour or more away. In severing the ties between regular pawners and their pawnbrokers, the PLS also fractured the traditional geographical ties that bound pawners to their local pawnshops.

Another essential part of the PLS's strategy to legitimate itself was simply to redefine pawnbroking as a gentile profession. While some of the PLS's key investors were Jewish (as were, undoubtedly, many of its customers), the public face—the managers, appraisers, and clerks—was primarily Irish Catholic, beginning with the very first appraiser, a Bowery pawnbroker named Joe Keane, whose adeptness in the field may have "influenced the hiring of so many Irish in later years."[93] In contrast, officers perceived Sol Glicksman, the PLS's only Jewish appraiser, as an eccentric who allegedly spent more time offering home remedies to the "many pledgers plagued with headaches, hangovers, hemorrhoids, and fallen arches" and running a "free dispensary" than doing prescribed PLS work.[94]

Enforced impersonality between regular pawners and their pawnbrokers, in addition to the systematized appraisal process, prevented customers from negotiating loan terms, a common practice in independent pawnshops. Regular and reliable pawners might be able to cajole a few extra bucks out of their local pawnbroker, who knew from experience that they were good for the money. Institutional pawnshops offered no such flexibility. The PLS reported customers' complaints "that loans were not sufficiently liberal and were not so large as other pawnbrokers have been accustomed to make upon the same property." Pawners used to getting more from their collateral "have been disappointed and some of them have inquired wherein the benevolence of the Society consisted if it would not loan more or at least as much as other pawnbrokers."[95] It was a fair point. Not only were semiphilanthropic pawnshops' loans very conservative, they were also extended only on limited kinds of collateral, objects whose value could be easily and accurately calculated according to the PLS's highly structured appraisal system. The first annual report stated, "The Society has thus far limited the classes of personal property on which it has made loans to clothing and to so-called 'jewelry,' including under that designation all articles of gold or silver, precious stones, opera glasses, eye glasses, etc."[96] A contemporary writer noted that "because of the necessary limitations the society has felt obliged to impose upon the character of goods received as security for loans," it "has scarcely reached as yet the poorer people who are perhaps most imposed upon."[97] Eventually realizing the inefficacy of collateral limitations, the organization relaxed its restrictions, but only at branches in impoverished neighborhoods.

Other aspects also made semiphilanthropic pawnshops less attractive to potential pawners. They could not be found in every city and dispensed only a small fraction of the country's total collateral loans. For example, in the 1930s independent pawnbrokers alone (not counting other sources of personal credit) carried about $400 million in outstanding loans, compared with $53 million for semiphilanthropic agencies.[98] In the 1880s the Pawners' Bank of Boston adopted "a more commercial method" of operation, reminiscent of early savings banks, limiting hours to between 9:00 a.m. and 2:00 p.m., thereby making it "less convenient for the use of the poorer classes than the regular pawnbrokers."[99] Perhaps most off-putting was the moralizing tone pervading many loan societies. Institutional policies were intended to uplift pawners by teaching them the value of hard work and the importance of meeting financial obligations. This philosophy was articulated in an 1895 issue of the *Charities Review*, which likened the poor to farm animals: "One who loans money to the needy and unfortunate poor, takes the ox out of the ditch, puts him on his feet and enables him to go on doing his humble duty and earning his living, but one who gives indiscriminately to the poor simply feeds the ox and leaves him in the ditch to require more food from the next passerby."[100] Similarly, of the PLS Katherine Louise Smith wrote, "Reports of this association state that those who obtain loans are rarely found on the records of charitable institutions, but are self-supporting persons that desire to tide over periods of misfortune or illness. The work is preventive rather than charitable."[101]

That pawners stood on more equal footing with their local independent pawnbrokers both economically and socially may explain why large institutional pawnshops could not put their smaller rivals out of business. Pawners and pawnbrokers may have viewed one another guardedly, but theirs was a *mutual* association of people who had more in common than not. In contrast, pawners must have been painfully aware of the condescendingly didactic purpose of the larger, organized institutions. By entering semiphilanthropic "loan societies," pawners bowed before the powerful, who doled out money only to people they deemed "worthy." "The pawnbroker estimates the poor with a juster and more experienced eye," wrote a defender of private pawnbrokers. "He is no stranger to the cruelty and selfishness by which they are actuated, and he is certain that his customers would, if they could, cheat him out of his last dollar."[102] And *Scientific American* remarked that customers of independent pawnbrokers "show a great deal of confidence in them, and . . . it is not uncommon for regular pledgers to leave articles without taking any receipt."[103] Tellingly, when the PLS was first established, some people derisively referred to it as the "Vanderbilt pawnshop."[104]

The PLS and other institutional pawnshops were successful on a scale the independents could not match. By drawing on investors' pooled funds, the organizations could offer low-interest loans to thousands of urban dwellers who needed ready cash. By the early 1930s, the PLS boasted over $32 million in assets. In 1931 alone it had loaned over $36 million to some 500,000 people—ten times the business logged by the Crédit Municipal in Paris. The loans were useful: 95% of borrowers weathered hard times and were able to redeem their collateral before it went up for public sale.[105]

Competing with independent pawnbrokers, the PLS and its sister institutions in other cities succeeded in driving down all interest rates, forcing pawnbrokers to charge less than the maximum allowed by law. While institutional pawnshops did not eradicate independent pawnbrokers, they did pose enough of a challenge to force pawnbrokers to rethink their own operations. As a result, the independent shops adopted some of the strategies used by big business. They began limiting forms of collateral, specializing in fine jewelry and precious metals. They also banded together and established professional organizations. All cities with thriving institutional pawnshops—including not only New York but also Chicago, Boston, St. Louis, and San Francisco—saw the emergence of pawnbrokers' societies like the State Pawners' Society in New York.[106]

Within the established PLS framework, pawning no longer seemed a stigmatized business if streamlined and capitalized so it became part of mainstream commerce overseen by supposedly reputable businessmen. An account of the PLS written in 1932 noted that "it has extended the same courteous treatment to its customers that they would expect from a commercial bank," continuing, with a clear disregard for the long history of collateral lending, "The Society has done much to popularize the use of jewelry and silverware as a source of credit. These are possessions of value just as much as stocks or bonds."[107] The PLS legitimized a practice that pawnbrokers had been engaged in for centuries. What was more, borrowing itself was no longer (in the eyes of the PLS, anyway) a moral failing, as it had been thought of in the past: "Financial distress is not merely a concomitant of industrial depression—it is a continuing and inevitable condition among members of all classes of society. . . . The range of borrowers is as large as society itself and the reasons for borrowing include all the unnumbered embarrassments, difficulties, emergencies and opportunities incident to the complex life of the modern metropolitan community."[108]

Like most charitable projects during the Progressive Era, the PLS's efforts proved equal parts philanthropic and entrepreneurial. It both offered a more affordable and convenient way to borrow money by driving down the independent pawnbroker's interest rates and (necessarily) destigmatized the pawning process—positive outcomes on the whole. Pawners could pay back their loans with less interest and walk away with more money in their pockets. As a byproduct of the PLS's charitable efforts, the consistent return on investment rewarded the organization's contributors.

Yet the officers themselves stressed that the institution was run on "business principles." This might explain why its first building was in a more upscale neighborhood, attracting a better class of people with more valuable things to pawn and generating more revenue. The PLS's third branch, at last in a poor neighborhood, could finally serve the very people it ostensibly set out to help. Business interests that maximized investor returns vied with the supposed philanthropic aims of the institution. Although semiphilanthropic lenders vilified private pawnbrokers, they too were making money off the poor. They simply tried to do it in a more acceptable fashion.

CHAPTER SEVEN

UNREDEEMED

Compared with other forms of credit available to us today, pawning seems down-right old-fashioned, a vestige of the distant past. Mortgages have been traded and sold from one bank to another, sliced and diced into mortgage-backed securities, and sold again. Banks themselves have been sold off and consolidated so often that it's hard to keep track of who services our checking account (to say nothing of the person behind the counter). Perhaps most abstract of all, credit cards (sur-prisingly recent additions to the credit economy), slick, convenient, and wholly anonymous, enable a form of borrowing that is pawning's mirror opposite.

Despite its pariah status as part of the fringe economy, pawning still plays a crucial role in today's postindustrial credit-based world, a testament to its ver-satility and the simple fact that as human beings who need physical objects to survive, we will always have collateral that is of value to someone.[1] Like the pawnbrokers who emerged and thrived during the formative years of capitalism and the boom and bust decades that followed, today's pawnbrokers continue to respond to shifts in the economy and society. Some will do well as the cur-rent recession takes hold, while others—tethered to the falling fortunes of their customers—will not.

The history of pawnbroking remains relevant today not only because pawn-broking as an institution still flourishes in many areas, but also because earlier responses to borrowing and lending among the underclass continue to reverber-ate. Professional pawnbroking emerged in this country at the dawn of capitalism, only a few decades after America won its independence. The business found its place in the interstices of an American economy and culture that were radi-cally changing and would create the foundations we continue to live with. Then as now, pawnbrokers carried out market transactions that existed somewhere beyond (or between) wholesale and retail exchange. Objects that carried sentimental value, that could be displayed as status symbols, or that were used as tools also served as collateral to secure loans. Pawners, too, were (and continue to be) caught in the middle, between yesterday's and next week's payday, autumn's labor season and the coming spring's, the last and inevitably the next family crisis. Workers increasingly lost control over their own labor, exploited by the owners and operators of manufactories who steadily consolidated their power and wealth. Today people continue to balance low wages against increasing expenses, working at minimum wage for multinational corporations that have attained a global presence. Fluctuating gas prices, a turbulent stock market, and escalating foreclosure rates occupy the headlines and monopolize our thoughts.

In the nineteenth century pawnbroking continued to thrive even as social and economic life changed radically. Hundreds of thousands of pawners kept pawnshops in business, evidence of an economic system that created some winners and many more losers—another legacy we continue to live with. Those who stood to gain the most championed industrial capitalism, selling it as an idea as much as an economic system. In doing so they characterized capitalist pursuits as "normal," "mainstream" economic activity and pawnbroking as anomalous. In their eyes pawnbrokers were amoral profiteers, pawners were spendthrifts, and pawnbroking was aberrant.

Average Americans remained vulnerable throughout the nineteenth century. With little access to capital and credit, they had no choice but to live under capitalism's constraints. No longer equal partners in transactions rooted in reciprocal exchange and collective obligation, people were subjected to the often relentless and inflexible demands of organized wage labor. Day after day, thousands of people struggled to work within, get out from under, or maneuver around capitalism's tight reins. And to varying degrees they succeeded. Some gained entry into the elite world of the upper classes or carved out comfortable livings as members of the growing middle class. But many others either did not move up or found themselves bankrupt and broke after one of the nation's many economic contractions. We have seen echoes of this recently as various economic bubbles have swelled and then, inevitably, burst.

Knowing what we know about the solidifying of power during the nineteenth century, it might be useful to examine the behavior of those controlling today's large consumer lending industry, who have perfected making money off the poor. Powerful lobbying groups acting for officers and stockholders of banks, subprime mortgage corporations, payday lending operations, and tax refund services have helped their clients win legislation that allows them to circumvent traditional usury and bankruptcy laws. The legislation itself (and the lack of government oversight) has resulted in individual consumers' often carrying tens of thousands of dollars of debt, made it more difficult for individuals to file for bankruptcy, and contributed to the collapse of the real estate market, bringing us fully into a recession. Formal processes for dealing with debtors continue to be punitive and, according to Katherine Porter, rooted more in "perception and politics than empirical reality."[2] Although lenders are forever deploring the financial habits of the so-called profligate, until very recently they have generously extended high-interest loans to people who were clearly bad risks. Subprime and "exotic" mortgages were sold to the very people who could least afford them.[3]

Along with these modern forms of credit marketed to the lower classes, traditional arms of the poverty industry continue to exist and in fact, since the 1990s, have flourished. Because of its ability to adapt to changing times, the Provident Loan Society is still around and now operates five branches.[4] But that organization too seems quaint and old-fashioned.

More sophisticated and better-capitalized outfits, including rent-to-own stores, rapid-refund tax shops, phone card outlets, and title loan companies, have tapped into the market potential of the economically disenfranchised, catering to their twenty-first-century needs, whether to communicate with family members in other countries, to have someone prepare their income taxes, or to outfit their apartments with the latest electronic equipment. This is the new "fringe economy," no longer comprising the small independent pawnshops and the corner money-order outlets so much as we tend to think. It is, rather, "an industry increasingly dominated by a handful of large, well-financed national and multinational corporations with strong ties to mainstream financial institutions."[5]

These entities are pawnbrokers' main competition. Corporations have stood to make huge profits by inducing customers to turn away from pawnbrokers' credit services and instead choose credit cards at high interest rates or the myriad other options available on the market, including home equity lines of credit and mortgage refinancing. There is no question that operators in this fringe economy exploit their customers as far as the law allows. And the laws are generous: fringe operators can legally charge significantly higher interest rates than loan sharks.[6] (In fact, some scholars consider payday lenders nothing more than modern loan sharks.)[7] People still frequent these places because, as members of the growing population of the "unbanked," they need money and have few other resources. Not even able to live paycheck to paycheck, they seek cash advances on money they have not yet earned, getting into debt *ahead* of their future wages. Often the loans themselves bury people so deep they cannot dig out of the hole. According to a recent study, a payday loan of $325 costs the average borrower $793 after fees and compounded interest. Extended for an additional two weeks, that loan will accrue annual interest of 417%, significantly higher than even the highest pawn-broking rates.[8] Desperation and ignorance together induce borrowers to accept loans that end up being "inescapable debt traps."[9] With the rise of home fore-closures and unemployment, propelled by the collapse of the real estate market, more needy people will come to the doors of fringe lenders.[10]

Like the nineteenth-century pawnbrokers who preceded them, today's fringe lenders follow the paths of economic need away from gentrified pockets and toward poorer neighborhoods. Because banks long ago abandoned depressed areas, payday lenders have become the key financial institutions there and tend to compete with pawnbrokers. Between 2000 and 2003, the number of payday lenders more than doubled to 20,000, a figure that counts only brick-and-mortar outlets and does not include the many instant-cash Web sites.[11] The poor pay dearly for the few such services offered to them. Much like convenience stores that have replaced grocery stores in depressed areas, fringe lending operations charge inflated prices for limited services, because they can.

The ability to tap into lines of credit is bound to our social identity and essen-tial to the function of our consumer-based service economy. "The significance of consumer credit," according to Lendol Calder, "is now measured by the fact that for middle-class people it has become virtually impossible to live the Amer-ican dream *without* access to credit payment methods, as anyone knows who has placed a phone order from a catalog or tried to pay cash for a rental car."[12] (He was writing before the new era of Internet shopping, a world from which the disenfranchised—lacking access to both technology and credit cards—are completely excluded.)

As I write, the contraction of credit internationally is creating a global finan-cial crisis. Here at home, employees are being laid off, consumers are cutting back, and people are losing their homes. Fringe lenders and their ilk, easy to criticize, are merely capitalizing on market opportunities, just as real estate spec-ulators and investment bankers did. Many Americans are getting closer to the pawnshop's door, glancing around the house and making a mental inventory of possessions that might serve as collateral. (As if to normalize the idea that many of us will soon be pawners, the media have recently offered a spate of stories on pawnshops around the country.)

The things we bought that maxed out our credit cards—iPods, DVD play-ers, video consoles, and gold jewelry—might very well be the same things we take to the pawnshop to secure a loan. In many cases these loans will cost less than using our plastic. Pawnbrokers charge simple interest, limited by the usury laws in their states. Credit card companies (typically, large banks) charge compound interest. Headquartered in states whose usury laws are the most lax, such as South Dakota and Delaware, they are free to hike interest to rates that were once considered usurious. Additionally, credit card companies tack on other fees that increase monthly balances but are not advertised as part of the annual percentage rate (calculations presented as opaquely as possible). Infractions such as making a single late payment, going over the credit limit, and taking out cash advances (offered as a "service" but treated punitively) often incur another set of finance charges and interest rate hikes. What is more, any balance that remains after paying the suggested minimum is cycled onto next month's bill and thus costs even more—compound interest compounded again. Charging interest on interest is a boon to companies counting on the customers who are just scraping by and can make only minimum monthly payments. The banks that oversee credit card accounts do not hesitate to turn debtors over to collection agencies, ruining credit ratings and making it much more expensive and difficult to secure credit in the future.

In contrast, pawnbrokers provide clear information about loan terms on their pawn tickets. They are strictly regulated by federal, state, and local laws. Pawners know in advance how much they are borrowing, the interest rate and any additional fees being charged, when the loan will come due, and how much money in total is required to retrieve collateral. They also know they are risking only the item they bring to the pawnshop to secure the loan. Collection agents do not hector, and credit rating companies are not informed if the loan is not repaid.

That is not to say that pawnbrokers, fringe economy entrepreneurs on a much smaller scale, are by any means heroic figures in this narrative. Daniel Feehan, chief executive officer of Cash America, admits that "during the early stages of a downturn in the economy we're gonna get a temporary boost as people use our lending services to try to adjust" to changing economic circumstances.[13] But it is important to consider that people are often better off being in hock to a pawnbroker than to a multinational corporation, because a pawnbroker will only keep the collateral and not come after major assets such as house or car.

The consolidation of fringe lending enterprises, whether into chain pawnshops or seasonal rapid-refund storefronts, signals a new phase in credit transactions and a distinct break with the past. In the eighteenth century people extended loans to their friends and neighbors and, when possible, relied on barter and exchange. Economic and social relationships were interlinked, whereas today we think it best not to mingle the two. During the emergence of industrial capitalism in the nineteenth century, more rigid economic systems and anonymous financial transactions gradually replaced informal and intimate yet inefficient and outmoded credit relationships. General brokers became specialists, and peddlers and used goods dealers worked their way up. As pawnbrokers, they met the particular needs of cash-strapped city dwellers who could no longer rely on friends and family. To regular pawners, the pawnbroker was a familiar figure in their lives. By forging relationships with "their" pawnbrokers, mixing the business with the personal, they enjoyed certain advantages when it came to securing more favorable loan terms and extended payment schedules. Thus the anonymous pawnbroker was not necessarily so anonymous, and the supposedly impersonal, atomistic credit relationships were perhaps not so impersonal either.

Today the individual family-run pawnshop, like so many other independently owned businesses, is disappearing, and with it goes one of our last modes of doing business personally. While many people might look on the diminishing number of pawnbrokers as a positive trend, it is also an indication of the alienation engendered by global capitalism. The shuttering of independent pawnshops that have been in business over several generations owing to competition from large chains is a result of these economic and demographic shifts. As formerly downscale neighborhoods become gentrified and local shops are taken over by conglomerates, longtime residents and businesses are uprooted, becoming disconnected from their traditional social and economic networks. Pawnbrokers in turn lose their reliable customer base and must either close or move to areas with new clientele, usually transplanting themselves to outlying strip malls and leaving faithful customers in search of other credit sources. Longtime Seattle pawnbroker Alan Goldman, for one, closed Central Loan and Gun recently because the First Avenue area, once home to twenty-seven pawnshops and "numerous XXX-rated places, plus plenty of smoky, old-time taverns," had gone upscale, with high-end boutiques and posh hotels. "Why should the customers go to a downtown pawnshop," he argued, "when there are all those brand-new ones in the suburbs, offering free parking?"[14]

Goldman's story is now a familiar one, and the survival of traditional pawnshops remains in doubt across the country. In early 2008 Louis Kimmel closed the oldest pawnshop in Buffalo, which first opened its doors in 1885. Kimmel followed the career path of old-school pawnbrokers. His father Jack was a Polish immigrant who grew up in the business, working for twenty-five years under an experienced pawnbroker. Kimmel purchased the shop after the original owner died, and his son Louis worked under him for fifteen years before the elder Kimmel died. Kimmel, now eighty, stayed on running the business, which is five blocks from his home. His wife's father and brother were also pawnbrokers. Like the country's very first pawnbrokers, those working today often have to combine businesses in order to compete, not only providing loans but also engaging in resale. According to Kimmel, "We couldn't exist just on items that came out of pawn. We developed a good trade with affluent people who bought big ticket items from us. They enjoyed buying diamonds out of pawn."[15]

Like their nineteenth-century predecessors, today's professional pawnbrokers tend not to resemble the two-dimensional stereotypes portrayed in popular culture. They are often engaged with in their communities. Like Buffalo pawnbroker Louis Kimmel and Seattle pawnbroker Alan Goldman, longtime North Carolina pawnbroker Leo Finkelstein was a bedrock of his hometown. He was among Asheville's "most highly respected people," and his oral history resides in the collection of the local university. Obituaries lionized Finkelstein when he died in 1999 at ninety-three, describing him as an "active force" in various fraternal and benevolent organizations including the Lion's Club, the Elks, the Masons, the Jewish Aid Society, and Temple Beth Ha Tephila, of which he was a founding member. His musical ensemble, "the Sanctimonious Seven," played charity gigs all around the area.[16]

Finkelstein mused, "The day of the old-time hockshop is over," its shelves no longer filled with false teeth, strange surgical appliances, and woolen overcoats. In some ways he was right. Ever adaptive to the times, pawnbrokers have replaced metal screens with bullet-proof glass and limited their inventory primarily to jewelry, electronics, leather jackets, and guns. Yet the spirit of the "old-time hockshop" lives on in many local communities. Pawnbrokers remain rooted there, patronized by generations of pawners, some of whom follow them to new shops. Take, for example, pawnbroker Jay Rosado, featured in a recent *New York Times* piece, who intended to work only a few weeks in the business but has been running his own shop in the South Bronx for twelve years. Reminiscent of PLS pawners who trailed clerks to new branch offices, one of Rosado's customers followed him when he opened Mr. Pawnbroker, pawning an engagement ring for $650 not because she needed the money but "to welcome him to the neighborhood."[17] Customers have invited the proprietor of McGarry's in Philadelphia, a shop that's been around since the 1850s, to countless weddings, funerals, and baptisms. She has seen many through good times and bad, has heard tragic stories she'd rather not retell, and does her best to make her people feel comfortable and welcome: they get "McGarryized." Of course this thoughtful service and reliability ensures that people will come back and is ultimately a good business strategy. But many pawnbrokers also allow personal gestures to cut into their profit margins. They grant leniency to certain loyal customers by freezing interest charges or holding collateral well beyond the expiration of the loan and, like Leo Finkelstein—who gave customers back their unredeemed coats during Depression winters—may subsidize them in particularly hard times.

Such personalized transactions are not possible in the chain pawnshops, independent pawnbrokers' most formidable competition. Extremely well capitalized and centrally organized, chains increasingly offer complementary fringe lending services such as payday lending, loans via the Internet, and instant refunds during income tax season. These places also do quite well in the resale businesses. Cash America, for example, started with one store in 1983 and now has over five hundred outlets in twenty-two states; the company posted a revenue of some $600 million in 2005 and has a listing on the New York Stock Exchange.[18] It is hard to imagine, though, going to a Cash America outlet hoping to pawn a rat trap or one's underwear, as Birmingham pawners did at Steel City, or writing to the owner of the company and asking for collateral to be held past the loan's expiration, as Hands Loan Company customers were able to do.

Big or small, most pawnbrokers are members of the National Pawnbrokers Association (NPA), a trade group that helps its constituency maintain market share and compete with other fringe lenders. The organization lobbies on behalf of members for favorable legislation. Just as important, it strives to burnish the profession's public image. The NPA urges its members to conduct themselves "in such a manner as to enhance and promote the positive and professional image of all pawnbrokers," and as an official trade organization one of its key missions is "to contribute to the professional and personal development of member pawnbrokers and member associates through the enhancement of the images and perceptions of the industry."[19] There is even a National Pawnbrokers Day, every December 6. A press release reminds the public that "today's pawnshops are attractive, welcoming places to do business. Most of them are family-owned and operated shops that offer superb customer service. . . . Need a television, diamond bracelet or tools? Your neighborhood pawnshop just may be the place to find a good deal!" Part of pawnbrokers' image campaign includes addressing misperceptions about their customers. "Did you know?" the NPA Web site asks,

- Nearly 8 out of 10 pawn customers return for their items.
- More than 92% of borrowers are employed.
- About 33% of pawn customers are homeowners.
- More than 25 million Americans annually use pawn services.[20]

The NPA and its members have a vested economic interest in promoting pawning as a "normal" activity and dispelling deep-seated stereotypes that have developed over centuries. Pawners are ordinary people who live in houses and have jobs, just like the rest of us. And pawnbrokers are not unscrupulous Shylocks but regular folks, possibly your own neighbors.

Trips to the pawnshop continue to be a regular part of the lives of millions of Americans. As the country hunkers down to face a financially uncertain future, the pawnshop will perhaps play an even more important role in helping people to make ends meet and to cope with the exigencies of postindustrial credit capitalism. After decades of decline, the pawnbroking industry has experienced rapid growth in recent years. In 1988 there were an estimated 6,900 pawnshops in the country.[21] Today there are about 12,000.[22]

While payday lenders and predatory mortgage companies are now the deserved subjects of public and government scrutiny (and bailouts), pawnbrokers continue to be the easiest to demonize. This is not only because of their long history in this country but also because, ironically, they are not as anonymous as corporate lenders. We can connect individual names and faces with many pawnbroking establishments, even though the commercial behemoths that operate today enjoy a much larger share of the personal credit market. Indeed, the credit and poverty industry profiteers reap the benefits of the work undertaken by nineteenth-century reformers, businessmen, politicians, and cultural critics who stigmatized pawnbrokers and marginalized pawnbroking at the same time as they themselves were capitalizing on people's need, directly and indirectly.

White-collar predatory lending is mirrored by thriving gray and black markets, which also constitute an important part of the fringe economy and are themselves undergoing a transformation resulting from advances in technology, population sprawl, and diffuse social networks. Again, it is easiest to target pawnbrokers, who are still assumed to be major traffickers in stolen goods ("slightly criminal," as it was recently put to me). As a matter of course, movies and television police dramas depict the pawnbroker as a receiver. Pawnshops cannot practically avoid taking in stolen goods on occasion, and undoubtedly there are some who are active receivers. Dayton, Ohio, pawnbroker Ric Blum has remarked that "only stupid thieves bring stolen property to pawnshops. It is a sure way to get caught."[23] But in an article on stolen goods that Blum wrote for the trade journal *Today's Pawnbroker*, he admitted, "It would be unfair of me to say that no stolen property ever winds up in pawnshops. It does. There are also some unethical pawnbrokers who encourage thieves to patronize them. We are not all angels."[24]

Yet many independent pawnbrokers work closely with police, developing relationships akin to those seen in the nineteenth century. Pawnbroker Louis Kimmel remarks that "the biggest misconception is that pawnshops were a hotbed for stolen merchandise. Our store was really a hotbed for recovering stolen property." He adds, "We had a good name. We always conformed with city ordinances on interest rates, never sold or lost any of our customers' stuff and were never called before the Better Business Bureau."[25] The owner of McGarry's introduced me to Philadelphia police officer Linda Fell of the Pawnshop Investigation Unit, with whom she is on good terms.

According to authorities, constant police surveillance (with daily and sometimes hourly reporting requirements) deters pawnbrokers from crime, whether selling firearms illegally or trafficking in stolen goods. Like other large cities, Philadelphia, where I live, has a Pawnshop Investigation Unit that is an integral part of the Police Department. According to the department's Web site, the unit "is responsible for coordinating the investigation of pawnshops and their operation to ensure compliance with the city ordinances and state banking regulations."[26] Part of its job is to conduct annual background checks on pawnbrokers and their employees before license renewal, investigate new license applicants, and monitor the city's precious metals dealers. In addition, the unit teams up with state and federal investigators on cases involving jewelry store robberies and thefts of art and artifacts.

As in the past, scrap and precious metals dealers, not pawnbrokers, are the main conduits of stolen goods, according to Officer Fell. With the recent rise in copper prices there have been more scrap metal scroungers stealing copper piping from construction sites. Precious metals dealers are more high-end, taking in gold, platinum, and silver.[27] Required to hold the items they buy for only five days, these dealers quickly melt down jewelry, silver services, and similar items, rendering them permanently beyond identification and recovery.[28] Although pawnbrokers in Pennsylvania, like scrap and precious metals dealers, can now buy goods over the counter, they are accountable for these purchases and have to hold them before they can resell them.

Officer Fell and her staff examine about a half a million pawn transactions each year (a fraction of the total number), looking for patterns—transactions with known criminals and certain kinds of goods being pawned in certain locations. "Follow the goods and you follow the criminals," Fell advises, not unlike the strategies employed by nineteenth-century law enforcement officers such as police inspector William Bell. Pawnbrokers' daily reports to police help track criminals who are suspected of theft and those with outstanding warrants. In fact, pawnbrokers' accounts often provide crucial personal information that police themselves do not have access to. If accurate, pawnbrokers' records, as I know from my own experience at Simpson's, contain identification numbers, addresses, telephone numbers, Social Security numbers, and sometimes even photos and fingerprints. With the increasing integration of technology into pawnbrokers' record-keeping systems, this information is much easier to record, manage, and make accessible to authorities.

Because only pawnbrokers and dealers in precious metals and scrap metals have to report their transactions to police (not, for example, wholesale and retail dealers), stolen goods are trafficked through a number of alternative markets—if money itself doesn't trickle down, the capitalist ethos of profit-making certainly does. Officer Fell points to the gas station that also sells tires, baby formula, car stereos, and even jewelry: a lot of this merchandise is stolen. Flea markets are notorious places to move stolen goods as well: "Maybe not the granny who's got crocheted pot holders; she probably didn't steal those," says Fell, "but that guy selling all those tools down at the end of the bargain mart? Those are probably stolen."[29] She doesn't mention the most immense flea market of all, eBay, but the tens of thousands of virtually anonymous transactions that take place on the Web site every day underscore her point—there are plenty of other stores, shops, institutions, and sites of informal transactions that are not accountable to authorities through licensing or regular reporting. Like nineteenth-century entrepreneurs of the underworld, today's participants in gray and black markets make a buck using the latest innovations (whether for producing fake gemstones or selling stolen goods over the Internet).

Certainly, a fair number of stolen goods *do* come through pawnshops—in the same year two of my friends have recovered their stolen property (tools in one case, a computer in the other) from pawnshops near where the thefts occurred. They were lucky. Most goods, whether cycled through eBay, flea markets, scrap metal dealers, or pawnshops, are not recovered because they cannot be identified. In order for stolen property to be recovered, the goods "have to be unique and unique to you." But few people take the time to compile property lists detailing product makes and models, serial numbers, special inscriptions, and anything else individuating possessions—whether heirloom brooches or electronics—describing the unique features of an item and establishing a clear chain of ownership. Our relationship to possessions in a throwaway culture is paradoxical. Material objects tend to mean a great deal to us in the aggregate. Yet we typically do not think enough about the individual things we own to bother to know them as intimately as our nineteenth-century predecessors did.[30]

For the wealthy, there remain a few high-end pawnshops to discreetly take care of financial embarrassments. The Beverly Loan Company, an upscale pawnshop in Beverly Hills, California, for example, offers valet parking, has fine art hanging on the walls, and features a gigantic hourglass filled with cascading diamonds in its showroom. It has been in the same family since it opened in 1938. Its Web site describes the business as "specializing in large collateral loans," apparent from the images of gemstone-studded Cartier watches and diamond-encrusted platinum rings that appear on the home page. Located in an office building just off of

Rodeo Drive, the shop pays an armed guard who sits behind bulletproof glass. Business is strictly confidential; pawners who need quick cash can conduct their affairs in private offices, and the well-screened employees sign agreements forbidding them ever to reveal customers' identities.[31] Accepting flashy collateral and serving an A-list clientele, Beverly Loan, featured in a *People* magazine article a few years ago, is perfectly palatable to mainstream consumers. Then-owner Jean Zimmelman explained that "a lot of customers come in after a divorce. Maybe a woman wants cosmetic work; she borrows against her wedding ring. Attorneys and plastic surgeons don't wait for their money."[32] Sanitized and spruced up, it is associated with the rich and famous rather than the down-and-out. (Indeed, collateral here is not "left unredeemed" but instead is "foreclosed.")

West Palm Beach pawnbroker Levi Touger calls Beverly Loan "one of the most successful pawnshops in the country," because the rich, too, have credit problems. He would know; his Royal Pawn and Jewelry has seen an increase in traffic by wealthy pawners since the Bernard Madoff Ponzi scheme came to light. Some of Madoff's victims have offered Touger as collateral a Ferrari, a Tiffany ring, a $17,000 seventy-two-inch plasma screen television, and a yacht worth over half a million dollars. Like the poor, the rich do not necessarily understand the true value of their possessions. According to Touger, "A customer may be shocked to learn, for example, that a diamond that cost $30,000 is worth only about $8,000 on the wholesale market.[33]

Perhaps an apt subject for feel-good puff pieces, upscale pawnshops, like the loan offices of the late nineteenth century catering to the elite, represent only a fraction of the pawnbroking industry as a whole. A more accurate picture of contemporary pawning comes from a recent issue of the *National Pawnbroker*, the trade journal of the NPA. It is filled with articles about navigating Bureau of Alcohol, Tobacco, and Firearms laws regarding gun dealing; pending legislation proposing to cap interest rates for loans to soldiers on active duty; growing competition from payday lenders; privacy issues arising from authorities' unencumbered access to databases with customers' information; and tips for spotting Rolex replicas. The magazine's advertisements also highlight the collective needs and concerns of today's pawnbrokers. PawnMaster is one of many computer software systems for "pawn management." Pawnguard offers several models of digital safes to hold jewelry and other valuable collateral. Several metal-refining services (Raising the Bar, We're Golden Retrievers) promise quick turnaround, no minimums, and the best prices for converting old jewelry into solid gold and silver. Other outfits buy diamonds and musical instruments, The Ring Man buys sports championship jewelry, and still others sell aftermarket watch accessories— two-tone watchbands, bezels with princess diamonds, refinished dials, and more.

There are also advertisements for gemstone appraisal courses and notices about the annual convention, which is often in Las Vegas.[34]

True to the logic of capitalism, if there is money to be made, people will find a way to make it. The poverty industry offers a surprising number of avenues for profit. People making money off the pawnbrokers include lobbyists working Capitol Hill on behalf of the NPA, insurance agents selling policies to pawnshops, diamond cutters and gold smelters, and purveyors of business management software. Pawnbrokers, of course, are making money off the pawners by collecting interest and selling unredeemed collateral.

It is easy for us to demonize pawnbrokers even today, because we have been doing so for centuries. Even though some, like the chain pawnshops, can be highly profitable and often resemble any other "big box" store, pawnshops still seem to inhabit a world we typically consider outside mainstream business. We have internalized the nineteenth-century campaigns launched by cultural critics, reformers, businessmen, and politicians. The stereotypes they helped create remain entrenched today, and they may continue to vex the profession as long as pawnbroking exists. But perhaps we should not be so quick to choose pawnbrokers to excoriate, of all the credit purveyors out there. In times of need, such as our current economic climate of shrinking budgets and contracted credit, "My Uncle" might be the only relative we can turn to for money.

NOTES

CHAPTER ONE

1. W. R. Patterson, "Pawnbroking in Europe and the United States," *Bulletin of the Department of Labor,* no. 21 (March 1899): 173–310.

2. In addition to rates' varying from state to state, sometimes, as in Arkansas, where pawnshop interest rates are not regulated, they can vary *within* a state. Sliding scales (lower rates based on higher loans), and additional processing, ticket writing, and storage fees make it difficult to accurately calculate individual state interest rates. John Caskey provides a suggestive, if dated, chart of various interest rates and loan terms in *Fringe Banking: Check-Cashing Outlets, Pawnshops, and the Poor* (New York: Russell Sage Foundation, 1994), 40–41. He also explains why pawnshops are concentrated in the South and why the rates charged there tend to be much higher than those assessed by pawnbrokers in the North; see esp. 48–52. For legal interest rates and usury laws in the eighteenth and nineteenth centuries, see J. B. C. Murray, *The History of Usury from the Earliest Period to the Present Time* (Philadelphia: J. B. Lippincott, 1866).

3. Scholars have traced the origins of systematized pawnbroking to fifth-century Chinese monasteries that oversaw funds referred to as "long life cash." Also called the "inexhaustible treasury," the pot of money came from estates of deceased nobility and from donations made in exchange for monks' prayers. In addition to offering lodging, caring for the sick, and burying the dead, monks also loaned money as a public service. Eventually the laity took control of pawnbroking, charging profit-yielding interest on loans secured by personal property. See T. S. Whelan, *The Pawnshop in China,* based on *Yang Chao-yü, Chung-kuo tien-tang yeh* (*The Chinese Pawnbroking Industry*), with a historical introduction and critical annotations (Ann Arbor: Center for Chinese Studies, University of Michigan, 1979), esp. 1–16. Pawnbroking in China may also have descended from the practice of exchanging political prisoners, often members of the aristocracy. According to Whelan, "The character *chih,* . . . 'a hostage,' came to mean 'an earnest' or 'a pledge' and subsequently became a general term for the Buddhist institution of pawning during the Six Dynasties and the T'ang" (*Pawnshop in China,* 3).

4. See, for example, "Pawns, Pawners, and Pawn-Brokers," *Once a Week* 10 (March 19, 1864): 340–41. Historian Raymond de Roover, though, has discredited this explanation of the pawnbroker's three balls because "the Church considered pawnbrokers as common or 'manifest' usurers. As such, they were not entitled to the protection of a patron saint." See de Roover, "The Three Golden Balls," *Bulletin of the Business Historical Society* 20, 4 (October 1946): 118. An intriguing but unsubstantiated story is that the symbol derives from the three branches of pomegranates that embellished the ancient silver shekel of Israel.

5. De Roover, "Three Golden Balls," 122, 124.

6. Kenneth Hudson, *Pawnbroking: An Aspect of British Social History* (London: Bodley Head, 1982), 22.

7. Murray, *History of Usury*, 42.

8. "Advances to the prince and feudal lords were for considerable amounts and were secured by collateral of great value," according to Raymond de Roover in *Money, Banking and Credit in Mediaeval Bruges: Italian Merchant-Bankers, Lombards and Money-Changers, a Study in the Origins of Banking* (Cambridge, Mass.: Mediaeval Academy of America, 1948), 119.

9. For a definitive study on the subject, see Joseph Shatzmiller, *Shylock Reconsidered: Jews, Money-Lending, and Medieval Society* (Berkeley: University of California Press, 1990).

10. For more on the origins and meanings of the mont-de-piété, see Patterson, "Pawnbroking in Europe and the United States," 174. Patterson provides a substantive overview of the development of modern pawnbroking. For the emergence of pawnbroking in other countries, see Jim Fitzpatrick, *Three Brass Balls: The Story of the Irish Pawnshop* (Doughcloyne, Wilton, Cork: Collins Press, 2001); Heiko Schrader, *Lombard Houses in Saint Petersburg: Pawning as a Survival Strategy of Low-Income Households?* Market, Culture and Society 10 (Hamburg: Lit, 2000); and Marie Eileen Francois, *A Culture of Everyday Credit: Housekeeping, Pawnbroking, and Governance in Mexico City, 1750–1920* (Lincoln: University of Nebraska Press, 2006).

11. Patterson, "Pawnbroking in Europe and the United States," 174, 182.

12. Patterson, "Pawnbroking in Europe and the United States," 174, 213.

13. Patrick Colquhoun, *A Treatise on the Police of London* (Philadelphia: Benjamin Davies, 1798), 20, 111. Population figures for London are from the 1801 census. See "A Population History of London: The Demography of Urban Growth, 1760–1815," http//www .oldbaileyonline.org/static/Population-history-of-london.jsp#a1760–1815.

14. The name had staying power. In the mid-nineteenth century a "gripe-fist" was a broker or a miser. See George W. Matsell, *Vocabulum, or The Rogue's Lexicon* (New York: George W. Matsell, 1859), 39.

15. Jenny Uglow, *Hogarth: A Life and a World* (London: Faber and Faber, 1997), 493.

16. *A Few Reasons in Favour of Vendues* ([Philadelphia: Henry Miller, 1772]).

17. Odd Langholm, *The Aristotelian Analysis of Usury* (Bergen, Norway: Universitetsforlaget, 1984), 56.

18. For a much more detailed account, see Benjamin Nelson, *The Idea of Usury: From Tribal Brotherhood to Universal Otherhood*, 2nd ed. enl. (Chicago: University of Chicago Press, 1969), xix.

19. Henry Smith, *The Examination of Usury: A Sermon Preached in the City of London* ([Boston?]: Booksellers, 1751), 11–13; quotation on 13.

20. Smith, *Examination of Usury*, 5.

21. Nelson, *Idea of Usury*, xxiii–xxiv.

22. Experts often make fine distinctions between interest and usury that are not apparent to laypeople. For example, usury, according to historian Eric Kerridge, "is the taking of payment over and above the amount lent merely and solely in return for a secured loan," while interest "is in compensation of a man's *verum interesse*, of his true interest in a business." See Kerridge, *Usury, Interest, and the Reformation* (Aldershot, Hants, UK: Ashgate, 2002), 5.

23. Susan L. Buckley, *Teachings on Usury in Judaism, Christianity and Islam* (Lewiston, NY: Edwin Mellen, 2000), 161.

24. Adam Smith, *An Inquiry into the Nature and Causes of the Wealth of Nations*, new ed. (Philadelphia: Printed for Thomas Dobson, 1789), 42.

25. Jeremy Bentham, *A Defence of Usury: Shewing the Impolicy of the Present Legal*

Restraints on the Terms of Pecuniary Bargains (London: Printed for T. Payne, and Son, 1787), 1; original emphasis.

26. Bentham, *Defence of Usury*, 6.

27. John A. Bolles, *A Treatise on Usury and Usury Laws* (Boston: James Munroe, 1837), vii.

28. Billy G. Smith, *The "Lower Sort": Philadelphia's Laboring People, 1750–1800* (Ithaca, NY: Cornell University Press, 1990), 200. For more on the lives of workers during the first half of the nineteenth century, see Paul Gilje, ed., *Wages of Independence: Capitalism in the Early American Republic* (Madison, WI: Madison House, 1997); Bruce Laurie, *Working People of Philadelphia, 1800–1850* (Philadelphia: Temple University Press, 1980); and Sean Wilentz, *Chants Democratic: New York City and the Rise of the American Working Class, 1788–1850* (New York: Oxford University Press, 1984).

29. Ann Fabian discusses the outsider status of nineteenth-century gamblers who engaged in moneymaking that was "the antithesis of both production and consumption." See Fabian, *Card Sharps, Dream Books, and Bucket Shops: Gambling in 19th-Century America* (Ithaca, NY: Cornell University Press, 1990), 11. Pawnbrokers too were not considered part of the rational economy (but in fact were central to it).

30. Scholars debate the true causes of the Panic of 1837, the worst of its kind up to that point, but many agree that it was brought about by Andrew Jackson's ill-advised banking policies. Distrusting banks in general and a national bank in particular (because it was seen as having monopolistic control over the nation's money), Jackson disbanded the national bank, funneling specie (hard currency) into local banks. Jackson's policies forced people to pay their taxes in gold or silver, which they did not have.

31. For a description of "The Times," see Bernard F. Reilly Jr., *American Political Prints, 1766–1876: A Catalogue of the Collections in the Library of Congress* (Boston: G. K. Hall, 1991), 102.

32. In her article on Jewish merchants and credit reporting, Rowena Olegario writes, "Arguably, much of what we term 'business culture' revolves around the question of what constitutes creditworthiness: Who deserves credit?" Her argument raises another issue: businessmen must also have been wondering who deserved to be a lender. See "'That Mysterious People': Jewish Merchants, Transparency, and Community in Mid-Nineteenth Century America," *Business History Review* 73 (Summer 1999): 162.

33. See Fabian, *Card Sharps*, 3.

CHAPTER TWO

1. Humphrey Humdrum, *Mother Midnight's Comical Pocket-Book, or A Bone for the Criticks* ([Boston]: Zechariah Fowle, 1763), 32.

2. "Poetics," *New-York Daily Gazette*, November 1, 1790.

3. Ellen Schiff, "Shylock's *Mishpocheh*: Anti-Semitism on the American Stage," in *Anti-Semitism in American History*, ed. David A. Gerber (Urbana: University of Illinois Press, 1986), 80.

4. Schiff, "Shylock's *Mishpocheh*," 80–81.

5. Robert Morris to Richard Butler, Philadelphia, August 26, 1782, in *The Papers of Robert Morris, 1781–1784*, vol. 6, ed. John Catanzariti and E. James Ferguson (Pittsburgh: University of Pittsburgh Press, 1984), 253–54.

6. Of the twenty-five brokers in Philadelphia during the Revolution, only two were Jewish: Haym Salomon and Moses Cohen, and both were highly respected. See Edwin Wolf 2nd and Maxwell Whiteman, *The History of the Jews in Philadelphia from Colonial Times to the Age of Jackson* (Philadelphia: Jewish Publication Society of America, 1956), 105.

7. John J. Appel, "Jews in American Caricature: 1820–1914," *American Jewish History* 71, 1 (September 1981): 108.

8. Appel, "Jews in American Caricature," 107.
9. Michael N. Dobkowski, *The Tarnished Dream: The Basis of American Anti-Semitism* (Westport, CT: Greenwood Press, 1979), 79. For more on the development of the Jewish stereotype over time, see Rudolf Glanz, *The Jew in Early American Wit and Graphic Humor* (New York: KTAV, 1973), and Avner Ziv and Anat Zajdman, eds., *Semites and Stereotypes: Characteristics of Jewish Humor,* Contributions in Ethnic Studies 31 (Westport, CT: Greenwood Press, 1993).
10. Leonard Dinnerstein, *Antisemitism in America* (New York: Oxford University Press, 1994), 14.
11. Dinnerstein, *Antisemitism,* 13.
12. As Glanz has written, "For a long time, the religious notions of the founders of the American civilization so dominated the Americans' image of the Jew that his appearance as a real member of a living contemporaneous community of people came to their consciousness only slowly and reluctantly. The contrast between the real subject, the Jewish people struggling for survival as a community of human beings in new times and on a new continent, and the unreal picture consisting of a mixture of the most diverse interpretations of Biblical literature, led to the wildest notions: the identification of the Indians as the Lost Ten Tribes of Israel, the importance of the conversion of the Jews as a preliminary to the redemption of the world, and continuous comparisons of various Christian sects with Judaism, all of which almost erased the real living Jew." *Jew in Early American Wit and Graphic Humor,* 13–14.
13. "Biblicus," "Queries respecting the Jews," *Monthly Magazine, and American Review* 3, 3 (September 1800): 184.
14. "Querist," "What Is a Jew?" *Monthly Magazine, and American Review* 3, 5 (November 1800): 324; original emphasis.
15. "Querist," "What Is a Jew?" 325.
16. "J. Sommers," *New York Evening Post,* August 25, 1817.

17. "J. Sommers," *National Advocate,* August 26, 1817; original emphasis.
18. "We did not observe," *New York Evening Post,* August 27, 1817; spelling as in the original.
19. "Had not a certain," *New York Flagellator,* September 6, 1828; original emphasis.
20. Dobkowski, *Tarnished Dream,* 80.
21. "The Jewish Sabbath," *Sunday Flash,* October 17, 1841.
22. Dinnerstein, *Antisemitism,* 15.
23. Dinnerstein, *Antisemitism,* 19. Historians have located the origins of Shylock (the "supervillain") in Judas, and have also seen the figure's reappearance in Chaucer's *Canterbury Tales,* in Shakespeare's *Merchant of Venice,* and as Dickens's Fagin in *Oliver Twist.* See in particular Louise A. Mayo, *The Ambivalent Image: Nineteenth-Century America's Perception of the Jew* (Rutherford, NJ: Fairleigh Dickinson University Press, 1988), 40.
24. "Crime among the Israelites," *National Police Gazette,* July 11, 1846.
25. Mayo, *Ambivalent Image,* 44.
26. Jerome V. C. Smith, "The Jew-Broker of Damascus," *Gleason's Pictorial Drawing-Room Companion* 5, 22 (November 26, 1853): 346.
27. Edwin T. Freedley, *A Practical Treatise on Business, or How to Get, Save, Spend, Give, Lend, and Bequeath Money, with an Inquiry into the Chances of Success and Causes of Failure in Business* (Philadelphia: Lippincott, Grambo, 1853), 95; passage reprinted in Freeman Hunt, *Worth and Wealth: A Collection of Maxims, Morals and Miscellanies for Merchants and Men of Business* (New York: Stringer and Townsend, 1856), 149.
28. "Bargains. Commerce, Trade, Barter, Swap, Exchange, Wrap, &c." *New England Artisan, Laboring Man's Repository* 2, 5 (January 31, 1833): 4; spelling as in the original.
29. John Beauchamp Jones, *The Winkles, or The Merry Monomaniacs* (New York: D. Appleton, 1855), 171–72; original emphasis.
30. William R. Simpson and Florence K. Simpson with Charles Samuels, *Hockshop:*

The Fabulous Story of the "Emperors of Pawnbroking" (New York: Random House, 1954),
3.

31. Simpson and Simpson, *Hockshop*, 4.

32. "Pawnbrokery in New York," *Hours at
Home* 7, 3 (July 1868): 251, 247, 248, 246.

33. Douglas Jerrold, "The Pawnbroker,"
New-York Mirror 19, 9 (February 27, 1841): 65.

34. Jerrold, "Pawnbroker," 65; "Pawn Brokers and Their Assistants," *Whip*, February 5,
1842.

35. Jerrold, "Pawnbroker," 65.

36. Stuart M. Blumin in the introduction to
the reprint edition of George Foster's *New
York by Gas-Light and Other Urban Sketches*
(Berkeley: University of California Press,
1990), 60.

37. George Foster, *New York in Slices* (New
York: William H. Graham, 1849), 22.

38. Foster, *New York in Slices*, 24.

39. Foster, *New York in Slices*, 30.

40. Foster, *New York in Slices*, 32–33.

41. *Estelle Grant, or The Lost Wife* (New
York: Garrett, 1855), 331.

42. Frank Luther Mott, *A History of American
Magazines*, vol. 2, *1850–1865* (Cambridge,
MA: Harvard University Press, 1938), 301.

43. Eliza Cook, "Obscure City Life," *Ladies'
Repository* 12, 1 (January 1852): 31.

44. Cook, "Obscure City Life," 31.

45. M. S. G. Nichols, "Cousin Fanny," *Graham's Magazine* 34, 6 (June 1849): 354.

46. "Pawnbrokers," *New Bedford Mercury*,
February 2, 1833.

47. "A great work," *Monthly Cosmopolite*,
April 1, 1850, and "H. Long & Brother . . .
have just published," *Godey's Lady's Book* 40,
1 (January 1850): 83.

48. For more on Bennett, see *The Dictionary of American Biography*, vol. 2, ed. Allen
Johnson (New York: Charles Scribner's Sons,
1929), 193–94.

49. Walter Sutton, *The Western Book Trade:
Cincinnati as a Nineteenth-Century Publishing
and Book-Trade Center* (Columbus: Ohio State
University Press, 1961), 205.

50. Emerson Bennett, *The Artist's Bride, or
The Pawnbroker's Heir* (New York: Garrett,
Dick and Fitzgerald, 1859), 13.

51. Bennett, *Artist's Bride*, 399–400.

52. Bennett, *Artist's Bride*, 399–400.

53. Bennett, *Artist's Bride*, 402.

54. "Literary Notices," *Godey's Lady's Book*
56, 1 (January 1858): 84–85.

55. Richard B. Kimball, *Undercurrents of Wall-
Street: A Romance of Business* (New York:
G. P. Putnam, 1862), 357; my emphasis.

56. Julia McNair Wright, *Our Chatham Street
Uncle, or The Three Golden Balls* (Boston:
Henry Hoyt, 1869), 80.

57. Wright, *Our Chatham Street Uncle*, 70.

58. Wright, *Our Chatham Street Uncle*, 132.

59. Wright, *Our Chatham Street Uncle*, 258.

60. Wright, *Our Chatham Street Uncle*,
326–27.

61. Wright, *Our Chatham Street Uncle*, 340.

62. H. Hastings Weld, "The Mourning Ring,"
Godey's Lady's Book 26, 6 (June 1843): 277–85.

63. See, for example, George Canning Hill,
"The Last Pawn," *Gleason's Pictorial Drawing-Room Companion* 2, 16 (April 17, 1852):
250–51.

64. It should not be surprising, then, that a
major theme appearing in both *The Three
Golden Balls* and *Our Chatham Street Uncle*
was the problem of marriage between Jews
and gentiles. Historian David Gerber has
described the relationship between these two
groups in the antebellum era as "freighted . . .
with a dual burden: the historic legacy of
religious and social prejudice and the more
general problem of business relations, across
a vast cultural and physical distance, between
strangers in a changing economy." See "Elite
Anti-Semitism in the Marketplace," in Gerber,
Anti-Semitism in American History, 211.

65. Quoted in Gerber, "Elite Anti-Semitism,"
219.

66. "Chatham Street Auctioneers," *Sunday
Flash*, September 19, 1841.

67. "Chatham Street," *Broadway Omnibus*,
November 1, 1858.

68. Wright, *Our Chatham Street Uncle*, 8.

69. Leslie A. Fiedler, "What Can We Do about Fagin? The Jew-Villain in Western Tradition," *Commentary* 7 (1949): 412.

70. "The Opera Excitement," *New York Picayune*, November 15, 1856.

71. Jones, *Winkles*, 32.

72. James W. Redfield, *Outlines of a New System of Physiognomy* (New York: J. S. Redfield, 1849), 10.

73. A "shave" was a popular term for someone who took more than a fair cut when exchanging money; a "sharp dealer," according to Webster, specifically when discounting notes of exchange. "To shave, is to cut off a portion of the outside; hence to strip, deprive, take away unjustly, as a robber or hard dealer; one who does this is a *shaver*," according to John Russell Bartlett's *Dictionary of Americanisms* (New York: Bartlett and Welford, 1848). Bartlett adds, "This word, in the United States, is applied to money brokers, who purchase notes at more than legal interest," 295. "Shave" also might have another meaning, referring more directly to "the Jew with the Knife," a murderous character willing to sacrifice even his own children for money. See Fiedler, "What Can We Do about Fagin?" 411–18.

74. James Redfield, *Comparative Physiognomy, or Resemblances between Men and Animals* (New York: W. J. Widdleton, 1866), 308.

75. "Notices of the Fine Arts," *Godey's Lady's Book* 38, 3 (March 1849): 219.

76. *The Illustrated Annuals of Phrenology and Physiognomy* (New York: S. R. Wells, 1873), 18.

77. "Our Fashions and Fancy Work," *Nick-Nax for All Creation* 1, 7 (November 1856): 224.

78. "The Pawn-Broker," *Nick-Nax for All Creation* 1, 3 (July 1856): 74.

79. "Love and Hard Times," *Nick-Nax for All Creation* 2, 10 (February 1858): 295.

80. "The Tendency of the Times: A Lesson to Heads of Families," *Harper's Weekly* 18, 891 (January 24, 1874): 88.

81. Names such as Bentley, Bohan, Hogan, Morton, and Norden appear in greater numbers in the various city directories under the pawnbroking profession. At the height of midcentury immigration, the Irish engaged in junk dealing. By the end of the century cities had greater call for pawnbroking, which required similar skills but was more lucrative than the junk business.

82. Michael N. Dobkowski, "American Anti-Semitism: A Reinterpretation," *American Quarterly* 29, 2 (Summer 1977): 171.

83. Mayo, *Ambivalent Image*, 85.

84. Frank Luther Mott, *A History of American Magazines*, vol. 3, *1865–1885* (Cambridge, MA: Harvard University Press, 1938), 528. *Judge's Library* circulation figure is from James H. Dormon, "Ethnic Stereotyping in American Popular Culture," *Amerikastudien* 30, 4 (1985): 490.

85. Mayo, *Ambivalent Image*, 85; *Judge* quoted in Dormon, "Ethnic Stereotyping," 490.

86. *Puck*, October 17, 1888, 117; June 14, 1893, 259; January 18, 1893, 348.

87. Dormon, "Ethnic Stereotyping," 490. He notes the special issue of *Judge*, "Our Friend: The Hebrew," published in 1890. Other special issues included one lampooning the Irish Aristocracy and several "black-oriented" issues such as one appearing in 1902 titled "Melon Time" (491).

88. Appel, "Jews in American Caricature," 111.

89. Eugene Zimmerman, *Cartoons and Caricatures, or Making the World Laugh* (Scranton, PA: Correspondence Institute of America, 1910), 20.

90. Appel, "Jews in American Caricature," 113.

91. Quoted in Appel, "Jews in American Caricature," 122.

92. Mark Twain, "Concerning the Jews," in *The Complete Essays of Mark Twain*, ed. Charles Neider (Garden City, NY: Doubleday, 1963), 237.

93. Twain, "Concerning the Jews," 239.

94. Historian Dave Cheadle notes that Philadelphia printer David Heston would provide advertisers with 10,000 trade cards for $20, while a New York City dry goods chain "bragged of their intention to distribute 100,000 trade cards in a single season." See Cheadle, *Trade Cards: Historical Reference and Value Guide* (Paducah, KY: Collector Books, 1998), 11. For more on the history of trade cards, see Robert Jay, *The Trade Card in Nineteenth-Century America* (Columbia: University of Missouri Press, 1987). For more on the rise of color printing, see Peter C. Marzio, *The Democratic Art: Chromolithography, 1840–1900* (Boston: David R. Godine, 1979).

95. Richard L. Bushman and Claudia L. Bushman, "The Early History of Cleanliness in America," *Journal of American History* 74, 4 (March 1988): 1228.

96. Quoted in Suellen Hoy, *Chasing Dirt: The American Pursuit of Cleanliness* (New York: Oxford University Press, 1995), 92. For more on the linkage between cleanliness and race in popular culture, see Jackson Lears, *Fables of Abundance: A Cultural History of Advertising in America* (New York: Basic Books, 1994), esp. chap. 6, "The Perfectionist Project."

97. George Miller and Dorothy Miller, *Picture Postcards in the United States, 1893–1918* (New York: Clarkson N. Potter, 1976), 22.

98. Miller and Miller, *Picture Postcards,* 206.

99. G. B. Brigham, *A New Comic Song: Hock Shop, or It's Over in the Hock Shop Now* (Chicago: G. B. Brigham, 1894). Digital images available from the Lester S. Levy Collection of Sheet Music, Special Collections at the Sheridan Libraries of Johns Hopkins University, http://levysheetmusic.mse.jhu.edu/.

100. Harry Koler, "Big Chief Dynamite" (Chicago: Will Rossiter, 1909), Lester S. Levy Collection of Sheet Music.

101. Harold Payne, "The Shylock Pawnbroker," *Beadle's Dime Library,* 68, 883 (New York: Beadle and Adams, 1895).

102. Internet Movie Database, www.imdb.com.

103. Griffith wrote the screenplay but did not direct.

104. Quoted in Patricia Erens, *The Jew in American Cinema* (Bloomington: Indiana University Press, 1984), 31.

105. "At the Pawnbroker," *Every Saturday* 2, 62 (March 4, 1871): 214.

106. "Pawnbrokers' Clerks," *Bismarck (ND) Daily Tribune,* August 18, 1888.

107. E. C. Matthews, *How to Draw Funny Pictures* (Chicago: Frederick J. Drake, 1928), 89.

CHAPTER THREE

1. John J. McCusker and Russell R. Menard, *The Economy of British America, 1607–1789* (Chapel Hill: University of North Carolina Press for the Institute of Early American History and Culture, 1985), 347.

2. Robert Morris to Richard Butler, Philadelphia, August 26, 1782, in *The Papers of Robert Morris, 1781–1784,* vol. 6, ed. John Catanzariti and E. James Ferguson (Pittsburgh: University of Pittsburgh Press, 1984), 253–54.

3. Quoted in Roy A. Foulke, *The Sinews of American Commerce* (New York: Dun and Bradstreet, 1941), 89–90.

4. "Hendrick Oudenaarde, Broker," *New-York Journal, or General Advertiser,* November 26, 1767. For more on early brokers, see McCusker and Menard, *Economy of British America,* 347, and Carl Bridenbaugh, *Cities in Revolt: Urban Life in America, 1743–1776* (New York: Knopf, 1955), 286–89.

5. "Jonas Phillips, Auctioneer and Broker," *New-York Journal, or General Advertiser,* June 21, 1770.

6. For more on the early American economy, see Robert Greenhalgh Albion, *The Rise of New York Port, 1815–1860* (New York: Charles Scribner's Sons, 1970); Bridenbaugh, *Cities in Revolt;* Thomas M. Doerflinger, *A Vigorous Spirit of Enterprise: Merchants and Economic Development in Revolutionary Philadelphia* (Chapel Hill: University of North Carolina Press for the Institute of Early American History and Culture, 1986); Cathy Matson, *Merchants and Empire: Trading in Colonial New York* (Baltimore: Johns Hopkins University

Press, 1998); Cathy Matson, ed., *The Economy of Early America: Historical Perspectives and New Directions* (University Park: Pennsylvania State University Press, 2006); and McCusker and Menard, *Economy of British America*.

7. T. H. Breen, *Tobacco Culture: The Mentality of the Great Tidewater Planters on the Eve of Revolution* (Princeton, NJ: Princeton University Press, 1985), 93.

8. For more on specie versus paper currency, see Cathy Matson, "The Revolution, the Constitution, and the New Nation," in *The Cambridge Economic History of the United States*, vol. 1, *The Colonial Era*, ed. Stanley Engerman and Robert E. Gallman (New York: Cambridge University Press, 1996), esp. 366–70. See also John J. McCusker, *Money and Exchange in Europe and America, 1600–1775* (Chapel Hill: University of North Carolina Press for the Institute of Early American History and Culture, 1978), esp. chap. 1, "Money, Rates of Exchange, and Bills of Exchange: An Introduction," 3–26.

9. According to Wm. P. M. Ross's *The Accountant's Own Book and Business Man's Manual* (Philadelphia: G. B. Zieber, 1848), brokers "negotiate sales of produce between different merchants, [and] usually confine themselves to some department or line of business" (68). Because early directories often lumped all sorts of businessmen under the title "broker," it is difficult to know for sure who was a pawnbroker. In later decades, when city directories listed people by occupation or profession, most brokering professions were listed under *B* ("broker, cotton" "broker, real estate," etc.) while pawnbroking had its own category in the *P* section.

10. John A. Paxton, *The Philadelphia Directory and Register, for 1813* (Philadelphia: B. and T. Kite, [1813]), printed matter pasted to inside of front board.

11. Albion, *Rise of New York Port*, 336.

12. Foulke, *Sinews*, 116.

13. *A Law to Regulate Pawnbrokers, and Dealers in the Purchase or Sale of Second-Hand Furniture, Metal or Clothes: Passed July 13th, 1812* (New York, 1812).

14. "Money! Money! Money!" *Baltimore American*, October 15, 1833. My thanks to Seth Rockman for pointing me to this advertisement and to Baltimore City Council Records.

15. Foulke, *Sinews*, 118. Baltimore City Council Records from 1819 contain a "supplement" to the ordinance on pawnbrokers, suggesting that regulations were already on the books. "Urban Danger," Baltimore City Council Records [1819] RG 16 S1, box 18, item 467. Collection of the Baltimore City Archives. Population statistics based on 1830 figures, Campbell Gibson, "Population of the 100 Largest Cities and Other Urban Places in the United States: 1790–1990," Population Division, U.S. Bureau of the Census, June 1998, Population Division Working Paper 27, table 6. http://www.census.gov/population/www/documentation/twps0027/twps0027.html.

16. "Urban Danger."

17. Petition to Jesse Hunt on behalf of Sarah Millem, Baltimore, November 6, 1832. Baltimore City Archives, RG 9 S2, box 9, 1832, 1170.

18. W. O. Stoddard, "Pawnbrokers and Loan-Offices," *Harper's New Monthly Magazine* 39 (June 1869): 125.

19. Samuel W. Levine, *The Business of Pawnbroking: A Guide and a Defence* (New York: D. Halpern, 1913), 52–53.

20. Sommer was convicted of charging his customers 65% interest rather than the legal 7%. His name probably made it into the 1818 city directory only because it was compiled in 1817. Sommer likely was out of business by the time the directory appeared in print.

21. See *Matchett's Baltimore Director, Corrected up to June 1829* (Baltimore, 1829); *Matchett's Baltimore Director, Corrected up to September, 1835* (Baltimore, 1835); *Matchett's Baltimore Director, Corrected up to May 1837* (Baltimore: Baltimore Director Office, 1837); and *Match-*

ett's Baltimore Director for 1853–54 (Baltimore: Richard J. Matchett, 1853).

22. John Adams Paxton, *The Philadelphia Directory and Register, for 1819* ([Philadelphia]: Editor, [1819]); Edward Whitely, *The Philadelphia Directory and Register, for 1820* ([Philadelphia]: M'Carty and Davis, [1820]); Edward Whitely, *The Philadelphia Directory and Register, for 1821* ([Philadelphia]: M'Carty and Davis, 1821); Edward Whitely, *The Philadelphia Directory and Register, for 1822* ([Philadelphia]: M'Carty and Davis, 1822); Robert Desilver, *The Philadelphia Index, or Directory, for 1823* ([Philadelphia]: Editor, [1823]); Robert Desilver, *The Philadelphia Index, or Directory, for 1824* ([Philadelphia]: Editor, [1824]); *The Philadelphia Directory and Stranger's Guide, for 1825* (Philadelphia: John Bioren, 1825); Robert Desilver, *Desilver's Philadelphia Directory and Stranger's Guide, for 1828* (Philadelphia: Robert De[s]ilver, 1828); Robert Desilver, *Desilver's Philadelphia Directory and Stranger's Guide, for 1829* (Philadelphia: Robert De[s]ilver, 1829); Robert Desilver, *Desilver's Philadelphia Directory and Stranger's Guide, for 1830* (Philadelphia: Robert Desilver, 1830); Robert Desilver, *Desilver's Philadelphia Directory and Stranger's Guide, for 1831* (Philadelphia: Robert Desilver, 1831); Robert Desilver, *Desilver's Philadelphia Directory and Stranger's Guide, for 1833* (Philadelphia: Robert Desilver, 1833); *Longworth's American Almanac, New-York Register, and City Directory* (New York: David Longworth, 1803); *Longworth's American Almanac, New-York Register, and City Directory* (New York: David Longworth, 1810); *The New-York Business Directory for 1844 and 1845* (New York: John Doggett Jr., 1844); *Longworth's American Almanac, New-York Register, and City Directory* (New York: Thomas Longworth, 1830–40); *Wilson's Business Directory of New-York City . . . for 1849* (New York: John F. Trow, 1849); *Harris's General Business Directory of the Cities of Pittsburgh and Allegheny* (Pittsburgh: A. A. Anderson, 1847); *The Boston Directory . . . for 1855* (Boston: George Adams, 1855); *Desilver's Philadelphia Directory and Stranger's Guide, for 1837* (Philadelphia: Robert Desilver, 1837); *McElroy's Philadelphia Directory, for 1850* (Philadelphia: Edward C. and John Biddle, 1850). For more on the occupational and social worlds of nineteenth-century clerks, see Brian Luskey, "Jumping Counters in White Collars: Manliness, Respectability, and Work in the Antebellum City," *Journal of the Early Republic* 26 (Summer 2006): 173–219, and Brian Luskey, *On the Make: Striving Clerks, Counter Jumpers, and the Quest for Capital in Nineteenth-Century America* (New York: New York University Press, 2010).

23. George Chaplin, interview by Dale Rosengarten, October 3, 1995, Charleston, South Carolina. Jewish Heritage Collection, College of Charleston Library, MSS 1035–41.

24. Alexander Keyssar, *Out of Work: The First Century of Unemployment in Massachusetts* (Cambridge: Cambridge University Press, 1986), 37.

25. See Foulke, *Sinews*, 117, 118. Population statistics based on 1830 figures for New York City from "New York (Manhattan) Wards: Population and Density 1800–1910," http://www.demographia.com/db-nyc-ward1800.htm.

26. Based on a work year of 313 days at 81¢ a day for unskilled laborers and $1.10 a day for skilled laborers for the year 1821. See Robert A. Margo and Georgia C. Villaflor, "The Growth of Wages in Antebellum America: New Evidence," *Journal of Economic History* 47, 4 (December 1987): 893, 894; figures from table 5, "Nominal Daily Wage Rates for Artisans, 1821–1856," and table 6, "Nominal Daily Wage Rates for Unskilled Labor, 1821–1856." See also Robert A. Margo, "Wages and Labor Markets before the Civil War," *American Economic Review* 88, 2 (May 1998): 51–56.

27. Quoted in Levine, *Business of Pawnbroking*, 22–23.

28. "The Pawnbroker," *New York Daily Times*, November 19, 1855.

29. W. R. Patterson, "Pawnbroking in Europe and the United States," *Bulletin of the Department of Labor*, no. 21 (March 1899): 275; figures rounded to the nearest hundred.

30. Levine, *Business of Pawnbroking*, 32.

31. Statistics regarding the number of pawnbrokers in 1911 from Levine, *Business of Pawnbroking*, 31 and 101. Population statistics for cities listed are for 1910, gathered from Gibson, "Population of the 100 largest Cities and Other Urban Places in the United States: 1790–1900," table 14, Population of the 100 Larges Urban Places: 1910," http://www.census.gov/population/documentation/twps0027/tabl4.txt; and Thirteenth Census of the United States: 1910, http://www.census.gov/prod2/decennial/documents/36894832v3_TOC.pdf.

32. For a detailed portrait of one such neighborhood in New York City, see Tyler Anbinder, *Five Points* (New York: Plume, 2002). He writes that although there were pawnshops throughout the city, "the neighborhood's dozens of 'second-hand' and junk shops located on Baxter Street served as informal pawnshops," 116.

33. James D. McCabe, *The Secrets of the Great City: A Work Descriptive of the Virtues and the Vices, the Mysteries, Miseries and Crimes of New York City* (Philadelphia: National, [1868]), 356.

34. Junius Henri Browne, *The Great Metropolis: A Mirror of New York* (Hartford, CT: American, 1869), 474.

35. *Wilson's Business Directory of New-York City . . . for 1849* (New York: John F. Trow, 1849); and New York (N.Y.) Common Council, *Manual of the Corporation of the City of New York* (New York, 1849).

36. George G. Foster, "'Philadelphia in Slices' by George G. Foster," with an introduction by George Rogers Taylor, *Pennsylvania Magazine of History and Biography* 93 (1969): 34–35.

37. This was especially true before consolidation in 1854. See Allen Steinberg, *The Transformation of Criminal Justice. Philadelphia,*

1800–1880 (Chapel Hill: University of North Carolina Press, 1989).

38. Emma Jones Lapsansky, *Neighborhoods in Transition: William Penn's Dream and Urban Reality* (New York: Garland, 1994), 140.

39. Lapsansky, *Neighborhoods*, 110.

40. *A Guide to the Stranger, or Pocket Companion for the Fancy, Containing a List of the Gay Houses and Ladies of Pleasure in the City of Brotherly and Sisterly Affection* (Philadelphia, 1849), 17.

41. See *Bywater's Philadelphia Business Directory and City Guide, for the Year 1850* (Philadelphia: Maurice Bywater, [1849]), 113.

42. Louise Marion Bosworth, *The Living Wage of Women Workers* (New York: Longmans, Green, 1911), 26.

43. For more on Baltimore, see James Silk Buckingham, *America, Historical, Statistic, and Descriptive* ([London]: Fisher, [1841]), vol. 1; and Sherry H. Olson, *Baltimore: The Building of an American City* (Baltimore: Johns Hopkins University Press, 1980).

44. Perry R. Duis, *Challenging Chicago: Coping with Everyday Life, 1837–1920* (Urbana: University of Illinois Press, 1998), 310.

45. "Wage Map No. 1," *Hull-House Maps and Papers: A Presentation of Nationalities and Wages in a Congested District of Chicago* (New York: Thomas Y. Crowell, 1895).

46. *Hull-House Maps and Papers*, 21.

47. Duis, *Challenging Chicago*, 311.

48. Stuart Blumin, *The Emergence of the Middle Class: Social Experience in the American City, 1760–1900* (New York: Cambridge University Press, 1989), 105. Here Blumin quotes William Sumner, who likened large retailers to "feudal chiefs."

49. "Pawnbrokers' Shops: Their Habituees and Characteristics," *San Francisco Daily Evening Bulletin*, December 5, 1872.

50. Browne, *Great Metropolis*, 475.

51. Douglas Jerrold, "The Pawnbroker," *New-York Daily Mirror* 19, 9 (February 27, 1841): 65.

52. Richard B. Kimball, *Undercurrents of*

Wall-Street: A Romance of Business (New York: G. P. Putnam, 1862), 357.

53. "The Night Hawk," no. 27, *Mechanic's Free Press,* July 4, 1829.

54. "Auction Sales: And Loan Office," *Business Journal and Traveller* (Philadelphia), April 12, 1856.

55. Frank H. Norton, "Up the Spout," *Harper's New Monthly Magazine* 19 (1859): 673.

56. Edmund Mottershead III, "Pawn Shops," *Annals of the American Academy of Political and Social Science* 196 (March 1938): 150.

57. Albert Bigelow Paine, "At the Sale of the Unredeemed," *Century Magazine* 47 (January 1905): 360.

58. For 1850 figures see J. J. Lee and Marion R. Casey, eds., *Making the Irish American: History and Heritage of the Irish in the United States* (New York: New York University Press, 2006), 14. For later figures see Kevin Kenny, *The American Irish: A History* (Harlow, UK: Pearson Education, 2000), 105–6. For 1860 figures see Gibson, "Population of the 100 Largest Cities and Other Urban Places in the United States: 1790–1900," table 9, "Population of the 100 Larges Urban Places: 1860," http://www.census.gov/population/documentation/twps0027/tab9.txt. For Chicago, see "Jews," in Chicago Historical Society, *The Encyclopedia of Chicago,* www.encyclopedia.chicagohistory.org.

59. *Hull-House Maps and Papers,* 91, 93.

60. See Edwin Wolf 2nd and Maxwell Whiteman, *The History of the Jews in Philadelphia from Colonial Times to the Age of Jackson* (Philadelphia: Jewish Publication Society of America, 1956), 185.

61. On the history of usury and religion, see Eric Kerridge, *Usury, Interest, and the Reformation* (Burlington, VT: Ashgate, 2002); Joseph Shatzmiller, *Shylock Reconsidered: Jews, Moneylending, and Medieval Society* (Berkeley: University of California Press, 1990); and Norman L. Jones, *God and the Moneylenders: Usury and the Law in Early Modern England* (Oxford: Blackwell, 1989).

The history of Jews in retail and resale trades can be found in Jacob Rader Marcus, *United States Jewry 1776–1985,* 4 vols. (Detroit: Wayne State University Press, 1989–93).

62. Marcus, *United States Jewry,* 1:157–58.

63. Jacob Rader Marcus, *Memoirs of American Jews, 1775–1865* (Philadelphia: Jewish Publication Society of America, 1955–56), 1:305.

64. According to the U.S. Census of 1850, auctioneer Moses Nathans and his wife supported seven children at their address in addition to four servants (three Irish women and a fourteen-year-old black boy).

65. Bruce Mann, *Republic of Debtors: Bankruptcy in the Age of American Independence* (Cambridge, MA: Harvard University Press, 2002), 7. See also Edward Balleisen, *Navigating Failure: Bankruptcy and Commercial Failure in Antebellum America* (Chapel Hill: University of North Carolina Press, 2001).

66. David A. Gerber, "Cutting Out Shylock: Elite Anti-Semitism and the Quest for Moral Order in the Mid-Nineteenth-Century American Marketplace," in *Anti-Semitism in American History,* ed. David A. Gerber (Urbana: University of Illinois Press, 1986), 213, 219, 223. The subjects of Gerber's study were Jews in Buffalo, but their economic life was similar to those in other cities. For a more favorable account of Dun and Bradstreet credit reports on Jewish businesses, see Rowena Olegario, "'That Mysterious People': Jewish Merchants, Transparency, and Community in Mid-Nineteenth Century America," *Business History Review* 73 (Summer 1999): 161–89.

67. Tony A. Freyer, *Producers versus Capitalists: Constitutional Conflict in Antebellum America* (Charlottesville: University Press of Virginia, 1994), 74.

68. *Matchett's Baltimore Director for 1853–4* (Baltimore: Richard J. Matchett, 1853), front matter, 27.

69. Petition to Jesse Hunt on behalf of Sarah Millem; newspaper advertisement, "Widow Sarah Millem," *Baltimore American,* October 10, 1833. See also *Matchett's Baltimore Director, Corrected up to May 1833* (Baltimore, 1833) and *Matchett's Baltimore Director, Corrected up to May 1837* (Baltimore: Baltimore Director Office, 1837).

70. Baltimore City Ordinances, 1828.

71. Virginia Penny, *Five Hundred Employments Adapted to Women* (Philadelphia: John E. Potter, 1868), 406.

72. *The Lakeside Annual Directory of the City of Chicago* (Chicago: Chicago Directory Company, 1880).

73. *Appleton's Dictionary of New York and Its Vicinity* (New York: D. Appleton, 1892), 193–94.

74. Norton, "Up the Spout," 673.

75. Boyden Sparkes, "Is Your Watch at Simpson's?" *Saturday Evening Post* 209, 35 (February 27, 1937): 31.

76. Eve Garrette, "The Hockshops of New York," *Good Housekeeping* 108, 1 (January 1939): 25.

77. William R. Simpson and Florence K. Simpson, with Charles Samuels, *Hockshop: The Fabulous Story of the "Emperors of Pawnbroking"* (New York: Random House, 1954).

78. For more on the Simpsons, see "Robert Simpson," *New York Times*, June 9, 1898; "William Simpson's Death," *New York Times*, April 10, 1879; and "A Family of Pawnbrokers," *St. Louis Globe-Democrat*, August 11, 1878. The quotation is from *Appleton's Dictionary*, 194.

79. *Appleton's Dictionary*, 194.

80. Simpson and Simpson, *Hockshop*, 4.

81. "A Millionaire's Death," *Milwaukee Sentinel*, August 13, 1872.

82. Philadelphia tax lists, Cedar Ward, for 1833, 1835–38, 1840, and Philadelphia census of 1840.

83. New York City Census, 1850.

84. Levine, *Business of Pawnbroking*, 36.

85. "Pawn-Brokers," *National Advocate*, December 31, 1828. Population statistics based on 1830 figures, from "New York (Manhattan) Wards: Population and Density, 1800–1910," http://www.demographia.com/db-nyc-ward1800.htm.

86. "Statistics of Poverty," *Hunt's Merchants' Magazine* 43 (1860): 343. Population statistics based on 1860 figures, from "New York (Manhattan) Wards: Population and Density, 1800–1910." Figures are based on geographic area of pawnbrokers surveyed. Those on the "eastern side of the city" were compared against population figures for wards 2, 4, 7, 10, 11, 13, and 17.

87. Provident Loan Society of New York, *Third Annual Report* (New York: Marion Press, 1898), 7.

88. Patterson, "Pawnbroking in Europe and the United States," 273–74. Statistics for other cities are Pittsburgh, 3,328 pawns totaling $17,113.35; Providence, 3,679 pawns totaling $11,574.97; Buffalo, 3,174 pawns totaling $18,615.65; and Boston, 16,113 pawns totaling $38,620.

89. Mottershead, "Pawn Shops," 149.

90. Champion Bissell, "A Study of Pawnbrokers," *Lippincott's* 53 (1894): 226.

91. Levine, *Business of Pawnbroking*, 67–69.

92. Frank A. Fetter, *The Principles of Economics with Applications to Practical Problems* (New York: Century, 1904), 132.

93. "Hard Times—the Run on the Pawnbrokers," *Newark Advocate*, October 6, 1876.

94. "A Talk with a Pawnbroker," *St. Louis Globe-Democrat*, February 5, 1877.

95. "Hard Times: What New York Pawnbrokers Say," *San Francisco Daily Evening Bulletin*, August 14, 1877.

96. "Failure of Pawnbrokers," *New York Times*, September 3, 1893.

97. "Business Troubles," *New York Times*, January 19, 1895.

98. Rolf Nugent, *The Provident Loan Society of New York: An Account of the Largest Remedial Loan Society* (New York: Russell Sage Foundation, 1932), 11.

99. Mottershead, "Pawn Shops," 151.

100. See Leo Finkelstein obituary and "Local businessman Finkelstein dies at 93," both in *Asheville (NC) Citizen-Times*, March 24, 1999; "Finkelstein Made Many Marks," *Asheville Citizen-Times*, March 26, 1999; and interview conducted on February 5, 1993, by Dorothy Joynes for the Voices of Asheville Oral History Collection, University of North Carolina at Asheville, Special Collections/University Archives, OH-VOA F56 Le.

101. M. R. Neifeld, *The Personal Finance Business* (New York: Harper and Brothers, 1933), 45.

102. Joseph Cantrell, Annette Watters, Ahmad Ijaz, et al., "Alabama's Economic Indicators," *Alabama Economic and Business Indicators*, University of Alabama, http://cber.cba.ua.edu/rbriefs/abl299.html.

103. Joe Williams to Ralph Hands, Salinas, CA, undated but ca. late February or early March 1938; "Friendly reminder" from Hands Loan Company to Lauren J. Williams, February 23, 1938. Hands Loan Company Records, Holt-Atherton Special Collections, University of the Pacific Library (hereinafter Hands Loan Company Records).

104. David Carr to Ralph Hands, Reno, November 29, 1937. Hands Loan Company Records.

105. Emma Mitchell to Ralph Hands, Stockton, CA, May 15, 1937. Hands Loan Company Records.

106. James H. Davis to Ralph Hands, Aspermont, TX, September 5, 1937. Hands Loan Company Records.

107. Mrs. W. J. Blackiston to Ralph Hands, Alameda, TX, June 3, 1937. Hands Loan Company Records.

108. Glenn Foley to Ralph Hands, San Francisco Loan Co. undated, ca. March 9, 1937. Hands Loan Company Records.

109. W. P. Holmes to Ralph Hands, no place and undated, ca. 1937. Hands Loan Company Records.

110. Steel City Pawnshop, Open Accounts Receivable, 1930 to 1931, Account Book, alphabetized *A* to *S*, 1930, Main Account Book, 1930, Records 298.1.1.1.1–298.1.3.2.9. Birmingham Public Library, Department of Archives and Manuscripts, Birmingham, Alabama. The ledgers are unbound and fragmentary; only parts of each ledger survive, and some pages are filed out of order. This list is compiled from both books.

111. Donald Paneth, "From the American Scene: Pawnbroker on Eighth Avenue, a Portrait," *Commentary* 17 (March 1954): 281.

112. Paine, "At the Sale of the Unredeemed," 366.

113. Stoddard, "Pawnbrokers and Loan-Offices," 128, 126.

114. *Appleton's Dictionary*, 194.

115. "'Up the Spout,'" *New York Times*, September 3, 1871.

116. "The Pawnbrokers of New York," *Great Republic Monthly* 2, 1 (July 1859): 26.

117. "Two Kinds of Pawnbrokers," *Atchison (KS) Champion*, February 8, 1890.

118. "Hard Times: What New York Pawnbrokers Say."

119. Richard Edwards, *The Industries of Philadelphia* (Philadelphia: Richard Edwards, 1881), 219.

120. Garrette, "Hockshops of New York," 107.

121. "Enterprising," *Cleveland Herald*, September 2, 1881.

122. "Enterprising."

123. "Enterprising."

124. "Enterprising."

125. "Enterprising."

CHAPTER FOUR

1. John Simpson Record Book, August 2, 1838, to February 22, 1839 (hereafter cited as Simpson Record Book), New-York Historical Society Manuscript Collection. The pawnshop was at 25 Chatham Street. I thank Ted O'Reilly, manuscript reference librarian, for locating this item.

2. The broader term "pledge" refers to all

forms of security, not only physical property but also real estate, stocks and bonds, and other assets put up as collateral for a loan. The narrower "pawn" applies specifically to a physical object used as loan security. In *A Treatise on the Law of the Contract of Pledge* (New Orleans: F. F. Hansell, 1898), Henry Denis elaborated on the various forms of the pledge: "It takes the shape of bills of lading. . . . It takes the shape of *margin* in the sale of futures, for money itself may be pledges. It takes the shape of bottomry bonds in maritime contingencies. It takes the shape of warehouse receipts when money is borrowed on merchandise at home. It takes the shape of policies of insurance either on life or property" (6).

3. James Schouler, *A Treatise on the Law of Bailments,* 3rd ed. (Boston: Little, Brown, 1897), 171.

4. Cathy Matson, *Merchants and Empire: Trading in Colonial New York* (Baltimore: Johns Hopkins University Press, 1998), 66.

5. John J. McCusker and Russell R. Menard, *The Economy of British America, 1607–1789* (Chapel Hill: University of North Carolina Press for the Institute of Early American History and Culture, 1985), 335.

6. See Roy A. Foulke, *The Sinews of American Commerce* (New York: Dun and Bradstreet, 1941), 111–13. For more on interest rates charged on private transactions, see Sidney Homer and Richard Sylla, *A History of Interest Rates* (New Brunswick, NJ: Rutgers University Press, 1996), 274–79.

7. The phrase "everybody but capitalists" comes from the article "'Uncle' of All Mankind," *Milwaukee Daily Republican-Sentinel,* October 22, 1882.

8. Elizabeth Blackmar, *Manhattan for Rent, 1785–1850* (Ithaca, NY: Cornell University Press, 1989), 240.

9. Robert A. Margo, "The Rental Price of Housing in New York City, 1830–1860," *Journal of Economic History* 56, 3 (September 1996): 605–25. He writes that the length of

contract "had a significant effect on rent" (612).

10. Christine Stansell, *City of Women: Sex and Class in New York, 1789–1860* (Urbana: University of Illinois Press, 1987), 6–7.

11. James Mease, *On the Utility of Public Loan Offices and Savings Funds, Established by City Authorities* ([Philadelphia? 1836]), 1.

12. "Pawnbrokers and Loan-Offices," *Harper's New Monthly Magazine* 39 (1869): 126.

13. People "employed in the building, textile, and other finishing trades, followed seasonal manufacturing calendars and adjusted their household economies to unpredictable turns in income," according to Blackmar, *Manhattan for Rent,* 239.

14. Lee J. Vance, "Banks for the People," *North American Review* 160, 460 (March 1895): 382.

15. "To My Valentine" ([New York?]: McLoughlin, ca. 1900). Author's collection.

16. Stansell, *City of Women,* 12.

17. Rolf Nugent, *The Provident Loan Society of New York: An Account of the Largest Remedial Loan Society* (New York: Russell Sage Foundation, 1932), 12.

18. John Truair, *A Call from the Ocean, or An Appeal to the Patriot and the Christian in Behalf of the Seamen* (New York: John Gray for "the American Seamen's Friend Society," 1826), 19n. I thank Peter Reed for bringing to my attention this aspect of early pawning in coastal cities.

19. Chester Whitney Wright, *Economic History of the United States* (New York: McGraw-Hill, 1949), 332.

20. Stansell, *City of Women,* 12. Women's names populate the Simpson Record Book in large numbers. Although most pawners were listed by surname only, it is safe to assume that many of these too were women.

21. Charles Barnard, "Pawnshops and Small Borrowers," *Chautauquan* 19 (April 1894): 72.

22. Melanie Tebbutt, *Making Ends Meet: Pawnbroking and Working-Class Credit* (New York: St. Martin's Press, 1983), 10.

23. Amy Dru Stanley, "Conjugal Bonds and Wage Labor," *Journal of American History* 75, 2 (September 1988): 496–97.

24. Suzanne Lebsock, *The Free Women of Petersburg: Status and Culture in a Southern Town, 1784–1860* (New York: W. W. Norton, 1984), 56.

25. For more on the disjuncture between the legal and lived worlds of women, see the work of Margot Finn, especially "Women, Consumption and Coverture in England, c. 1760–1860," *Historical Journal* 39, 3 (1996): 703–22.

26. Tebbutt, *Making Ends Meet*, 46–47.

27. Margaret Winkle to Ralph Hands, Tulsa, July 20, [1937]. Holt-Atherton Special Collections, University of the Pacific Library, Stockton, California.

28. G. Frank Brockway to "Friend Jones," May Port East Florida, January 26, 1875. Collection of the Connecticut Historical Society, Hartford.

29. Mathew Carey, "Essays on the Public Charities of Philadelphia, Intended to Vindicate the Benevolent Societies of This City from the Charge of Encouraging Idleness," in *Miscellaneous Essays,* 5th ed. (Philadelphia: Carey and Hart, 1830), 191, 193. For more on wages and the cost of living during the early nineteenth century, see Donald R. Adams Jr., "Wage Rates in the Early National Period: Philadelphia, 1785–1830," *Journal of Economic History* 28 (1968): 404–26.

30. Julia McNair Wright, *Our Chatham Street Uncle, or The Three Golden Balls* (Boston: Henry Hoyt, 1869), 91–92.

31. Louise Bolard More, *Wage-Earners' Budgets: A Study of Standards and Cost of Living in New York City,* Greenwich House Series of Social Studies 1 (New York: Henry Holt, 1907), 147.

32. "Two Kinds of Pawnbrokers," *Atchison (KS) Champion,* February 8, 1890.

33. W. R. Patterson, "Pawnbroking in Europe and the United States," *Bulletin of the Department of Labor,* no. 21 (March 1899): 276–77. Redemptions recorded in the Simpson ledger

also bear this out. Madelon Powers describes Saturday payday as "the social highlight of the week for many workers," who took some of their wages home to cover family expenses (including, no doubt, repaying loans) and then spent the rest of the night and their money drinking in saloons. See *Faces along the Bar: Lore and Order in the Workingman's Saloon, 1870–1920* (Chicago: University of Chicago Press, 1998), 53.

34. Working Women's Protective Union, *Twelfth Annual Report of the Working Women's Protective Union* (New York: Working Women's Protective Union, [1875?]), [3].

35. Proprietor of McGarry's, Philadelphia, in discussion with the author, January 2004.

36. "The Pawnbrokers of New York," *Harper's Weekly* 11, 558 (September 7, 1867): 561.

37. Simpson Record Book, August 15, 1838. Mrs. McKnight, listed at "Reed" (i.e., Reade) is entry 64; Hanah Gold, at "Center" (i.e., Centre) is entry 91.

38. John Beachamp Jones, *The Winkles, or The Merry Monomaniacs* (New York: D. Appleton, 1855), 33.

39. *Harper's Weekly* 1, 36 (September 5, 1857): 576. See also "Pawnbrokers and Loan-Offices," which observed, "More than one fashionable leader has been known to procure the means for her summer trip to Newport or Saratoga by depositing with a 'broker' or an auctioneer such articles of value as she would not require in her absence" (128).

40. Edward Howland, "The Bankers of the Poor," *Galaxy* 3 (1867): 662.

41. "The Night Hawk," no. 33, *Mechanic's Free Press,* October 3, 1829.

42. "Who'd a Thought of Seeing You?" sheet music (New York: Atwill, ca. 1830). Collection of the American Antiquarian Society, Worcester, Massachusetts.

43. T. H. Breen, *The Marketplace of Revolution: How Consumer Politics Shaped American Independence* (Oxford: Oxford University Press, 2004), 55. Paul G. E. Clemens describes the "consumer revolution" from 1760 to

1820 as one that brought status and comfort to households of the Middle Atlantic. See Clemens, "The Consumer Culture of the Middle Atlantic, 1760–1820," *William and Mary Quarterly* 62, 4 (October 2005): 577–624.

44. Breen, *Marketplace of Revolution*, 102–3.

45. "Pawn-Brokers," *National Advocate*, December 31, 1828.

46. "By Whiteley and Bevan," *Baltimore Patriot*, December 15, 1831.

47. For other auction advertisements for unredeemed goods, see, for example, M. Thomas and Son's ads in the *Mechanic's Free Press*, October 24, 1829, and March 27, 1830.

48. Representative entries from pages of Simpson Record Book.

49. "Pawn-Brokers," *National Advocate*.

50. "The Number of Articles Received," *Saturday Evening Post*, January 17, 1829; "Pawn-Brokers," *Atlas*, January 10, 1829. Probably owing more to a lack of statistics than for any other reason, these figures were cited repeatedly throughout the nineteenth century. Some writers even appropriated the figures as their own, such as John F. Watson, who in his *Annals of Philadelphia*, published in 1905, quoted them verbatim, failing to mention that "the city" referred to was New York, not Philadelphia, and that the figures were seventy-seven years old. Watson, *Annals of Philadelphia* (Philadelphia: Edwin S. Stuart, 1905), 239.

51. Carey, "Essays on the Public Charities," 160. According to a pawnbroker-informant working today, this is a realistic number and would be even higher if it included loan renewals.

52. Simpson Record Book. Total number of pawns recorded from August 2, 1838, to February 22, 1839.

53. "Pawn-Brokers," *National Advocate*. Calculated on annual loan terms, these rates were inflated. Typically a pawner would repay his loan within a month, and often loan durations were even shorter and loan amounts smaller.

54. Carey, "Essays on the Public Charities," 161.

55. See U.S. Federal Census, 1830, High Street Ward, Philadelphia, and U.S. Federal Census, 1840, Southwark Ward, Philadelphia. The William M'Clean appearing in the directories during this time moves from north Philadelphia to south Philadelphia and could plausibly be the head of household represented in the two Philadelphia wards.

56. Horace Mann, *Remarks upon the Comparative Profits of Grocers and Retailers, as Derived from Temperate and Intemperate Customers* (Boston: Ford and Damrell, 1834), 8.

57. McLean did not redeem his watches, since his pawn tickets were never forfeited to pawnbroker Holmes but instead found their way into a collection of miscellaneous financial instruments at the Historical Society of Pennsylvania in Philadelphia. Holmes mistakenly inscribed 1834 on ticket no. 36.

58. Carey, "Essays on the Public Charities," 158–59.

59. George Foster, *New York in Slices* (New York: W. F. Burgess, 1849), 32–33; spelling as in the original.

60. Foster, *New York in Slices*, 33.

61. Pawners' Bank of Boston, *Pawners' Bank Sale: Sixth Semi-annual Sale* (Boston: Morrill and Son, [1863?]).

62. Campbell Gibson, "Population of the 100 Largest Cities and Other Urban Places in the United States: 1790 to 1900," Population Division Working Paper 27. U.S. Census Bureau, 1998. http://www.census.gov/population/www/documentation/twps0027.html.

63. See Edgar W. Martin, *The Standard of Living in 1860: American Consumption Levels on the Eve of the Civil War* (Chicago: University of Chicago Press, 1942), esp. 393–417.

64. "Life in Philadelphia," *Christian Recorder*, January 23, 1869.

65. Barnard, "Pawnshops and Small Borrowers," 72.

66. Provident Loan Society, *Sixth Annual Report* (New York: De Vinne Press, 1901), 9.

67. First State Pawners Society of Chicago, *Report of the President to the Stockholders at the Annual Meeting, November 17, 1908* (Chicago: Kendig and Hitchings, 1908), 10.

68. *Hull-House Maps and Papers: A Presentation of Nationalities and Wages in a Congested District of Chicago* (New York: Thomas Y. Crowell, 1895), 21–22.

69. Michael O'Malley writes that in the early 1830s "watches were still too expensive for most people," yet pawning data suggest that pocket watches were in common circulation by then. See O'Malley, *Keeping Watch: A History of American Time* (New York: Viking, 1990), 41.

70. Based on the week of August 15 to August 22, 1838.

71. Patterson, "Pawnbroking in Europe and the United States," 278–79.

72. For more on "singularizing" commodities, see Igor Kopytoff, "The Cultural Biography of Things: Commoditization as Process," in *The Social Life of Things: Commodities in Cultural Perspective*, ed. Arjun Appadurai (New York: Cambridge University Press, 1995), 64–91.

73. Timothy J. Gilfoyle, *A Pickpocket's Tale: The Underworld of Nineteenth-Century New York* (New York: W. W. Norton, 2006), 144.

74. M. L. Booth, *New and Complete Clock and Watchmakers' Manual* (New York: John Wiley, 1860), 275.

75. Figures cited in Martin, *Standard of Living*, 213–14, and taken from United States, Register of the Treasury, *Commerce and Navigation Report, 1860–61* (Washington, DC: George W. Bowman, 1861), 76–77, 198–99, and United States, Census Office, *Manufactures of the United States in 1860* (Washington, DC: GPO, 1865), 742.

76. *The Watch and Jewelry Trade of the United States* (New York: Wm. F. Bartlett, 1860), front matter, 8.

77. *Watch and Jewelry Trade*, 51.

78. J. W. Benson, *J. W. Benson's Illustrated Pamphlet of Watches, Clocks, Chains, Brooches, etc.* (London, 1860), 14. Guineas were then equivalent to £1.05, or $4.85 according to the exchange rates calculated on the Economic History Services Website: http://eh.net/hmit/.

79. John Fries and Son, *Now Established No. 822 Spring Garden St.* ([Philadelphia]: Sherman, [ca. 1869]).

80. Alexander Keyssar has written, "Nonagricultural occupations were becoming more common, household manufacturing was beginning to decline, and the population's dependence on the market was growing. Some jobs were becoming more specialized, and large-scale manufacturing ventures began to appear in towns like Waltham and Dudley." See Keyssar, *Out of Work: The First Century of Unemployment in Massachusetts* (Cambridge: Cambridge University Press, 1986), 14.

81. Display advertisement in *The St. Louis Directory for the Years 1854–5* (St. Louis: Chambers and Knapp, 1854), 45. See "Pawn Ticket," December 23, 1857, in *The Papers of Ulysses S. Grant*, vol. 1, *1837–1861*, ed. John Y. Simon (Carbondale: Southern Illinois University Press, 1967), 339–40. The original is in the Abraham Lincoln Presidential Library, Springfield, Illinois, item #SC 587.

82. Ulysses S. Grant, *Personal Memoirs of U. S. Grant* (New York: Charles L. Webster, 1885), 1:210, 211.

83. "American Jewelry," *Scientific American*, n.s., 3, 1 (July 2, 1860): 3. The article explained that "massive jewelry" was solid gold plate on inferior metal, "filled-in work" was made of thin sheets of gold stuck together with solder, and "plated" was inferior metal covered with a thin sheet of gold.

84. Martin, *Standard of Living*, 215.

85. David Jaffee, "Peddlers of Progress and the Transformation of the Rural North, 1760–1860," *Journal of American History* 78, 2 (September 1991): 511.

86. "Seeing Your Uncle," 8.

87. Robert Orr, *A Great Business in the Heart of the Great Metropolis* ([New York, ca. 1890]), 4.

88. Orr, *Great Business*, 6.

89. Gold, Coleman and Company, *Fall and Winter, 1905–1906* ([New York, 1905]).

90. "How New-Yorkers Live: Visits to the Homes of the Poor in the First and Fourth Wards," *New York Times*, June 20, 1859.

91. Rebecca Yamin, "Lurid Tales and Homely Stories of New York's Notorious Five Points," *Historical Archaeology* 32, 1 (1998): 74–85.

92. "The Pawnbroker," *New York Daily Times*, November 19, 1855. Pawnbrokers were offering redemption-by-mail services by the end of the century.

93. Hamilton Andrews Hill, *An Inquiry into the Relations of Immigration to Pauperism* (Boston: Alfred Mudge and Son, 1876), 6.

94. Jaffee, "Peddlers of Progress," 513.

95. Alexis de Tocqueville, *Democracy in America*, trans. Henry Reeve, 4th ed. (New York: J. and H. G. Langley, 1841), 2:229.

96. Karen Halttunen, *Confidence Men and Painted Women: A Study of Middle-Class Culture in America, 1830–1870* (New Haven, CT: Yale University Press, 1982), 61–62.

97. "A Talk with a Pawnbroker," *St. Louis (MO) Globe-Democrat*, February 5, 1877.

98. Tocqueville, *Democracy in America*, 137.

99. Tocqueville, *Democracy in America*, 137.

100. "Five Dollars Reward," *Kentucky Reporter*, July 5, 1820.

101. Jackson Lears, *Fables of Abundance: A Cultural History of Advertising in America* (New York: Basic Books, 1994), 46.

102. William Ellery Channing, *Lectures on the Elevation of the Laboring Portion of the Community* (Boston: Crosby and Nichols, 1863), 18.

103. In "The Cultural Biography of Things," Igor Kopytoff, posits that "schemes of valuation and singularization [are] devised by individuals, social categories, and groups" and that they "stand in unresolvable conflict with public commoditization as well as with one another," 80.

104. "The Pawnbroker's Window," *Hunt's Merchants' Magazine* 20 (1849): 92–93.

105. Richard B. Kimball, *Undercurrents of Wall-Street* (New York: G. P. Putnam, 1862), 356, 358.

106. William James, *The Principles of Psychology* (New York: Henry Holt, 1890), 1:291–92; original emphasis. See also Russell W. Belk, "Possessions and the Extended Self," *Journal of Consumer Research* 15 (September 1988): 139.

107. Thomas J. Schlereth, "Country Stores, County Fairs, and Mail-Order Catalogues," in *Consuming Visions: Accumulation and Display of Goods in America, 1880–1920*, ed. Simon J. Bronner (New York: W. W. Norton, for the Henry Francis du Pont Winterthur Museum, 1989), 364.

108. For more on the deployment of material culture to assert social status, see Kenneth Ames, *Death in the Dining Room and Other Tales of Victorian Culture* (Philadelphia: Temple University Press, 1992).

109. Simon J. Bronner, "Reading Consumer Culture," in Bronner, *Consuming Visions*, 26; William Leach, *Land of Desire: Merchants, Power, and the Rise of a New American Culture* (New York: Pantheon, 1993), 3.

110. Thorstein Veblen, *The Theory of the Leisure Class* (1899; New York: American Library, 1953), 35.

111. Veblen, *Theory of the Leisure Class*, 38.

112. Jonathan Gilmer Speed, "Pawnbrokers and the Poor," *Harper's Weekly* 36, 1863 (September 3, 1892): 862.

113. More, *Wage-Earners' Budgets*, 147.

114. *Papers of Ulysses S. Grant*, 339–40.

115. William R. Simpson and Florence K. Simpson with Charles Samuels, *Hockshop: The Fabulous Story of the "Emperors of Pawnbroking"* (New York: Random House, 1954), 16. On the Hope diamond, see also Harold Dambrot, "The History of Pawnbroking," pt. 6, "The Hope Diamond," *National Pawnbroker*, February 2008, 50.

116. "Statistics of Poverty," *Hunt's Merchants' Magazine* 43 (1860): 344.

117. This, in fact, proved the financial downfall of many pawnbrokers who went out of business during depressions. A common misconception was (and is) that pawnbrokers thrived during hard times. Since their capital was cash, if their customers could not redeem their pawns, pawnbrokers had no money to lend to others. They were often forced to obtain bank loans at much higher interest rates than they could legally lend at, making their financial situations untenable. And when seeking bank loans, the collateral they had in store—physical representations of the hard money they had loaned out—did not count toward their assets.

118. Data taken from sample week August 15 to August 22, 1838.

119. "'Uncle' of All Mankind."

120. Provident Loan Society, *First Annual Report* (New York: De Vinne Press, 1896), 21; *Second Annual Report* (New York: De Vinne Press, 1897), 5; *Third Annual Report* (New York: Marion Press, 1898), 7.

121. First State Pawners Society of Chicago, *Report of the President*, 10.

122. Quoted in Howland, "Bankers of the Poor," 665.

123. Mary C. Jackson, "Mrs. Jackson's Fund," typescript account of the Emergency Loan Fund, April 10, 1911, 2. Schlesinger Library, Radcliffe Institute for Advanced Study, Harvard University.

CHAPTER FIVE

1. "Lost or Stolen," *Georgia Gazette* (Savannah), October 25, 1764.

2. "Stolen or Taken Away," *South-Carolina Gazette and General Advertiser* (Charleston), June 24–26, 1784.

3. See representative ads in the *Pennsylvania Gazette*, December 16, 1729; January 5, 1731; December 5, 1734; July 8, 1736; October 26,

1738; April 3, 1755; September 13, 1764; September 18, 1766; May 21, 1767; and December 14, 1769. For other examples see "Lost or Stolen"; "Stolen or Taken Away"; and "Stolen," *South-Carolina Gazette and General Advertiser* (Charleston), March 30, 1785.

4. T. H. Breen, *The Marketplace of Revolution: How Consumer Politics Shaped American Independence* (New York: Oxford University Press, 2004), 104.

5. Quoted in Roy A. Foulke, *The Sinews of American Commerce* (New York: Dun and Bradstreet, 1941), 114–15.

6. "Notice," *City Gazette and Daily Advertiser*, July 20, 1790; original emphasis.

7. Peter Thompson, *Rum Punch and Revolution: Taverngoing and Public Life in Eighteenth-Century Philadelphia* (Philadelphia: University of Pennsylvania Press, 1999), 3.

8. Thompson, *Rum Punch*, 72.

9. George Washington to John Quincy Adams, Philadelphia, September 12, 1796, in *The Writings of George Washington*, vol. 35, ed. John C. Fitzpatrick (Washington, DC: Government Printing Office, 1940), 207–8.

10. Thompson, *Rum Punch*, 73.

11. Patrick Colquhoun, *A Treatise on the Police of London: Containing a Detail of the Various Crimes and Misdemeanors by Which Public and Private Property and Security Are, at Present, Injured and Endangered* (Philadelphia: Printed for Benjamin Davies, 1798), vii. For Colquhoun's entire enumeration of human depravity, see vi–x.

12. Colquhoun, *Treatise*, 10.

13. New York City Common Council, *A Law to Regulate Pawn-Brokers, and Dealers in the Purchase or Sale of Second-Hand Furniture, Metals or Clothes: Passed July 13th, 1812* (New York: Hardcastle and VanPelt, 1812), 4–5; original emphasis.

14. *Report of the Library Committee of the Pennsylvania Society for the Promotion of Public Economy* (Philadelphia: Printed for the Society, 1817), 19.

15. *Report of a Committee on the Subject of Pauperism* (New York: Samuel Wood and Sons, 1818), 7.

16. W. A. H. Hows, *A History of Pawnbroking, Past and Present* (London: W. Jackson, 1847), 88.

17. Managers of the Society for the Prevention of Pauperism, in the City of New-York, *Second Annual Report* (New York: E. Conrad, 1820), 11.

18. See especially *A Digest of the Ordinances of the City of Philadelphia* (Philadelphia: S. C. Atkinson, 1834); *A Digest of the Acts of Assembly, and the Ordinances, of the Commissioners and Inhabitants of the Kensington District of the Northern Liberties* (Philadelphia: Joseph Rakestraw, 1832); *A Digest of the Acts of Assembly and of the Ordinances of the Inhabitants and Commissioners of the District of Spring Garden* (Philadelphia: Thomas B. Town, 1841); and *A Digest of the Acts of Assembly and Ordinances of the District of Moyamensing, with the Rules of Order* (Moyamensing, PA: Bernard J. M'Cann, 1848).

19. "Pawn Brokers, &c.," *Democratic Press*, July 10, 1823.

20. "Pawnbrokers," *New Bedford (MA) Mercury*, February 1, 1833.

21. "To the Mayor's Court of the City of Philadelphia," *Philadelphia Gazette*, April 8, 1835.

22. "Communication," *Saturday Evening Post*, July 3, 1830.

23. James Mease, *On the Utility of Public Loan Offices and Savings Funds, Established by City Authorities* ([Philadelphia? 1836]), 1–2.

24. Published in the *Pennsylvania Journal of Prison Discipline* 7, 1 (January 1852): 35.

25. "A bill was passed," *New York Daily Times*, February 11, 1856.

26. "A Peep at the Pawnbroker," *Ariel: A Semimonthly Literary and Miscellaneous Gazette* 4, 4 (June 12, 1830): 29.

27. "One Evil of Great Cities," *New York Times*, August 26, 1866.

28. "Money Advanced," *Freeman's Journal and Philadelphia Mercantile Advertiser*, March 13, 1809.

29. Edward Crapsey, "Our Criminal Population," *Galaxy* 8 (September 1869): 353.

30. "$10 Reward," *National Police Gazette*, December 6, 1845.

31. "New-York, July 21: Police," *Independent Chronicle and Boston Patriot*, July 28, 1821.

32. "Robbery by a Dry Goods Clerk— Villany of Pawnbrokers," *National Police Gazette*, March 14, 1846.

33. "Tables Covered with Watches: The Stock of a Chatham-Street Pawn-Broker," *New York Times*, November 27, 1879.

34. William Bell, "Diary of William Bell, Inspector of Second-Hand Dealers, and Junk Shops," December 4, 1850. New-York Historical Society Manuscript Department (hereafter cited as Bell Diary).

35. Wilbur R. Miller, "Police Authority in London and New York City, 1830–1870," *Journal of Social History* 8 (Winter 1975): 85.

36. Miller, "Police Authority," 86.

37. Bell Diary, December 14, 1850.

38. "Pawnbrokers and Loan-Offices," *Harper's New Monthly Magazine* 39 (1869): 126.

39. Timothy J. Gilfoyle, *A Pickpocket's Tale: The Underworld of Nineteenth-Century New York* (New York: W. W. Norton, 2006), 150–51.

40. "Pawnbroking.—To the Editor of the N.Y. Daily Tribune," *New York Daily Tribune*, March 28, 1853. Very few original copies of this newspaper still exist. The microfilm version is hopelessly illegible, and I have tried to decipher the text as accurately as possible.

41. "Laying Up Treasure in the Pawnshop," *New York Times*, March 29, 1880.

42. "A Boarding-House Robbery," *New York Daily Times*, August 21, 1852.

43. Miller, "Police Authority," 85.

44. "Daring Robbery and Prompt Detection," *Eastern Argus Semi Weekly*, November 5, 1830.

45. "Stopped," *National Police Gazette*, October 11, 1845.

46. "Brooklyn Legislation," *New York Times*, April 23, 1876.

47. "Tracing Stolen Ribbons," *New York Times*, October 30, 1879.

48. "The Staten Island Murders," *Brooklyn Eagle*, January 2, 1844; original emphasis.

49. "The examination of Polly Bodine," *Brooklyn Eagle*, January 23, 1844.

50. George Washington Walling, *Recollections of a New York Chief of Police* ([Denver]: Denver Police Mutual Aid Fund, 1890), 402–3.

51. "Tracing the Criminal," *New York Times*, June 24, 1879.

52. Supreme Court of New York, Appellate Division, First Department, 73 A.D. 428; 1902 N.Y. App. Div. LEXIS 1579, June 1902, Decided; Supreme Court of Minnesota, 108 Minn. 174; 121 N.W. 905; 1909 Minn. LEXIS 664, June 18, 1909.

53. Crapsey, "Our Criminal Population," 353.

54. "Detectives Recovering Stolen Goods," *Harper's Weekly* 32, 1650 (August 4, 1888): 569.

55. "Arrested for Receiving Stolen Property," *National Police Gazette*, March 14, 1846.

56. "Two More *Fences* in Trouble," *National Police Gazette*, July 4, 1846; "Arrest for Receiving Stolen Goods," *National Police Gazette*, August 8, 1846.

57. "Sentence of Vantine, the Philadelphia Receiver," *National Police Gazette*, February 20, 1847.

58. "Licensing Receivers of Stolen Goods," *New York Times*, May 2, 1871.

59. Bell Diary, November 25, 1850; spelling as in the original.

60. Bell Diary, August 30, 1851.

61. Bell Diary, May 3, 1851.

62. "One Evil of Great Cities," *New York Times*, August 26, 1866.

63. "Police Reports: The Victims of a Woman," *New York Times*, October 19, 1860.

64. "Libby O'Brien's Robberies," *New York Times*, November 6, 1877.

65. "An interesting but wayward," *Brooklyn Eagle*, December 10, 1846; "City Intelligence," *Brooklyn Eagle*, March 19, 1846.

66. "Monthly Table of General Information. A Detective's Strategy: The Disappearance and Recovery of a Diamond Pin—a Long but Successful Chase," *Detective's Manual and Officer's Guide* 1, 2 (September 1868): 143, 145.

67. "A Son Robbing His Father," *New York Times*, May 23, 1878.

68. "Seduction," *Brooklyn Eagle*, April 6, 1849.

69. "There's No Fool Like an Old Fool," *National Police Gazette*, July 9, 1881.

70. William R. Simpson and Florence K. Simpson with Charles Samuels, *Hockshop: The Fabulous Story of the "Emperors of Pawnbroking"* (New York: Random House, 1954), 11–12.

71. Stephen Mihm, *A Nation of Counterfeiters: Capitalists, Con Men, and the Making of the United States* (Cambridge, MA: Harvard University Press, 2007), 210.

72. James D. McCabe, *The Secrets of the Great City: A Work Descriptive of the Virtues and the Vices, the Mysteries, Miseries and Crimes of New York City* (Philadelphia: National, [1868]), 491–93.

73. "Sham Champagne—a Pawnbroker Outwitted," *New York Daily Times*, February 7, 1854.

74. "The extraordinary passion of the lower classes in America for jewelry suggested a new field, and consequently Bohemian glass, or chrystals [*sic*], well mounted in gold, took the place of heavier wares," asserted the author of the article "Swindlers and Adventurers in the City of New York," *New York Illustrated News*, January 1, 1853.

75. "Swindlers and Adventurers." Electroplating techniques, described in popular periodicals, were no secret. In the early 1850s *Scientific American*, for one, published a slew of articles on the processes. See, for example, "Useful Receipts," 5, 20 (February 2, 1850): 153; "Gilding—No. 1," "Gilding—No. 2," "Gilding—No. 3," "Gilding—No. 4," 9, 10–

9, 13 (November 19–December 10, 1853): 80, 88, 96, 104; "Depositing Alloys on Metals," 9, 3 (October 1, 1853): 18; "Galvanic Plating with Metals," 7, 22 (February 14, 1852): 176; "Original Recipes for Electro-plating, Gilding, and Brassing," 12, 18 (January 10, 1857): 142; and "Plated Goods," 13, 8 (October 31, 1857): 57.

76. "History of Pearls, Natural and Artificial," *Godey's Lady's Book* 48, 6 (June 1854): 536. Four years later *Scientific American* referred to the production of imitation pearls as a "vast workshop." "Artificial Jewels," *Scientific American* 14, 8 (October 30, 1858): 63. See also "Imitating Ivory and Bone," *Scientific American* 6, 22 (February 15, 1851): 169, for recipes for making artificial ivory and bone out of gypsum and limestone; "Artificial Gems," *Scientific American* 4, 48 (August 18, 1849): 384; and "Artificial Sapphires and Rubies," *Scientific American* 12, 40 (June 13, 1857): 317.

77. "American Jewelry," *Scientific American*, n.s., 3, 1 (July 2, 1860): 3.

78. "Preparation of Precious Stones," *Harper's Weekly* 13, 660 (August 21, 1869): 535.

79. "Seeing Your Uncle," *Cleveland Herald*, December 3, 1883.

80. "Police," *Brooklyn Eagle*, January 31, 1844.

81. "Robbery of Jewelry," *Brooklyn Eagle*, December 19, 1849.

82. "A Detective's Good Bit of Work," *New York Times*, December 14, 1879.

83. "Courts," *Brooklyn Eagle*, August 22, 1850.

84. "Robbing His Benefactor," *New York Times*, September 15, 1878.

85. "Swallowing Pawn-Tickets," *New York Times*, February 20, 1879.

86. "City Intelligence: Arrest of Counterfeiters," *Brooklyn Eagle*, August 2, 1845.

87. "Profitable Speculation," *Broadway Dandy*, February 20, 1855.

88. "Profitable Speculation."

89. "Suspicious Circumstances," *Brooklyn Eagle*, January 11, 1847.

90. Ignatz Leo Nascher, *The Wretches of Povertyville: A Sociological Study of the Bowery* (Chicago: Jos. J. Lanzit, 1909), 29–30.

91. "A Pawnbroking Swindle," *New York Times*, July 14, 1875.

92. Champion Bissell, "A Study of Pawnbrokers," *Lippincott's Monthly Magazine* 53 (February 1894): 227–28.

93. According to Jenna Weissman Joselit, "Close to 80 percent of all felony charges brought against Jews between 1900 and 1915 had to do with the commission of property crimes: burglary, larceny, arson, horse-poisoning, and receiving stolen goods." See Joselit, *Our Gang: Jewish Crime and the New York Jewish Community, 1900–1940* (Bloomington: Indiana University Press, 1983), 33.

94. "Many Lives Imperiled," *New York Times*, July 7, 1880.

95. "Yorkville Police Court," *New York Times*, November 11, 1874.

96. A. J. McGarry, "Expense Book," entry for February 9, 1876. Private collection.

97. "A Day's Record of Crime," *New York Times*, December 6, 1880.

98. "Doing a Pawnshop," *National Police Gazette*, September 5, 1846.

99. "Between 5 and 6 o'clock yesterday evening," *New York Times*, July 26, 1874.

100. Pawnbrokers often lost court battles with insurance companies, which employed loopholes in the law and granted policies with limited benefits. For example, one pawnbroker's claim was denied because during a robbery his clerk, at gunpoint and under threat of death, told the robber the combination to the safe. The insurance policy covered only thefts occurring when the safe was forcibly entered. See Samuel Komroff (Merchants National Bank, Executor) vs. The Maryland Casualty Company. Supreme Court of Errors of Connecticut, Third Judicial District, Bridgeport, October Term, 1926 (105 Conn. 402; 135 A.

388; 1926 Conn. LEXIS 45; 54 A.L.R. 463), November 4, 1926, Argued, December 16, 1926, Decided.

101. "Heavy Haul in a Pawnbroker's Shop," *National Police Gazette*, November 1, 1879.

102. "Tavern Keepers Look Out," *Independent Chronicle and Boston Patriot*, July 28, 1824.

103. "Absconding Watchmaker," *National Police Gazette*, August 15, 1846.

104. New York State Legislature, *Report and Proceedings of the Senate Committee Appointed to Investigate the Police Department of the City of New York*, vol. 1 (Albany, NY: James B. Lyon, 1895), 40–41.

105. "Pawnbrokers, Detectives and Stolen Property," *Morning Oregonian* (Portland), August 11, 1886.

106. Bell Diary, August 21, 1851.

107. "Pawnbrokers in Trouble—Recovery of Stolen Property," *New York Times*, July 4, 1871.

108. Allan Pinkerton, *Claude Melnotte as a Detective* (Chicago: W. B. Keen, Cooke, 1875), 72.

109. "Detectives Recovering Stolen Goods."

110. This line is argued by William J. Novak in *The People's Welfare: Law and Regulation in Nineteenth-Century America* (Chapel Hill: University of North Carolina Press, 1996), 1.

111. Novak, *People's Welfare*, 14.

112. "The Pawnbroking Business," *New York Times*, June 12, 1881.

CHAPTER SIX

1. James Mease, *On the Utility of Public Loan Offices and Savings Funds, Established by City Authorities* ([Philadelphia? 1836]), 1.

2. James Mease, "Bank of Industry," *Archives of Useful Knowledge* 1, 2 (October 1810): 126–27.

3. Mease, *On the Utility*, 1.

4. W. R. Patterson dates the first charitable pawnshop to 1534 Belgium, when "a Flemish priest gave a small sum to establish a pawn bank at Ypres, and in 1572 a similar bank was founded in Bruges." See Patterson, "Pawnbroking in Europe and the United States," *Bulletin of the Department of Labor* 21 (March 1899): 174.

5. The term "mont-de-piété" has various translations. Patterson enumerates many of the possible meanings but concedes that neither "mountain of pity" nor "mountain of piety" quite conveys its true nature. He wrote, "It seems best not to attempt a translation, but employ it as a new word in our vocabulary." Patterson, "Pawnbroking," 174.

6. Mease, *On the Utility*, 1.

7. Philadelphia Saving Fund Society, *Articles of Association . . . with an Explanation of the Principles of the Institution, and Its Objects* (Philadelphia: Printed for the Society by W. Fry, 1817), 3.

8. *First Report of the Bank for Savings in the City of New-York* (New York: Clayton and Kingsland, 1820), 7, 9.

9. *The Brothers, or Consequences, a Story of What Happens Every Day, with an Account of Savings Banks* (Boston: Cummings, Hilliard, 1823), 56–57.

10. "Sixpenny Savings Banks in New York," *Hunt's Merchants' Magazine* 29 (1853): 740.

11. *Brothers*, 60; original emphasis.

12. Philadelphia Saving Fund Society, *Articles*, 6.

13. See, for example, the table of professions listed in the *First Report of the Bank for Savings in the City of New-York*, 4. It includes clerks (65), seamstresses (34), porters (15), oystermen and -women (8), students (6), peddlers (4), ladies' maids (2), and one coal measurer. The report noted that "even . . . public tavern keepers . . . have brought their money to the bank for safety and increase," 5.

14. American Seamen's Friend Society, *Second Annual Report* (New York: J. Seymour, 1830), 10.

15. "Lombard Association," *Independent Chronicle and Boston Patriot*, December 8, 1824.

16. New-York City Temperance Society, *An Address to the Inhabitants of the City of New-York by the Board of Managers of the New-York City Temperance Society* (New York: J. Seymour, 1829), 5.

17. William Ellery Channing, *Lectures on the Elevation of the Laboring Portion of the Community* (Boston: Crosby and Nichols, 1863), 14.

18. "Pawnshops as They Should Be," *New York Daily Tribune*, March 28, 1853.

19. "Memorial of Citizens of the City of Philad[a]. Requesting Authority to Establishment [*sic*] of a Lombard Association for the Benefit of the Necessitous Poor of the City and County of Philadelphia," Philadelphia, 1838. Manuscript in the John A. McAllister Papers, Library Company of Philadelphia.

20. "Benevolent Pawning Establishment," *Brooklyn Eagle*, September 9, 1848.

21. John W. Corson, *Loiterings in Europe. or Sketches of Travel* (New York: Harper and Brothers, 1848), 361, 362.

22. Corson, *Loiterings*, 362–63.

23. "Benevolent Pawning Establishment."

24. Chattel Loan Company, *The Chattel Loan Co. Was Incorporated* [Philadelphia, ca. 1855]; original emphasis.

25. "The Pawnbrokers and the Savings Banks," *Hunt's Merchants' Magazine* 20 (1849): 669.

26. "Pawnbrokers and the Savings Banks," 669.

27. Chattel Loan Company, *Chattel Loan Co.*

28. *An Act to Incorporate the Chattel Loan Company of Philadelphia* ([Philadelphia, 1855]).

29. Daniel Horowitz, *The Morality of Spending: Attitudes toward the Consumer Society in America, 1875–1940* (Chicago: Ivan R. Dee, 1992), 8.

30. "Savings Banks and Pawnbrokers," *DeBow's Review* 18, n.s., 1 (1855): 651.

31. "Savings Banks and Pawnbrokers," 651.

32. Chattel Loan Company, *Chattel Loan Co.*; original emphasis.

33. *Act to Incorporate the Chattel Loan Company.*

34. Morris R. Neifeld coined this term in *The Personal Finance Business* (New York: Harper and Brothers, 1933).

35. Collateral Loan Company, *Extract from the Report of the Committee That Advised the Establishment of Such a Bank* ([Boston? 1871]).

36. *Boston Directory . . . for 1863.* (Boston: Adams, Sampson, 1863), 404.

37. Collateral Loan Company, *Copy of the Charter of the Collateral Loan Company* ([Boston? 1871]).

38. Collateral Loan Company, *Copy of the Charter.*

39. Edward Howland, "The Bankers of the Poor," *Galaxy* 3 (March 15, 1867): 665.

40. "She Will Start a Pawnshop," *New York Times*, January 26, 1894.

41. Champion Bissell, "A Study of Pawnbrokers," *Lippincott's Monthly Magazine* 53 (February 1894): 224.

42. Howland, "Bankers of the Poor," 666.

43. Charles Barnard, "Pawnshops and Small Borrowers," *Chautauquan* 19 (April 1894): 74.

44. Emerson W. Peet, "A Review of Provident Loan Societies," *Charities Review* 4 (February 1895): 187.

45. Roy Lubove, *The Professional Altruist: The Emergence of Social Work as a Career, 1880–1930.* (Cambridge, MA: Harvard University Press, 1965), 5.

46. Alexander Keyssar, *Out of Work: The First Century of Unemployment in Massachusetts* (Cambridge: Cambridge University Press, 1986), 37.

47. Anthony F. C. Wallace, *Rockdale: The Growth of an American Village in the Early Industrial Revolution* (New York: W. W. Norton, 1978), 334.

48. Provident Loan Society of New-York, *First Annual Report . . . May 21, 1894–December 31, 1895* (New York: De Vinne Press, 1896), 5; original emphasis. Hereafter referred to as PLS.

49. Lubove, *Professional Altruist*, 6.

50. Robert H. Bremner, *American Philanthropy*, 2nd ed. (Chicago: University of Chicago Press, 1988), 96.

51. Bremner, *American Philanthropy*, 102. He notes that "wise administration of wealth was an antidote for radical proposals for redistributing property and a method of reconciling the poor and the rich."

52. PLS, *First Annual Report*, 13–14.

53. David Wagner, *What's Love Got to Do with It? A Critical Look at American Charity* (New York: New Press, 2000), 94.

54. According to Wagner, the professional management of wealth, which is what some charities seemed to offer, "provided a strong buffer between the origins of the money in the schemes of oil consolidation or big steel monopolies, and those representatives who would appear before the press and public to announce new grants or research studies" (*What's Love Got to Do with It?* 96).

55. See Larry Schweikart, ed., *Encyclopedia of American Business History and Biography: Banking and Finance to 1913* (New York: Facts on File, 1990), 288–91.

56. PLS, *First Annual Report*, 15.

57. Provident Loan Society of New-York, *Second Annual Report . . . 1896* (New York: De Vinne Press, 1897), 8.

58. Rolf Nugent, *The Provident Loan Society of New York: An Account of the Largest Remedial Loan Society* (New York: Russell Sage Foundation, 1932), 14.

59. Provident Loan Society of New-York, *Fourth Annual Report . . . 1898* (New York: Marion Press, 1899), 8.

60. *The Provident Loan Society of New York: Twenty-fifth Anniversary, 1894–1919* ([New York]: Provident Loan Society, 1919), 11–13, 25.

61. *Provident Loan Society of New York: Twenty-fifth Anniversary*, 15.

62. "Bread on the Waters," *Brooklyn Daily Eagle*, February 13, 1896.

63. Amos Griswold Warner, Stuart Alfred Queen, and Ernest Bouldin Harper, *American Charities and Social Work* (1894; New York: Thomas Y. Crowell, 1930), 177.

64. PLS, *Second Annual Report*, 6.

65. Provident Loan Society of New-York, *Third Annual Report . . . 1897* (New York: Marion Press, 1898), 10.

66. PLS, *Third Annual Report*, 9.

67. Provident Loan Society of New-York, *Fifth Annual Report . . . 1899* (New York: Knickerbocker Press, 1900), 1.

68. Bissell, "Study of Pawnbrokers," 229.

69. *Provident Loan Society of New York: Twenty-fifth Anniversary*, 11.

70. Peter Schwed, *God Bless Pawnbrokers* (New York: Dodd, Mead, 1975), 93.

71. Schwed, *God Bless Pawnbrokers*, 94.

72. Schwed, *God Bless Pawnbrokers*, 95.

73. Schwed, *God Bless Pawnbrokers*, 102.

74. Schwed, *God Bless Pawnbrokers*, 117.

75. *Provident Loan Society of New York: Twenty-fifth Anniversary*, 15.

76. *Provident Loan Society of New York: Twenty-fifth Anniversary*, 21.

77. Nugent, *Provident Loan Society*, 16.

78. First State Pawners Society of Chicago, *Report of the President to the Stockholders at the Annual Meeting, November 27, 1917* (Chicago: Kendig and Hitchings, 1917), 2.

79. "Philanthropic Pawnbroking," *New York Times*, May 21, 1888.

80. Bissell, "Study of Pawnbrokers," 229.

81. Barnard, "Pawnshops and Small Borrowers," 74.

82. "Pawnbrokers Plan a War on Philanthropists," *Brooklyn Daily Eagle*, January 12, 1902.

83. Barnard, "Pawnshops and Small Borrowers," 75.

84. *The Emergency Loan Fund*, ([Boston, 1894]), [6–7]. Collection of the Schlesinger Library, Radcliffe Institute for Advanced Study, Harvard University.

85. "Bread on the Waters."

86. Katherine Louise Smith, "Benevolent Loan Associations," *Arena* 24, 1 (July 1900): 89.

87. Jonathon Gilmer Speed, "Pawnbrokers and the Poor," *Harper's Weekly* 36, 1863 (September 3, 1892): 862.

88. Plot summary taken from www.siffblog.com/reviews/griffith_and_the_yiddish_silents_003471.html.

89. Nugent, *Provident Loan Society,* 8.

90. James Schouler, *A Treatise on the Law of Bailments,* 3rd ed. (Boston: Little, Brown, 1897), 164–65; my emphasis.

91. Schwed, *God Bless Pawnbrokers,* 81.

92. Schwed, *God Bless Pawnbrokers,* 81–82.

93. Schwed, *God Bless Pawnbrokers,* 79. For the presence of xenophobia in the junk trades, see Carl Zimring, "Dirty Work: How Hygiene and Xenophobia Marginalized the American Waste Trades, 1870–1930," *Environmental History* 9, 1 (January 2004), www.historycooperative.org/journals/eh/9.1/zimring.html.

94. Schwed, *God Bless Pawnbrokers,* 83, 84.

95. PLS, *First Annual Report,* 14.

96. PLS, *First Annual Report,* 13.

97. "Sociological Notes," *Annals of the American Academy of Political and Social Science* 14 (July 1899): 151, 150.

98. Neifeld, *Personal Finance Business,* 57–58.

99. "Pawns and Loans," *Boston Daily Advertiser,* March 1, 1884.

100. Peet, "Review of Provident Loan Societies," 182.

101. Smith, "Benevolent Loan Associations," 90.

102. Bissell, "Study of Pawnbrokers," 227.

103. "Pawnbroking," *Scientific American* 81, 8 (August 19, 1899): 115.

104. Frank Dekker Watson, *The Charity Organization Movement in the United States* (New York: Macmillan, 1922), 228.

105. Nugent, *Provident Loan Society,* 16.

106. "Pawnbrokers Plan a War."

107. Nugent, *Provident Loan Society,* 15.

108. *Provident Loan Society of New York: Twenty-fifth Anniversary,* 19.

CHAPTER SEVEN

1. For more on today's "fringe economy," see Howard Karger, *Shortchanged: Life and Debt in the Fringe Economy* (San Francisco: Berrett-Koehler, 2005).

2. Katherine Porter, "Profiting from 'Profligates': The Credit Industry's Business Model for Postbankruptcy Lending," paper presented at the Conference on Empirical Legal Studies, New York University, November 10, 2007.

3. Katherine Porter writes that the "reforms" Congress enacted in cutting back on bankruptcy relief, at the credit industry's behest, "were supposed to dampen prodigality and encourage consumers to make prudent financial decisions." But, she notes, "The credit industry's lending decisions were not subjected to similar scrutiny to that imposed on debtors' borrowing or bankruptcy decisions. Nor were lenders held to the same moral standard for evaluating the appropriateness of their financial practices as debtors were." Porter, "Profiting from 'Profligates,'" 3.

4. In the 1950s the organization took collateral lending services on the road with its "Loanmobile," a bus equipped with a counter and a small safe, as described in Peter Schwed's *God Bless Pawnbrokers* (New York: Dodd, Mead, 1975), 203. Today the business has an active Web site (www.pls.org) containing FAQs, a gloss of its history, reasons to use it instead of patronizing independent pawnbrokers, an online loan calculator, and a loan-by-mail program.

5. Karger, *Shortchanged,* x.

6. See Karger, *Shortchanged,* xiii.

7. See, for example, Christopher L. Peterson, "Usury Law, Payday Loans, and Statutory Sleight of Hand: An Empirical Analysis of American Credit Pricing Limits," paper presented at the Conference on Empirical Legal Studies, New York University, November 10, 2007. Peterson explains that because so many loopholes in state usury laws have emerged since the mid-1990s, there are few controls over interest rates not only for banks and credit card companies but for fringe lenders as well. He writes, "Emboldened by this new regulatory environment, salary-assignment

loansharks, now using the more colloquial appellation of 'payday lender,' reappeared" (10).

8. Peterson, "Usury Law, Payday Loans, and Statutory Sleight of Hand," 13, 11.

9. Peterson, "Usury Law, Payday Loans, and Statutory Sleight of Hand," 11.

10. For more on Americans' precarious personal finances, see Karger, *Shortchanged,* and Elizabeth Warren and Amelia Warren Tyagi, *The Two-Income Trap: Why Middle-Class Mothers and Fathers Are Going Broke* (New York: Basic Books, 2003). For the impact of policy decisions on consumer credit, see the monographs and working papers published by the George Washington University's School of Business Financial Services Research Program (http://www.gwu.edu/~/business/research/centers/fsrp).

11. Michelle Leder, "How the Other Half Banks," *Slate,* May 10, 2004, www.slate.com.

12. Lendol Calder, *Financing the American Dream: A Cultural History of Consumer Credit* (Princeton, NJ: Princeton University Press, 1999), 291; original emphasis.

13. Vicki Mabrey and Talesha Reynolds, "Pawn Shop Prosperity: One Industry That's Booming Despite the Sagging Economy," *ABC News,* aired April 21, 2008. Transcript at http://www.abcnews.go.com/business/story?id=4695868.

14. Erik Lacitis, "Classic Old Downtown Pawnshop Calls It Quits," *Seattle Times,* May 22, 2007.

15. Tom Buckham, "Pawn of Changing Times," *Buffalo News,* February 25, 2008.

16. See Leo Finkelstein obituary and "Local businessman Finkelstein dies at 93," both in *Asheville (NC) Citizen-Times,* March 24, 1999, and "Finkelstein made many marks," *Asheville (NC) Citizen-Times,* March 26, 1999. Finkelstein's oral history is at the University of North Carolina at Asheville, D. Hiden Ramsey Library Special Collections/University Archives, recorded February 5, 1993, by Dorothy Joynes for the Voices of Asheville Oral History Collection (OH-VOA F 56 Le).

17. Manny Fernandez, "Cash to Get By Is Still a Pawnshop's Stock in Trade," *New York Times,* September 14, 2007.

18. Mabrey and Reynolds, "Pawn Shop Prosperity"; Rob Walker, "Off the Skids: How the Familiar Lessons of Retail Growth Are Building Yet Another Chain—of Pawnshops," *New York Times Magazine,* June 11, 2006, 22.

19. National Pawnbrokers Association home page, www.nationalpawnbrokers.org.

20. National Pawnbrokers Association, "Industry News," www.nationalpawnbrokers.org/news.htm.

21. John P. Caskey, "Pawnbroking in America: The Economics of a Forgotten Credit Market," *Journal of Money, Credit, and Banking* 23 (February 1991): 87; cited in Robert W. Johnson and Dixie P. Johnson, "Pawnbroking in the U.S.: A Profile of Customers," George Washington University School of Business Financial Services Research Program Monograph 34 (July 1998), 7.

22. Fernandez, "Cash to Get By."

23. Ric Blum, e-mail message to author, May 26, 2004.

24. Ric Blum, "Where Does Stolen Property Go?" *Today's Pawnbroker* 16, 3 (Fall 2003): 9–10.

25. Buckham, "Pawn of Changing Times."

26. Philadelphia Police Department, "Police Unit Profiles," http://www.ppdonline.org/hq_profile_majcrimes.php.

27. In 2004 there were 809 precious metals dealers in Pennsylvania and only 53 pawnbrokers (33 concentrated in the Philadelphia area).

28. Like pocket watches of the nineteenth and early twentieth centuries, today's fine watches are almost always more valuable as functional timepieces than as scrap metal and loose gemstones, so they make their way into gray and black markets intact.

29. Linda Fell (officer, Major Crimes Unit, Philadelphia Police Department), in discussion with the author, Philadelphia, March 5, 2004.

30. Police departments today likely would approve of the suggestion offered by their brethren over a century ago: "All owners of watches should make it a point, immediately upon their purchase, to transcribe their number and the maker's name upon some private memorandum, so that upon their loss by theft or inadvertence, they may furnish a description which may lead to the detection of the thief or the recovery by other means. This rule would be a wise precaution, if applied to all other kinds of valuable property." "Owners of Watches," *National Police Gazette*, October 16, 1845. (As an exercise, Officer Fell asked me to provide a detailed physical description of the possession most precious to me, my grandmother's wedding ring. I couldn't.)

31. "Hollywood's Pawnshop," first aired April 11, 2008, and available at CNN Video, http://cnn.com/video.

32. "Pawn Star: Jean Zimmelman Runs the Beverly Loan Co., an Haute Hock Shop for Celebs Whose Cash Isn't Flowing," *People* 58, 15 (October 7, 2002): 120.

33. "Florida Pawn Shop Booming after Madoff Revelation," NPR, *All Things Considered*, aired December 15, 2008 (http://www.npr.org/templates/story/story.php?storyid=98293155). See also Paulo Prada, "In Palm Beach, Investors Assume Worst," *Wall Street Journal*, December 15, 2008.

34. See, for example, *National Pawnbroker*, November 2008.

INDEX

Page numbers in italics refer to pages with figures.

African Americans: as pawners, 80, *95*, 133; stereotypes of, 24, 44

anti-Semitism: affecting credit, 38, 72–73; within the business community, 17, 199 n 64; and capitalism, 22, 52; in illustrated magazines, 42, 44–46; in mid-nineteenth century, 36; and pawnbroking, 5, 24; in popular literature, 30–37, 40–41; rise of in United States, 17. *See also* Jews, stereotypes of; Shylock

appraisal: challenge of making accurate, 84–85, 109, 119, 142–43; as a learned skill, 58–60, 168–70; standardization of, 162, 169–71, *171*, *172*, 177

arson, 147–48

Asheville, NC, 188

auctioneers: as also pawnbrokers, 55, 71, 72, 83, 132; Jews as, 25, 38

auctions: in New York City, 70; redistributing goods, 70, 110, 113; selling stolen goods, 129; of unredeemed collateral, 70, 100–101, 104, 105, 110

Baltimore, MD: female pawnbroker in, 73; interest rates in, 58; pawnbrokers in, 57, 59, 65, 202 n 15; pawnbroking families in, 73; population of, 57

Bank for Savings of the City of New York, 156

banks: anonymity of, 190; consolidation of today, 182; depositors' occupations, 217 n 13; distrust of, 3; flight from poor neighborhoods, 185; lending practices of, 2, 17, 77, 156–57; the "unbanked," 184. *See also* savings banks

Barnard, Charles, 162, 163

Bell, William, 131, 132, 138–39, 150

benevolent organizations. *See* pawnshops, philanthropic; pawnshops, semiphilanthropic; Provident Loan Society (PLS); *and under individual names*

Bennett, Emerson, 35, 40

Bentham, Jeremy, 14

Berg, Irving (pawnbroker), 82

Beverly Hills, CA, 192–93

Beverly Loan Company, 192–93

Bibles, 32, 100, 101, 109–10, 123, 140

Birmingham, AL, 79

Blatchford, Stephen (pawnbroker), *16*, 57

Blum, Ric, 190

Bolles, John, 14

Boston: description of, 65; number of pawns in hock, 206 n 88; pawnbrokers in, 61, 62, 63, 65, *108*, 161–63, 175 (*see also* Pawners' Bank of Boston)

Boston Society on Pauperism and Crime, 128

boys, 27, 65, 130, 139

Bradford, Cornelia (pawnbroker), 163

brokers: becoming pawnbrokers, 15, 58, 59; in early America, 54–56, 197 n 6; elite, 23; specialization of, 56, 202 n 9

Brooker, Elizabeth (pawnbroker), 73, 75

Buffalo, NY, 58, 187–88, 205 n 66, 206 n 88

Calder, Lendol, 185

capitalism: championed, 2–3, 20, 160, 183; consolidation of, 183, 184; and consumption, 66, 104–5, 109, 113–18, 160; and crime, 128, 145–46; inflexibility of, 60, 182; and labor, 52–53, 164, 211 n 80; normalization of, 19, 20, 22, 28–29, 33, 36, 40, 46, 52, 182–83; reliance on credit, 88, 89; reliance on pawnbroking, 3, 9, 15, 20, 21, 54, 60, 87, 104–5; and secondary markets, 5, 145–46; and spread of pawnshops, 16, 60

Carey, Mathew, 102, 103, 112

Cash America, 186, 189

Channing, William Ellery, 114, 158

Charleston, SC, 73, 108, 124

Chattel Loan Company, 150, 160, 161

Chest of Savings, 155

Chicago: economic conditions of, 105; Jews in, 71; number of pawns in hock, 76, 105; pawnbrokers in, 62, 65, 66, 71, 73, 74, 174 (see also First State Pawners Society); used goods dealers in, 65

China, 7, 195 n 3

Church Missions House, 171–72

Cincinnati, OH, 62, 72

clothing: Jews dealing in, 62, 71, 72–73; pawnbrokers dealing in, 59, 62–63; as pawns, ii, 68, 70, 76, 83, 90, 94, 100; resale of, 27, 38, 64, 70, 101, 110, 111; retail sale of, 66; and stereotypes of Jews, 24, 45, 48; value of, 30, 113, 123. See also pawns; used goods

collateral. See pawns

collateral loans. See loans, collateral

Colquhoun, Patrick, 9, 125–26

Colwell, Stephen, 159–60

consumer culture: championed, 30; after the Civil War, 117–18; credit as essential to, 185; in eighteenth century, 99, 123, 209 n 43; effect on pawnbrokers, 119; effect on pawning, 82–83, 97–117; in nineteenth century, 4, 18, 87; normalized, 113, 114, 160–61; and personal identity, 99–100, 109, 112, 114, 116; and stolen goods, 124; Webster, Daniel, on, 160; and women, 142

consumer goods: benefits of spending on, 160; and capitalism, 118; changing roles of, 112–13; changing meanings of, 115, 212 n 103; circulation of, 123, 125, 135, 144; conspicuous consumption of, 117–18; distinguishing class, 113–14; egalitarianism of purchasing, 118; and Industrial Revolution, 82–83, 104, 105–7, 117, 147; as latent capital, 100; obtained through hard work, 112; as pawns, 16, 97–98, 100, 104, 109, 120–21; purchased by poor, 113; and self identity, 116–18; sentimental value of, 140–41; spurious, 143–44; as status symbols, 116; strictures about purchase and use, 114; Alexis de Tocqueville on, 113; Veblen, Thorstein, on, 117–18. See also pawns; used goods; and under individual items

Cook, Eliza, 31–32

Crash of 1893, 78, 119, 163

credit: assessment of, 38, 83, 197 n 32; card interest rates, 182, 185–86; and collateral loans, 76; compared with cash purchases, 30, 55; current forms of, 182–85; among elite, 54–55, 88, 89, 96, 121; effect on purchase price, 55; in eighteenth century, 54–55; essential to capitalism, 88, 183; essential today, 185; formalization of, 15, 56, 81, 121, 182, 186–87; global contraction of today, 185; informality of, 55, 88; Jews' limited access to, 17, 38, 72–73; poor's limited access to, 56, 70, 87, 88–89, 90, 91–92, 93, 103, 118, 126, 156, 158, 183–84, 186–87, 190; reporting agencies, 38; and reputation, 30, 55, 72, 88, 96; terms of, 88. See also interest; loans, collateral; loans, payday

crime, 134, 137, 139, 140, 143, 146–47; caused by poverty, 126, 128; in cities, 11, 31, 125–26; and Jews, 27, 28, 44, 148; pawnbrokers accused of causing, 17, 22, 26, 57, 126–29; pawnbrokers as victims of, 148–49; pawnbrokers engaged in, 122, 130, 133; pawnbrokers helping to solve, 134–37, 139; pawn tickets as evidence of, 144–46; philanthropic pawnshops as antidote to, 155; in popular literature, 33, 35, 51. See also markets, black; stolen goods; thieves

Cunningham, Ellen (pawnbroker), 73

Dayton, OH, 190

debt. *See* credit

De Forest, Robert W., 166

Dickens, Charles, 97, *99*

Dodge, William E., 165

economic conditions, urban, 14, 89, 102–4, 105, 110; of pawners, 102–4

Emergency Loan Fund, 120–21, 175

Fahnestock, Harris C., 165

Farwell, John V., 174

females. *See* women

Finkelstein, Leo (pawnbroker), 79, 188

First State Pawners Society, 105, 120, 174

Fell, Linda Officer, 2, 191–92

Ford, Benjamin (pawnbroker), 59

Foreman, Edwin G., 174

Foster, George, 30–31, 64, 104

Freedley, Edward, 28

gemstones: appraising, 113, 169–72, *171, 172;* as pawns, 70, 78, 79, 80, 83, 96, 101, 119, 169–70, 176; resale, 70, 110; spurious, 109, 143–44, 516 n 76; value of, 79, 101, 193

Germans: pawning habits of, 111–12; peddlers, 28; stereotypes of, 29, 42

Glicksman, Sol (pawnbroker), 178

Godey's Ladies' Book, 32, 33–34, 36, 37, 40, 109, 143

Goldman, Alan (pawnbroker), 187

Grant, Ulysses S., 107–9, 118

Great Depression, 79–82, 174

Hands, Ralph (pawnbroker), 80–81

Hands Loan Company, 80–81, 92–93

Hart, Elizabeth (pawnbroker), 73

Hogarth, William, 9, *10,* 11, 17

Hume, David, 13

humor, pawnbroking: in advertising, 47, *48;* in cartoons, 41–46, *43,* 96, *97,* 148; in postcards, 47–48, *49;* regarding interest rates of, 45, *45;* in sheet music, 48–49, *50,* 97, *98;* in verse, 22–23, 90

Hunt's Merchants' Magazine: critique of pawning, 115; pawnbroking statistics in, 76, 104, 119; on philanthropic pawnshops, 160; on savings banks, 156–57

illustrated magazines, *39,* 41–46, *42, 43, 45*

immigrants, 56, 176, 187; in Chicago, 65–66, 71; Germans, 28, 29, 42, 111–12; Irish, 24, 42, 44, 46, 71, 200 n 81; as pawners, 111, 115; possessions as pawns, 14, 15, 112; as untrustworthy, 175; and xenophobia, 47

income: pawnbrokers', 75–77; personal, 65, 77, 90, 92, 93, 103–4, 105, 203 n 26

innkeepers, 54, 55, 124–25, 128

intelligence offices, 54, 56, 59

intemperance, 3, 17, 22, 24, 125, 127, 128, 158

interest: and banking reform, 5; calculated on loans, 77, 102, 145; charged by Monts-de-Piété, 9, 155; charged by pawnbrokers, 6, 29, 58, 88; charged by philanthropic pawnshops, 155, 160, 161, 162, 163; charged by PLS, 174; charged during Revolution, 23; charged in early republic, 54; of credit cards, 185–86; distinguished from usury, 11–14, 196 n 22; economic theories about, 13–14; in eighteenth century, 23; in Great Britain, 13; history of rates, 7; humor regarding, 45, *45;* lack of uniformity of, 6, 195 n 2; paid by merchants, 88; under Richard I, 7; Smith, Adam, on, 196 n 24; terms of, 88. *See also* credit; usury

Irish: as junk dealers, 71; lineage of Simpsons, 74–75; occupations of, 71; as pawnbrokers, 42, 71, 73–74, 200 n 81; at PLS, 177, 178; stereotypes of, 24, 42, 44, 46

Jackson, Mary C., 121

jewelers, 70, 130

jewelry: domestic manufacture of, 109; frauds involving, 147; as pawns, 30, 56, 70, 84, 100, 101, 109, 110, 129, 141–41, 180; spurious, 109, 119, 143, 211 n 83, 215 n 75, 516 n 76; stolen, 135, 137; varieties of, 109. *See also* gemstones; pawns

Jews: ambivalence toward in early America, 24, 25, 198 n 12; barred from artisanal work, 71–72; in Buffalo, 205 n 66; in Cincinnati, 72; credit denied to, 38, 72–73; deemed

Jews (*continued*)
    good businessmen, 40, 205 n 66; defense
        of, 36, 46; expulsion from Great Britain,
        7; family alliances of, 72–73; history as
        moneylenders, 72; legal discrimination
        of, 27; marrying gentiles, 199 n 64; in
        Maryland, 27; as minorities, 24, 25; in
        New York City, 72; occupations of, 17, 24,
        27, 71; as outsiders in business, 26, 27, 40;
        as perceived business rivals, 24; in Phila-
        delphia, 72, 197 n 6; PLS not employing,
        177–78; population of, 23, 25; property
        crimes among, 148; questions about, 25;
        reactions against anti-Semitism, 46, 52;
        regard for in eighteenth-century America,
        23; success of in business, 27, 52; Sunday
        commerce of, 26–27, 38; in used goods
        trades, 17, 25–26. *See also* Jews, stereo-
        types of; usury
Jews, stereotypes of: as "acquisitive," 40;
        as alien, 24; as arsonists, 46, 147–48;
        British origins of, 22; in business 27, 40;
        in cartoons, *39, 45;* as Christian-hating,
        35–37; in credit reports, 38; as criminals,
        28, 44; as deceptive, 27; dialect of, 29,
        37; in eighteenth-century America, 21; as
        exploiters, 24; as goats, 40, 41; as greedy
        pawnbrokers, 32–33; in illustrated maga-
        zines, 42, 44–46; as moneylenders, 24; as
        murderous, 35; normalization of, 52; odor
        of, 38–39; as pawnbrokers, 21–53; physical
        characteristics of, 24, 27, *34,* 35, 36, 38–39,
        39, 45, 46, 47, *48,* 49, *49, 50,* 51; role of
        physiognomy and phrenology in creating,
        39–41; as sharp traders, 44; as "shaves,"
        40, 200 n 73; as thieves, 130, *140;* as tribal-
        istic, 72; as uncaring, 33; as usurers, 24, 26,
        28, 29, 46. *See also* pawnbrokers; Shylock
Jones, John Beauchamp, 39
Judge, 44, 200 n 87
junk: dealers as receivers, 128–29, 137, 191;
        dealing and capitalism, 3; Irish as dealers,
        71, 200 n 81; regulation of dealers, 57

Kennedy, John Stewart, 65
Kimmel, Louis (pawnbroker), 187, 190

labor: in Birmingham, AL, 79; elevating ef-
        fects of, 158; and ethnicity, 26, 27, 71;
        and fraud, 94; and industrialization, 16, 60,
        90, 106, 107, 118, 164, 170, 183; seasonality
        of, 16, 89, 90, 208 n 13; and unemploy-
        ment, *10,* 17, *18,* 60, 90, 164, 185; women's,
        73–74, 91
Ladies' Repository, 32
loan brokers: appearance of, 83, 84; in New
        York City, 96; prevalence of, 132; profits
        of, 84; as unlicensed, 83
loans. *See* loans, collateral; loans, payday
loans, collateral: amounts outstanding from, 76,
        79; average profits on, 76–77; for business-
        men, 70, 85; caps on, 167, 193; cost of, 102,
        145, 210 n 53; discrete nature of, 88; and
        downward mobility, 32; efficacy of, 12–21,
        183; immediacy of, 87, 94; informality of
        in early America, 88; and moral turpitude,
        124, 127, 128 (*see also* crime; intemperance);
        necessity of, 4, 15, 20, 21, 79–80, 87, 118,
        159, 186; from nonprofit pawnshops, 9,
        160, 161–62, 167, 178, 179; pawnbrokers'
        caps on, 78; percentage of all consumer
        credit, 76; and time, 83, 88–91, 120; terms
        compared with credit cards, 186; uses of,
        87–96, 102–4, 141; for the wealthy, 7, 83,
        96, 192–93. *See also* interest; pawnbrokers;
        pawners; pawning; pawns; pawnshops,
        chain; pawnshops, independent; pawnshops,
        philanthropic; pawnshops, semiphilan-
        thropic; pawnshops, unlicensed
loans, payday, 2–3, 184–86
loan societies. *See* pawnshops,
        semiphilanthropic
Locke, John, 13
Loeb, Solomon, 165
Lombards, 7–8

Mandelbaum, Fredericka, 132–33
markets: economic theories regarding, 13–14;
        fluidity of various, 88, 114; inflexibility of,
        20; informal, 55, 124, 132; mainstream, 89;
        pawnbrokers' knowledge of, 58–59, 84,
        119, 142–43; reconciled with religion, 14
        (*see also* usury); retail, 1; shift from infor-

mal to formal, 15; skills within various, 58, 59, 71, 119. *See also* used goods

markets, black, 31, 62, 84, 122, 134; activities within, 139–53, *140;* and capitalism, 128, 145–46; fluidity of, 123–24; "fringe," 183–84; pawn tickets traded in, 145–46; today, 190, 192. *See also* crime; police; stolen goods; theft

markets, resale: and capitalism, 3, 5, 78–82; enterprise within, 145–46; in pawnshops, 187–88, 189, 191; pawn tickets traded in, 145–46; unredeemed pawns in, 59, 64, 70, 78, 104, 110, *111*, 120, 129, 159. *See also* junk; used goods

McCabe, James, 139, *140*, 142

McGarry's (pawnshop): cooperation with police, 191; description of 1, 5–6; private entrance of, 68; relationships with pawners, 188; security vaults installed at, 149; watchman for, 148

Mease, James: proposal for Chest of Savings, 155; proposing a philanthropic pawnshop, 89, 128, 154–55, 156, 158

merchants: Christian compared with Jews, 27, 28, 41, 46; Christian compared with pawnbrokers, 29, 33; compared with moneylenders, 28; and credit, 17, 54, 55, 88, 89; economies of scale of, 54; involved with semiphilanthropic pawnshops, 158, 159, 162, 165, 174; location of stores compared with pawnshops, 64; as pawners, 90; and rent, 89; wholesale and retail compared with pawnbrokers, 27–29, 30, 33, 38, 40, 51–52

Millem, Sarah (pawnbroker), 57, 73

Mills, D. O., 166

Milwaukee, WI, 120

Monthly Cosmopolite, 33–34

Monte-de-Piété, 155

monts-de-piété, 8–9, 19, 155–56, 217 n 5

Morgan, J. Pierpont, 165

Morris, Robert, 23, 54

motion pictures, 21, 44, 51

Nathans, Moses (pawnbroker), 72, 205 n 64

National Pawnbroker, 193

National Pawnbrokers Association, 189–90, 193, 194

New York, NY: auctions of unredeemed collateral in, 70; cost of rent in, 89; descriptions of, 31, 62; economic conditions in, 56, 89, 105, 110–11; license fees in, 60; pawnbrokers in, 26–27, 29, 56, 57, 59, 60, 62, 73–75, 83, 86, 96, 100, 131, 139–40, 141–42, 150, 188; pawnbrokers per capita, 60; police in, 131–39, 148–52; regulation of pawnbrokers, 56–58, 126–27, 128; semiphilanthropic pawnshops in, 158–59, 163–81; statistics of pawning in, 76, 83, 100, 102, 104–5, 119; used clothing dealers, 110, *111*, 130

New York City Temperance Society, 158

New York Lombard Association, 158–59

New York State, 58

nonprofit pawnshops. *See* Monte-de-Piété; monts-de-piété; pawnshops, philanthropic; pawnshops, semiphilanthropic

Old Isaacs, the Pawnbroker (movie), 51, 176

Oppelman, L. (pawnbroker), 119

Panic of 1837, 17, *18*, 38, 119, 197 n 30

Panic of 1857, 36, *43*, 96, 107

Panic of 1873, *43*

Panic of 1907, 79, 167

Pawnbroker, The (movie), 21

pawnbrokers: abetting crime, 9, 125, 128, 129, 131, 137, 146–58, 190 (*see also* police; stolen goods); accused of receiving, 127–28, 130–31, 133–34; and appraising, 58–60, 84–85, 109, 119, 142–43, 168–70; assessment of pawners, 85, 94–95, 168, 175; assets of, 75, 77–78, 179; in Baltimore, 57, 59, 73, 202 n 15; as benefit to neighborhoods, 61, 64, 65–66, 174, 188; in Boston, 61, 62, 63, *108*, 161–63, 175; in Chicago, 62, 66, 71, 73, 74, 174; in Cincinnati, 62, 72; compared with merchants, 27–29, 30, 33, 38, 40, 51–52, 68; competition from semiphilanthropic pawnshops, 9, 155, 158, 163, 174–75, 179; cooperation with police, 2, 19, 122, 129, 134–37, 139–40, 149–50, pawnbrokers (*continued*)

151–52, 190–92; as crime victims, 122, 133–34, 143–44, 148–49, 216 n 100; critiqued by William Hogarth, 9, *10*, 11; cynicism regarding pawners, 142; defended, 51–52, 119, 127, 133–34, 153, 179; discretion of, 54, 83–84, 96–97; distinct from brokers, 54–56, 202 n 9; diversity of, 42, 71–74, 200 n 81; duties of, 169 (*see also* appraisal); earliest in America, 56; economic vulnerability of, 76–82, 85, 167, 188, 213 n 117; expenses of, 76, 77; family connections of, 1, 29, 61, *69*, 72–73, 74–75, *108;* fictionalized, 29, 30–37, 39; former occupations of, 59–60, 72–73; gender of, 15, 57, 73–74; during Great Depression, 79–82; honest, 129, 132, 137, 152; illustrations of, *10, 18, 34, 45, 48, 49, 50, 69, 108, 138, 140;* income of, 75–76, 77; innkeepers as, 54, 55, 124–25, 128; as intermediaries, 123, 152; Irish, 42, 71, 73–74; Jewish, 7, 16–17, 23, 26–27, 71–73, 178; knowledge of markets, 58–59, 84–85, 119, 142–43; leniency of, 80–81, 88–89, 178, 188; licensing of, 9, 57–62, 126, 131, 132, 152–53; locations of today, 187; in New York City, 26–27, 29, 56, 57, 59, 60, 73–75, 83, 86, 96, 100, 131, 139–40, 141–42, 150, 188; as "nonproducers," 16, 22; number per capita, 61–63; objectivity of, 114–15; personal relationships with pawners, 2, 80–81, 93, 133, 176, 177, 179, 187, 188; in Philadelphia, 5, 57, 59, 68, 72, 73, 83, 102, 125, 129, 149, 157, 188, 221 n 27; in Pittsburgh, 59, 72; at the PLS, 177, 178; and police (*see* police); in Providence, 62, 63; and rate of population growth, 61, 63; and record keeping, *ii,* 6, 57, 80, 129, 131, 135, *138,* 191; regulation of, 56–58, 60–61, 126–27, 202 n 15; and reward money, 129, 130, 134–35, 150, 151; sign of (*see* three balls, sign of); and spurious goods, 119, 143–44; stereotyped as Jewish, 21–53; stereotypes of (*see* anti-Semitism; Jews, stereotypes of; Shylock); and stolen goods, 127–42; surveillance of, 6, 130, 131–32, 138, *138,* 191; tavern

keepers as, 54, 55, 124–25, 128; today, 1–3, 5–7, 182, 184, 187–90; trade associations of, 148, 180, 189–90; training of, 1, 58–60, 73, 170–72, 187; unlicensed, 66, 83–84, 132, 174 (*see also* loan brokers); for upper classes (*see* loan brokers); vilified, 4, 115, 120, 124, 126–28, 158, 190; wealthy, 74–75. *See also under individual names*

pawnbroking: adaptability of over time, 18, 20, 54; and capitalism, 3, 9, 20, 54, 60, 85, 87; in China, 7, 195 n 3; and the church, 7; critiques of, 2, 3, 4–5, 22; emergence in Europe, 7–11; emergence in United States, 4, 54–60; and the European aristocracy, 7; in fiction, 30–37; in London, 9; as "marginal," 2, 3, 21, 22; in the Middle Ages, 7; necessity of, 60; philanthropists' opinions, 19, 127, 128; popular critiques of, 18–19; regulations of, 58, 73; seen as Jewish profession, 33, 42–53, 71–72, 74–75; today, 3, 58, 182, 193–94; and the working poor, 3, 19

pawners: African Americans as, 80, *95,* 133; as bad risks, 81–82; compared to retail customers, 29–30, 66, 68; as consumers, 70, 109, 115 (*see also* consumer culture; consumer goods); critiques of, 4, 17, 57, 114–15, 120, 156, 184, 220 n 3; dishonesty of, 133, 134, 136, 139–40, 141–42, 143–44; dissatisfaction with PLS, 178; economic conditions of, 89, 102–5, 110–11; economic decisions of, 87–96, 112, 115, 118; fictional portrayals of, 32–33, 93; good credit of, 80, 97; Grant, Ulysses S., as, 107–9; during Great Depression, 80–82; illustrations of, *10, 18, 34, 43, 49, 69, 95, 98, 99;* as majority of population, 20, 60, 76, 86, 102, 105; neighbors as, 61, 62, 64–66, 95, 174, 188; personal identification required of, 6; personal relationships with pawnbrokers, 2, 79, 80–81, 93, 176, 177, 179, 187, 188; poor as, 4, 14, 15, 56, 61, 65–66, 77, 79, 83, 86, 87, 89, 90–91, 102–5, 110, 112–14, 158–59, 166–67, 174, 178–79; privacy of, 2, *34,* 68, *69,* 84, 96, 97, *98, 99,* 107, 193; redemption rates of, 84, 94, 119–20, 179,

189; as repeat customers, 1–2, 61, 73, 118, 133–34, 143–44, 177, 178, 179, 188; restrictions on, 57, 88, 126; sailors as, 91, 156, 157; self-esteem of, 29–30, 68–69, 118; as small businessmen, 2, 70, 90; temporal pawning cycles, 83, 88–91, 93, 120; today, 2, 184–85, 187–90, 193; untrustworthy, 124, 133–34, 139–40, 142, 148–49, 175; wealthy as, 69, 78, 83, 84, 95–96, 97, 196 n 8, 209 n 39; women as, 80, 81, 90, 91–95, 95, 208 n 20; working poor as, 14

Pawners' Bank of Boston: auction of unredeemed collateral, 104, 105; dividends for investors, 162; hours of, 178; loan terms of, 162; organization and operation of, 161–63; as a profitable business, 163, 175; redemptions at, 120

pawning: accepted, 159, 162–63, 180; and capitalism, 20, 30, 60, 87, 104, 105, 116 (see also capitalism); and consumer culture, 4, 82, 97–117; criticized, 4, 17–18, 19, 90, 114, 119, 125; decisions of pawners, 87–96, 112, 118, 121; degradation from, 163; and dispossession, 112; in early America, 55–57, 124–27; embarrassment from, 29–30, 68–69, 118; as essential part of economy, 3, 4, 5, 15, 20, 21, 55, 79–80, 87, 104, 159, 190; explained, 5; flexibility of, 81, 87, 178, 182–83; and intemperance, 17, 125, 128, 158; in popular culture, 10, 18, 29, 30–37, 34, 41, 43, 49, 69, 90, 93, 96–97, 98, 99; records of, ii, 86, 101; and redemption rates, 84, 94, 119–20, 179, 189; and resale markets, 110–11, 111; and selfhood, 116–18; and sloth, 127; statistics of, 100, 101, 104–5, 129; temporal cycles of, 76–77, 83, 89, 91, 93, 94, 120; today, 58, 182, 188–94; women and, 91–95

pawns: Bibles as, 32, 100, 101, 109–10; and class distinctions, 29, 98–99, 101, 112–14, 116–19; clocks, 49, 51, 80, 100; clothing as, ii, 68, 70, 76, 83, 90, 94, 100; coats, 77, 79, 80–81, 101, 110, 139, 188; and consumer culture, 16, 18, 82–83, 97–117, 120–21; definition of, 5, 87–88, 176–77, 207 n 2; different spheres of value of, 30, 87, 98, 104, 114–15, 118, 121, 183; as economic

expedients, 114–15; embodying credit history, 94; high-end, 78, 119; general variety of, 55, 77, 80, 86, 94, 97, 99–102, 104, 105, 108, 111, 119, 123–24, 125, 135, 159, 178, 185, 188, 193; husbands' possessions as, 92, 93; immigrants' possessions as, 15, 71, 111–12; jewelry as, 30, 56, 70, 84, 100, 101, 109, 110, 129, 141–41, 180; limited by the PLS, 169–70, 176, 178; linking people, 37, 109, 192, 222 n 30; monetary value of, 86, 101, 141–42; not counted as pawnbrokers' assets, 77–78, 213 n 117; pawn tickets necessary for redemption, 6, 92, 102–3, 105, 109, 144–47; of the poor, ii, 11, 105, 91–95, 101, 105, 110, 111–12; resale markets of (see auctions; used goods); sentimental value of, 18, 31, 32, 81, 112–16, 159; spurious, 119, 142–44; statistics for, 76, 87, 100, 102, 206 n 88; stolen goods as (see under stolen goods); stored in pawnshops, 61, 67, 69, 98, 99, 108, 115, 138; tools as, 89, 90, 101, 112, 120, 139, 159–60; unacceptable, 88; used in early America, 54–55; watches as (see watches); wedding rings as, 92–93, 193; and women, 94. See also consumer culture; consumer goods; gemstones; jewelry; watches

pawns, unredeemed: auctions of, 70, 75, 100–101, 104, 105, 110; definition of, 6; and Great Depression, 81; losses from, 15; proceeds from, 76, 155, 167, 168; resale of, 64, 66, 70, 104, 110, 111, 129, 159; statistics on (see redemption rates); stolen goods as, 129, 134. See also redemption rates

Pawnshop Investigation Unit (Philadelphia), 2, 191

pawnshop loans. See loans, collateral

pawnshops, chain, 186, 189

pawnshops, independent: in African American neighborhoods, 66; amount of outstanding loans from, 76, 78, 79, 101–2, 178; in Asheville, 188; in Baltimore, 57, 59, 73; in Birmingham, 79; in Boston, 61, 62, 63, 108, 161–63, 175; in Buffalo, 58, 187; and capitalism, 16, 60–62; causing social ills, 3, 17, 126–29, 158; in Charleston, 73, 108,

pawnshops, independent (*continued*)
124; in Chicago, 65, 174; as community
fixtures, 61, 64, 65–66, 81, 174, 188;
compared to retail spaces, 66; compared
to savings banks, 156–57; compared to
semiphilanthropic pawnshops, 19, 161–62,
168–69, 172, 174, 176, 180; in Dayton, 190;
described generally, 17, 32, 33; exteriors
of, 9, *10, 18, 43, 50, 61, 67, 95,* 115, *173,*
176; family ownership of, *69,* 72–73, *108,*
187–88; first appearance of in cities, 60;
hours of operation, 27, 94; interiors of, 2,
5–6, 31, *34,* 37, *45, 49,* 51, 66, 68, *69,* 70,
83, *98, 99, 108, 138,* 172; locations generally, 15, 31, 62, 64–66, 81, 96, 148, 171,
177, 195 n 2; in Milwaukee, 120; in movies,
51; in New York City, 26–27, 29, 56, 57,
59, 60, 62, 73–75, 83, 86, 96, 100, 131,
139–40, 141–42, 150, 188; not displaced by
semiphilanthropic pawnshops, 159, 174–75;
number of, 62, 63, 190; oldest in United
States, 1; in Philadelphia, 5, *16,* 57, 59, 62,
64, 68, 72, 73, 83, 102, 125, 129, 149, 157,
188, 221 n 27; in Pittsburgh, 59, 63, 72;
privacy cubicles in, *34,* 68, *69,* 96–97, *98,*
99; private entrances of, 68, 83, 107; in
Providence, 62; retail trade conducted in,
1, 187–88, 191; in Seattle, 187; security in,
148, 149; staffing of, 66; in St. Louis, 107;
in Stockton, 80–81; surveillance of, 130,
131–32, *138,* 191 (*see also* police); today,
187; for upper classes 192–93 (*see also* loan
brokers); and westward expansion, 16, 60,
61. See also under individual names
pawnshops, philanthropic: distinguished from
semiphilanthropic pawnshops, 162, 163;
failure of in Great Britain, 9; history of,
155, 217 n 4; *Hunt's Merchants' Magazine*
on, 160; interest rates charged by, 155; poor
and, 155; proposals for in United States,
89, 128, 154–55, 156; resistance to, 154. *See
also* Mont-de-Piété; monts-de-piété
pawnshops, semiphilanthropic: advocated by
reformers, 89, 128, 154–56, 159; as antidote
to crime, 155; bureaucracy of, 176; Chattel
Loan Company, 159–61; collateral limited

by, 178, 180; compared with independent
pawnshops, 19, 161–62, 168–69, 172, 174,
176, 180; competing with independent
pawnbrokers, 9, 155, 158, 163, 174–75, 179;
conservative loans of, 178; and Crash of
1893, 163; didacticism of, 160, 164–65;
disadvantages of, 178–79; discrimination of pawners, 175–76; distinguished
from philanthropic pawnshops, 162, 163;
dividends paid by, 160, 162, 167; failure to
displace independent pawnshops, 174–75;
First State Pawners Society, 105, 174, 175;
hours of, 178–79; in Jersey City, 163; loan
terms of, 155, 161, 162, 163; in movies,
51, 176; New York Lombard Association, 158–59; number of loans in 1932,
174; Pawners' Bank of Boston, 104, 105,
161–63; as profitable businesses, 118, 164;
resistance to, 178–79; rise of in the United
States, 4–5, 19, 162–81. *See also* Provident
Loan Society (PLS)
pawnshops, unlicensed, in cities, 60–61, 66, 83,
84, 132, 174, 204 n 32. *See also* loan brokers
pawn tickets: belonging to Ulysses S. Grant,
109, 118; in black markets, 145–46; commerce in, 144–46; dealers conspiring
with pawnbrokers, 146–47; described,
144; essential for redemption, 144, 145;
as evidence of crimes, 133, 141, 144–45,
148; examples of, 102, *103,* 210 n 57; fees
for writing, 58, 76, 102, 195 n 2; forged,
122, 146; frauds involving, 144–47; safely
stored, 92, 97, *98;* today, 6; transferability
of, 6, 41–47; value of, 144
peddlers: becoming pawnbrokers, 58, 60, 71,
72, 186–87; and consumer culture, 71, 99,
113; German-Jewish, 28; Jews as, 71; selling in hinterlands, 14, 15
Pennsylvania Society for the Promotion of
Public Economy, 127
Philadelphia: auction sales in, 101; brokers
in, 56, 197 n 6; description of, 64–65;
economic conditions in, 102, 103–5; Jews
in, 72; ordinances regarding pawnbrokers,
127–28; pawnbrokers in, 5, *16,* 57, 59, 62,
64, 68, 72, 73, 83, 102, 125, 129, 149, 157,

188, 221 n 27; semiphilanthropic pawn-shops in, 89, 128, 154, 159, 160. *See also* McGarry's (pawnshop)

Philadelphia Saving Fund Society (PSFS), 156, 157

philanthropic organizations. *See* pawnshops, philanthropic; pawnshops, semiphilanthropic; Provident Loan Society; *and under individual names*

philanthropists: approval of pawning, 162; efforts after the Civil War, 163–64; intentions of, 165, 167, 180, 219 n 51, 219 n 54; and loan societies, 154–81; organizing savings banks, 156; paternalism of, 164–65. *See also under individual names*

Pittsburgh, PA, 59, 63, 72, 206 n 88

pledges. *See* pawns

police: arrest of pawnbroker, 131; authority of, 131–32, 135, 152; cooperation with pawnbrokers, 2, 19, 122, 129, 134–37, 139–40, 149–50, 151–52, 190–92; lack of enforcement, 61, 64; pawnbrokers' resistance to, 131–32, 134; Pawnshop Investigation Unit, 2, 191–92; and reward money, 150; surrender of stolen goods to, 76, 130; surveillance of pawnbrokers, 6, 130, 131–32, 138, *138*, 191; surveillance of used goods dealers, 138–39; use of pawn tickets to track crimes, 144. *See also* Bell, William; stolen goods

poor: access to credit, 56, 70, 87–93, 103, 118, 126, 156, 157, 158, 183–84, 186–87, 190; and banking, 3, 4, 14, 19, 60, 184–85; collateral loans as essential to, 3, 4, 5, 15, 20, 21, 55, 79–80, 87, 104, 159, 190; as consumers, 110, 113; controlled by reformers, 127, 154–81; economic conditions of, 14, 89, 102–4, 105, 110; ennobling effects of being, 157; helped by PLS, 174; like farm animals, 179; maligned, 91, 120, 156–57, 184, 220 n 3; as pawners, 3, 4, 14, 15, 19, 56, 60, 61, 65–66, 77, 79, 83, 86, 87, 89, 90–91, 102–5, 110, 112–14, 158–59, 166–67, 174, 178–79; pawns of, *ii*, 11, 105, 91–95, 101, 105, 110, 111–12; and payday loans, 185; and philanthropic pawnshops, 155, 160; PLS branches

for, 167; possessions of, 110; profits from, 183–85; "worthy," 160, 164, 179

postcards, 47–48, *49*

Providence, RI, 62–63, 206 n 88

Provident Institution for Savings, 156, 157

Provident Loan Society (PLS): accepted collateral limited, 170, 176; appraisals at deskilled, 168–70; architecture of, 171–72, *173*, 174; assets, 179; average loans, 105, 179; benefiting the poor, 174; branches of, 166–67, 171–72, *173*, 174, 180; bureaucracy of, 164, 166–74, 176, 177, 178; capital of, 167; compared with independent pawnshops, 168–69, 172, 174, 176, 180; during depressions, 78–79, 174; founding of, 163; impersonality of, 178; initial capitalization of, 167; interest rates charged by, 174; investors' returns on, 167; Jews not hired at, 177–78; "Loan-mobile," 220 n 4; loans capped, 167; organizers of described, 165–66; pawnbrokers working for, 177, 178; pawners' dissatisfaction with, 178; pawners' relationships with pawnbrokers negated, 177; pawners' use of loans from, 90–91; redemption rates recorded by, 94, 120; success of, 179; surplus of, 167; today, 184, 220 n 4; total annual loans, 167; as "Vanderbilt" pawnshop, 179

Puck, 44–46, *45*

redemption rates, 119–20; comparison of daily, 94; during economic decline, 119; recorded by First State Pawners Society, 120; recorded by PLS, 94, 120, 179; recorded by William Simpson, 119, 209 n 33; today, 189; among upper classes, 84

Reed, Carver (pawnbroker), 83

reformers: advocating semiphilanthropic pawnshops, 159; attempts to control the poor, 127; attempts to eliminate pawnbroking, 126; De Forest, Robert W., 166; as distanced from pawners, 165; intentions of, 164; Mills, D. O., 166; on "worthy" poor, 164. *See also* pawnshops, philanthropic; pawnshops, semiphilanthropic; philanthropists; Provident Loan Society

rent, 89, 91, 93
retail trade, 30, 66, 68, 116. *See also* consumer culture; markets
reward money, 129, 130, 134–35, 150, 151
Rosado, Jay (pawnbroker), 188

sailors, 91, 156, 157
savings banks: Bank of Savings of the City of New York, 156; Chest of Savings, promoted by James Mease, 155; compared with pawnshops, 157; number of compared with pawnshops, 157; operations of, 156; organized by philanthropists, 156; Philadelphia Saving Fund Society (PSFS), 156, 157; Provident Institution for Savings, 156, 157; Sixpenny Saving Bank, 156–57. *See also* banks
Schwed, Peter, 169–70, *171*, *172*, 177
Seattle, WA, 187
Shouler, James, 176–77
Shylock, 17, 21, 24, 40, 198 n 23. *See also* anti-Semitism; Jews, stereotypes of
Simpson family (pawnbrokers): amount in outstanding loans, 78; defended, 133; fame of, 74–75; family connections of, 74–75; ledger of John, *ii*, 91, 94, 105; Protestantism of, 29; redemption rates recorded, 119, 209 n 33; theft at shop, 149; transactions quantified, 86, 102; wealth of, 75; William recollecting pawning scam, 141–42; William specializing in high-end goods, 119
Sixpenny Saving Bank, 156–57
Sloane, John, 165–66
Smith, Adam, 13–14, 196 n 24
Sommer, John (pawnbroker), 26, 57, 59, 202 n 20
specie, 55, 156, 197
Speyer, James, 165
State Pawners' Society, 180
Steel City Pawnshop, 79, 80, 81–82
St. Louis, MO, 107
Stockton, CA, 80–81
stolen goods: circulation of, 125, 136–37; and consumer culture, 124; as evidence of crime, 136–37; Fredericka Mandelbaum as noted receiver of, 132; notices for, 123–24,

130; and pawnbrokers, 127–42; pawnbrokers as receivers of, 4, 17, 130–31, 192; pawnbrokers avoiding, 94–95; pawnbrokers' forfeiture of, 149–50; pawns as, 3, 123–42; recovery of, 124, 125, 130, 131, 134–42, *138*, 141, 151, 192, 222 n 30; regulations to control, 57; today, 190, 191–92; types of, 123–24, 131, 135, 139, 141; as unredeemed collateral. *See also* markets, black; police; theft; thieves

tavern keepers, 54, 55, 64–65, 124–25, 128, 137
theft: within families, 140–41; pawnbrokers as victims of, 149; women as victims of, 134, 135, 141. *See also* police; stolen goods; thieves
thieves: activity of, 106, 130, 132–36; avoiding pawnshops, 137; caught with pawn tickets, 144–45; clerk as, 131; relationships with victims, 140; women as, 133, 134, 135–36, 139, 145
Thompson, Mary Clark, 166
three balls, sign of: in advertising, 47, *48*, *108*; in early America, 15, *16*, *18*; humorous use of, 41, *42*; origins of, 7, *8*, 195 n 4; referred to, 128; on storefronts, *61*, *67*, *95*; as symbol of all Jews, 24; ubiquity of in Great Britain, 9; universally recognized, 176
Touger, Levi (pawnbroker), 193
trade cards, 47, *48*, 200 n 94
Twain, Mark, 46

United Charities Building, 171, *173*
upper classes: as pawners, *69*, 78, 83, 84, 95–97, *97*, 196 n 8, 209 n 39; philanthropy of, 156–68; possessions as status symbols, 116; possessions pawned, 78, 83–84, 119, 192–193. *See also* loan brokers; pawners: wealthy as
used goods: dealers and crime, 125–26, 128, 132; dealers in Chicago, 65–66; dealers in New York City, 62, 110, *111*, 130; dealers in Philadelphia, 221 n 27; dealers of becoming pawnbrokers, 71; dealers selling unredeemed collateral, 159; dealing and capitalism, 3, 70; general locations of, 62,

64–66; Jewish dealers in, 17, 25, 38, 72–73; and the lower classes, 110; markets affected by depressions, 78–82; in pawnshop windows, *50, 61, 66, 67,* 68, *108;* police surveillance of, 138–39; regulation of dealers, 57; and resale markets, 110, *111, 113;* types of, 130; as unredeemed collateral, 70, 104. *See also* junk; markets, resale; pawns

usury: Aristotle's philosophy regarding, 11; Biblical injunctions against, 12; Bolles, John, on, 14; clerical objections against, 12; current laws regarding, 184; distinguished from interest, 196 n 22; early theories regarding, 11–14; Hume, David, on, 13; and Jews, 12, 24; laws repealed, 220 n 7; Locke, John, on, 13; pawnbroker's conviction for, 26; popular reactions against, 14; Smith, Adam, on 13; Sommer, John, convicted of, 26, 59, 202 n 20. *See also* interest; Jews, stereotypes of

Vanderbilt, Cornelius, 165, 179
Veblen, Thorstein, 117

Washington, D.C., 76
Washington, George, 125
watches: cartoon about, 41, *42;* domestic manufacture of, 106–7; illustrations of, *49, 108;* importation of, 106–7; makers, 70; monetary value of, 106, 145, 146–47; pawned by Ulysses S. Grant, 107; as pawns, *43,* 74, 77, 81, 83, 86, 96, 97, 100, 101, 102–3, 105–9, 129, 141; physical char-

acteristics of, 106; as popular consumer good, 105–6, 211 n 69, 220 n 28; price of nineteenth century, 107; recorded in Simpson ledger, 105; retailers of, 106–7; sentimental value of, 113, 115, 116, 159; spurious, 119, 143; stolen, 106, 124, 130, 131, 135, 136, 137, 139, *139, 140, 141,* 144, 146, 149, 150, 151

Webster, Daniel, 160
West, 60, *61*
women: and coverture, 92; economic freedom enabled by pawning, 92; fictional portrayals of as pawners, 93; and household economies, 90–95; and husbands' possessions, 92, 93; income of, 91; income of 1830, 93; and knowledge of pawns' value, 94; occupations of, 65; as pawnbrokers, 15, 57, 73, 163; as pawners, 80, 81, 90, 91–95, *95,* 208 n 20; pawning strategies of, 92; as pawnshop clerks, 131; perpetrating frauds, 141–42; and poverty, 90–95; private entrances for pawners, 68; as thieves, 133, 134, 135–36, 139, 141–42, 145; as victims of theft, 134, 135, 141; weekly pawning cycles of, 94; and widowhood, 91
Workingmen's Loan Association, 175, 176
Working Women's Protective Union, 94
Wright, Julia McNair, 38–39, 93

xenophobia, 23, 220 n 93

Zimmelman, Jean (pawnbroker), 193
Zimmerman, Eugene ("Zim"), 46, 52, 46